century of the city no time to lose

D1444755

Commuters board a crowded Delhi Transport Corporation (DTC) bus, New Delhi, India

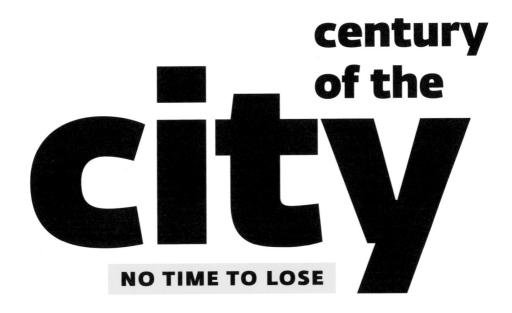

century of the city

NO TIME TO LOSE

THE ROCKEFELLER FOUNDATION

Neal R. Peirce and Curtis W. Johnson
with Farley M. Peters

Copyright © 2008 by
Neal R. Peirce and Curtis W. Johnson
All rights reserved.

Published by

New York
United States of America

ISBN: 0-89184-072-9

The views expressed in this publication
are not necessarily those of the
Rockefeller Foundation.

References to Internet Web sites (URLs)
were accurate at the time of writing.
Neither the authors nor the Rockefeller
Foundation is responsible for URLs that
may have expired or changed since the
manuscript was prepared.

Book design by Abbott Miller, John Kudos,
and Susan Brzozowski at Pentagram

Contents

Laundry drying at a multi-story prefabricated housing project, Hong Kong, China

Foreword

ALMOST A HALF CENTURY HAS PASSED since the Rockefeller Foundation
helped create the field of urban design and theory. One of the Foundation's
initial grants in that effort was to the young author, activist, and urbanist Jane Jacobs, whose life's work, especially her classic, *Death and Life of Great
American Cities* (1961), continues to shape perspectives about cities, planning,
and city planning. "In order for a society to flourish," Jacobs wrote all those
years ago, "there must be a flourishing city at its core." This bedrock recognition informs and inspires the Rockefeller Foundation's enduring commitment to and investment in "flourishing cities."

Today that commitment is more important than ever because the
world's population is moving to and growing in cities at an astonishing rate.
One of every ten people lived in urban areas a century ago. This year, for the
first time, a majority of people live in cities. By 2050, the United Nations
projects, almost three-quarters of the world's population will call urban areas
home. Most of this growth is centered in the developing countries of the
Global South. In these emerging economies, nearly three of every five people
will live in urban areas by 2030.

These are not cities with postcard skylines. Accelerating, unplanned
urban growth multiplies populations of slum dwellers, overburdens housing,
transportation, and infrastructure systems, and leaves hundreds of millions
vulnerable to new environmental and health threats. In fact, UN-HABITAT
projects that within three decades, one of every three human beings will live
in near total squalor—lacking sanitation and clean water, fueling the spread
of disease, and possibly igniting the next global pandemic.

To help shape our shared response, the Foundation convened the
Global Urban Summit at the Rockefeller Foundation Bellagio Center in July
2007. This month-long colloquy featured a diverse ensemble of voices from
around the world: government officials, finance experts, urban thinkers,
and other leaders from every walk of life. It explored new approaches to

solving 21st century urban challenges. It identified the gaps in our knowledge and fashioned an agenda to fill them.

For our part, the Foundation is already supporting substantial work to address new urban vulnerabilities. In the United States, we are helping to frame smarter, more sustainable 21st century transportation policies and to elevate the stature of transportation and infrastructure challenges on the national agenda. Efforts to strengthen urban planning, financing, and governance in the Global South will soon follow.

This volume emerges from the seminal Rockefeller Foundation Global Urban Summit and in the proud tradition of Jane Jacobs and urbanism, the field she pioneered and personified. It shares the valued perspectives of our partners: the Center for Sustainable Urban Development at Columbia University, University of Pennsylvania Institute for Urban Research, Brookings Institution Metropolitan Policy Program, and Regional Plan Association, among others. It supplies crucial, intellectual bricks and mortar with which more communities in more places can build sustainable futures. And it reflects the Rockefeller Foundation's continuing commitment to help more societies "flourish" by strengthening the cities — and the lives of *citizens* — at their core.

Judith Rodin
President
The Rockefeller Foundation

Cyclists cross a busy street, central Beijing, China

Aerial image of northern favelas, São Paulo, Brazil

A Call for Leadership in an Urban World

Why don't our leaders talk about cities? In my own country, the United States, most Americans live in city regions. The 100 largest U.S. metropolitan areas generate 75 percent of our GDP. Most of the Fortune 1000 companies and our nations' universities, research centers, hospitals, arts centers, and sports franchises are in urban areas. American culture—remarkably influential and potently felt around the globe—is imbued with an urban sensibility. Urbanist, writer, and activist Jane Jacobs said it best: "Without cities we would all be poor."

And, yet, our political leaders don't talk about their vision for cities. This may be partly because for some Americans, the mention of cities brings to mind negative images, such as the horrific urban racial strife of the 1960s, the subsequent decaying of urban centers (populated by minorities and the poor), and the growth of exclusive suburbs (primarily populated by middle-class and affluent whites). But this was a lifetime ago and recent evidence suggests that this paradigm has been turned on its head as our suburbs grow more diverse and large numbers of suburbanites, especially baby boomers and singles, are returning to central cities. Between 1990 and 2000, racial and ethnic diversity in America's suburbs increased from 19 to 27 percent.

In the developing world (or Global South), urbanization is inevitable and irreversible because of two profound trends—globalization and population growth in urban and rural areas. Here as in the Global North, agricultural development and urbanization are inextricably linked. For most of the last century, however, leaders in the Global South and many development institutions did not work effectively to integrate this economic reality into development priorities. Rural development practice was often disconnected from a focus on developing urban infrastructure and markets.

The result has been urban mal-development, manifested in the Global South acutely in the proliferation of urban slums. For most of the 20th century, urban leaders in the developing world regarded slums as temporary and slum dwellers as transients who would eventually return to the rural villages from whence they came. But as we cross the mark of 1 billion slum dwellers in the world, it is painfully clear that the face of poverty in this century will be increasingly urban and we must tackle this phenomenon head on to change it.

Fortunately, discussion of the critical role that cities can and must play in a country's dynamism, resilience, and economic growth is increasing around the world, particularly in developing regions where urbanization is occurring most quickly. For example, Zhou Xiaochuan, governor of the People's Bank of China (which is equivalent to the Reserve Bank of India or the U.S. Federal Reserve) noted in a 2008 submission to the Commission on Growth and Development that "10 or more years ago, the Chinese central government resisted urbanization, because the authorities thought its pace was too rapid...this policy [of slowing urbanization] should be part of the list of 'bad ideas' because of the importance of agglomeration efficiencies....The Chinese government has now reversed policy and understood the key role of urbanization in structural transformation."

OUR URBAN FUTURE

Recognizing the profound trend of urbanization and motivated by our mission to expand access to opportunity for poor and vulnerable people around the world, the Rockefeller Foundation in 2007 began a broad exploration of urban issues in the developing world and in the United States. We initiated our engagement by organizing a Global Urban Summit, an unprecedented convening of an array of urban leaders from six continents: more than 250 urban scholars, practitioners, NGOs, public officials, and foundation and corporate leaders. They gathered at the Foundation's Bellagio Center in Italy. For more than four decades, this Center has been a venue for framing contemporary international debates and devising creative responses to some of the most pressing issues of our time, from public health to food security to human rights.

The Rockefeller Foundation Global Urban Summit, consisting of eight conferences over four weeks, highlighted a set of actionable opportunities and solutions to the challenge posed by rapid urbanization. As you will see in the pages that follow, the Summit provided a platform for an in-depth examination of financing infrastructure for shelter, water, and sanitation; building climate change resilience; promoting urban population health; and developing urban planning and design, all in the Global South; and, in the United States, creating a national policy agenda for transportation reform; and improving regional policy and planning. While participants discussed many innovative ideas and models during the conferences, one sentiment was particularly strong: These new models must be designed for the broadest application possible so that they can address systemic, not just individual, problems.

Participants agreed that the challenges facing cities in this century demand multi-sectoral and multidisciplinary approaches, rather than the traditional reliance on "silos" of policy and practice (such as the "stovepiped" work of the public health, environmental, and finance fields). New models for meaningfully and effectively working in this integrated manner are required at local, regional, and international scales.

With cities confronting a complex overlay of problems, the brightest and most creative minds must apply their skills and knowledge to make urban areas more vibrant, inclusive, and environmentally sound. Poor public health and lack of infrastructure in existing urban settlements—both of which severely hamper economic and social vitality—have been long-standing problems. Today these issues are further complicated by 21st century challenges: While improving health and infrastructure, we must also help communities become more resilient to the inevitable devastating impacts of climate change and slow the production of greenhouse gases. We must combat new health threats resulting from environmental changes and increased demographic mobility. We must tap financial intermediaries to help catalyze private sector capital to enable lower-income households to gain access to shelter and water and sanitation services.

Summit participants agreed that in the United States the next few years offer a critical opportunity to help craft and inform new policy that addresses a variety of urban needs: A reimagined surface transportation system that reduces pollution, decreases foreign energy dependence, creates jobs, and improves equity and access to housing, employment, and education. Building climate change resilience must be elevated in public discourse. National economic development policies must incorporate demographic shifts among central city and suburban populations as well as the growth of megaregions.

From entrepreneurial NGOs and creative businesspeople to resourceful public officials, Summit participants shared new approaches, inventive strategies, and promising solutions that are now addressing the challenges of urbanization in every part of the world. Shack/Slum Dwellers International, a federation-based organization with operations in more than 26 countries, is helping inhabitants of informal settlements galvanize financial and political resources. In regions such as sub-Saharan Africa, nascent urban planning associations are expanding the exchange of ideas and best practices by strengthening professional networks. To better quantify urban expansion and slum development, new mapping technologies and community-based enumeration techniques are being combined. And in the face of rising energy costs in the United States, new policies are being crafted to eliminate incentives that favor building more roads and extending urban sprawl.

THE ROCKEFELLER FOUNDATION'S URBAN AGENDA

Armed with new partners, networks, and ideas, the Rockefeller Foundation continues to build on its efforts to expand opportunities for poor and vulnerable urban residents. For example, as part of our Climate Change Resilience initiative, the Foundation is supporting the development of climate adaptation plans for several cities in Asia. We have made a major multiyear investment in advancing equitable and environmentally sustainable transportation policy in the United States. A grant to Shack/Slum Dwellers International is assisting the organization in helping residents generate savings, housing, and political power. Support for UN-Habitat is helping the group hone its model for a finance fund for urban housing organizations. Our funding of the African Cities Network at the University of Cape Town is fostering a network of African urban planners. And we are exploring a new field, urban health, which will bring together some of the best minds in the fields of public health and urban policy.

It is through cities that the dreams and aspirations of many millions of people have been realized. We urge leaders in the United States and around the world to join in a global movement to invest in the ideas, institutions, and individuals at the forefront of forging solutions to the urban challenge of this century.

Darren Walker
Vice President, Foundation Initiatives
The Rockefeller Foundation

lack of capacity

the globe's wealth builders

dynamism

traffic

CHAPTER 1

Vast Challenges, Startling Opportunities

North–South commonality

interdisciplinary approaches

innovators

global city dialogue

cities make countries rich

energy demand

Bathers at Brighton Beach, Brooklyn, New York, U.S.A.

A CENTURY OF THE CITY, an urban future for mankind, has dawned. The year 2008 marked the first time in history that a majority of the world's people lives in cities—a percentage projected to rise to 70 percent by 2050. In the most massive population movement the world has ever seen, millions of people continue to pour out of rural villages each year, hoping for fresh economic opportunity in the world's cities. The populations of many of today's metropolises—Tokyo at 35.7 million, Mexico City at 19 million, Mumbai at 19 million—would have defied imagination just a few decades ago.

At the same time, some cities of the developed world are recovering from the initial impact of suburbanization, their urban cores thriving as centers of finance and new technology, which have given cities their dynamism since the first of significant size emerged in Mesopotamia between 3,500 and 4,000 B.C. Modern day electronic communications and easier travel, which many had thought could spell the doom of cities, are actually making them more vital than ever as they connect the capital markets of the developed world, also known as the Global North, with the human capital and new economic vigor of such nations as India and China.

dynamism

Throughout human history, cities have provided the world's great ideas and economic innovations. Indeed, the words *cities* and *civilization* both spring from the common root of *civitas,* a Latin word that reflected both citizenship and human settlements in ancient Rome.

Global Urban Summit

At an opening session of the July 2007 Global Urban Summit at the Rockefeller Foundation Bellagio Center in Italy, Rakesh Mohan, deputy governor of the Reserve Bank of India, underscored the dramatic possibilities of 21st century urbanism. Today's cities, he noted, are creating a continuous increase in people's access to water, sanitation, education, health services, and economic opportunity. It is true that islands of severe urban poverty in developing countries, collectively referred to as the Global South, may be as dehumanizing as the most severe rural poverty. Yet it is also true, he stressed, that never before in history have such large numbers of human beings had access to electricity, water, sanitation, schools, and telecommunications.

efficiency

And don't underestimate cities' immense efficiency, Mohan added. It is no accident that corporations large and small, banks and investment houses, universities and research laboratories, and specialized manufacturing all congregate, in overwhelming measure, in cities. Cities are great magnets

innovators

for the world's best thinkers and innovators. The proximity of roadways, rails, ports, and airports in urban areas reduce time, travel, and energy costs in a way that rural areas simply cannot match. And cities do satisfy the universal need for face-to-face contact to foster new products, processes, and intellectual capital.

As UN-HABITAT, the U.N. agency charged with promot-

cities make countries rich

ing adequate shelter for all, has noted, "Cities make countries rich. Countries that are highly urbanized have higher incomes,

Pedestrians crossing a street, Shibuya Ward, Tokyo, Japan

Rockefeller Foundation Global Urban Summit

THE DILEMMAS AND OPPORTUNITIES of the ever-increasing urban populations in the developing world were a major focus of the July 2007 Rockefeller Foundation Global Urban Summit:

- **Water, Sanitation, and Shelter: A Fresh Look at Finance** (Chapter 2) Given the entrepreneurial spirit—despite dire circumstances—in many Global South slums, how can global financial sources be tapped to help low-income communities invest in the basic water, sanitation, and housing they need?

- **Climate Change Resilience: An Urgent Action Agenda** (Chapter 3) While the world works on methods of mitigating greenhouse gas emissions and preventing the worst potential effects of climate change, the big challenge in the Global South is building resilience and fostering ways to deal with inevitable impacts. How can Global South cities prepare, with meaningful global assistance?

- **Urban Health: Learning From Systems That Work** (Chapter 4) Slums may be the epicenter of the world's most critical health problems, but the repercussions of poor health among the economically disadvantaged can be seen worldwide. What steps can improve disease-fighting and monitoring while tapping the community-based social capital and networks of those most in danger?

- **Designing the Inclusive City** (Chapter 5) How can the disciplines of urban planning and design recruit and train enough broad-minded professionals to think across narrow jurisdictional boundaries and fortify the vital urban building enterprise of the Global South?

Other Summit sessions delved into the United States' capacity to become a more resourceful and future-oriented society:

- **America 2050: U.S. Strategy for the Next Half Century** (Chapter 6) What new policies and investments should the United States undertake to assure protection of its infrastructure and natural areas, promote social and economic equity, and reduce its climate footprint as its population rises 120 million more by 2050, mostly in the nation's ten vast urban "megaregions"?

- **U.S. Transportation Challenge: Better Outcomes for Billions Spent** (Chapter 7) The United States' federal and state governments expend impressive sums yearly on transportation, yet their policies are fragmented, insensitive to environmental and safety needs, unfair to the disadvantaged, and often hostile to cities' health. What is a better prescription for the immediate future—and for this century?

- **U.S. Metros: Building Blocks of American Prosperity?** (Chapter 8) Metro regions are home to most of America's population and represent the heartbeat of the economy, yet federal policy routinely disregards them. How can their strengths be tapped for a more prosperous American future?

The final chapters summarize Summit highlights and look toward the future:

- **Building Evidence to Sustain an Urban Future** (Chapter 9) Informal city-to-city contacts can spread the word of urban policy innovations. But what are the ways that focused academic research can be fostered (and connected) across the globe to identify key questions and measure and compare innovations?

- **New Frontiers for a Global Urban Commons** (Chapter 10) What policies and approaches might world cities—Global South and Global North alike—share and learn from to enhance urban opportunities during this century of the city?

more stable economies, stronger institutions, and are better able to withstand the volatility of the global economy than those with less urbanized populations."

THE GLOBAL URBAN BOOM

Throughout the 20th century, cities all over the world grew in population, from 250 million to 2.8 billion—unprecedented expansion, and one that is accelerating, as cities have absorbed four times as many people in the second half of the century as in the first. Overall global population rose from 2.2 billion inhabitants of the world in 1950 to most recent estimates of 6.7 billion, with 9.2 billion now the projection for 2050. The growth rate will fall far short of 20th century levels, but the added billions of people will be highly significant. The most rapid increase in sheer numbers will switch from Latin America to Africa and Asia. Indeed, two-thirds of the added world inhabitants anticipated in the next 30 years will be in Asia, and overwhelmingly in cities.

There is no question that cities are top players in their nations' economies. As *The Economist* reports, Mumbai accounts for 40 percent of India's tax revenues, Tokyo alone accounts for a third of Japan's GDP, and more than three-quarters of Senegal's industrial production originates around Dakar.

None of the Summit participants dismissed the weight of 21st century problems and potential crises tied closely to cities. climate change Climate change triggered by two centuries of fossil fuel burning raises fears of drowned metropolises, parched highlands, and

GLOBAL POPULATION IN TRANSITION

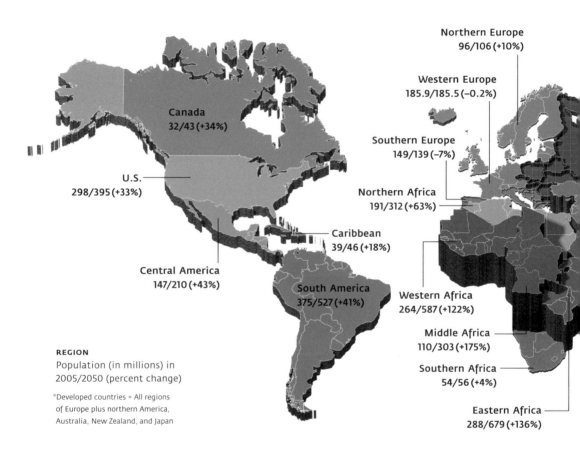

Northern Europe
96/106 (+10%)

Western Europe
185.9/185.5 (−0.2%)

Southern Europe
149/139 (−7%)

Canada
32/43 (+34%)

U.S.
298/395 (+33%)

Northern Africa
191/312 (+63%)

Caribbean
39/46 (+18%)

Central America
147/210 (+43%)

South America
375/527 (+41%)

Western Africa
264/587 (+122%)

Middle Africa
110/303 (+175%)

Southern Africa
54/56 (+4%)

Eastern Africa
288/679 (+136%)

REGION
Population (in millions) in
2005/2050 (percent change)

°Developed countries = All regions
of Europe plus northern America,
Australia, New Zealand, and Japan

Source: *Population Division, Department of Economic and Social Affairs of the United Nations Secretariat,* World Population Prospects: The 2004 Revision and World Urbanization Prospects: The 2003 Revision, *http://esa.un.org/ unpp; July 7, 2005*

Credit: Scientific American, September 2005; the Bryan Christie Studio

Eastern Europe
297/224 (−25%)

Russian Federation
143/112 (−22%)

China
1,316/1,392 (+6%)

Japan
128/112 (−13%)

Eastern Asia
1,524/1,587 (+4%)

Southeastern Asia
556/752 (+36%)

South-Central Asia
1,611/2,495 (+55%)

Western Asia
214/383 (+79%)

Oceania
33/48 (+45%)

Uneven growth will further shift the population balance between rich and poor nations. In 2005 developed* countries were home to 1.2 billion of the world's 6.5 billion people; less developed countries were home to the other 5.3 billion. In 2050 the rich countries will still have about 1.2 billion people, but the poor countries will grow to 7.9 billion. Falling fertility rates will cause some rich nations to begin losing population from 2010 onward. Fertility will also drop, on average, in developing countries, to a replacement level of 2.1 children per woman by around 2035, although birth rates in some of the poorest countries will remain higher.

CITISTATES OF THE WORLD

RANK	CITY/URBAN AREA	COUNTRY	POPULATION IN 2006 (MILLIONS)	RANK	CITY/URBAN AREA	COUNTRY	POPULATION IN 2006 (MILLIONS)
1	TOKYO	JAPAN	35.53	28	LONDON	UK	7.61
2	MEXICO CITY	MEXICO	19.24	29	TEHRAN	IRAN	7.42
3	MUMBAI (BOMBAY)	INDIA	18.84	30	HONG KONG	CHINA	7.28
4	NEW YORK	USA	18.65	31	CHENNAI (MADRAS)	INDIA	7.04
5	SÃO PAULO	BRAZIL	18.61	32	BANGALORE	INDIA	6.75
6	DELHI	INDIA	16.00	33	BANGKOK	THAILAND	6.65
7	CALCUTTA	INDIA	14.57	34	DORTMUND, BOCHUM	GERMANY	6.57
8	JAKARTA	INDONESIA	13.67	35	LAHORE	PAKISTAN	6.57
9	BUENOS AIRES	ARGENTINA	13.52	36	HYDERABAD	INDIA	6.34
10	DHAKA	BANGLADESH	13.09	37	WUHAN	CHINA	6.18
11	SHANGHAI	CHINA	12.63	38	BAGHDAD	IRAQ	6.06
12	LOS ANGELES	USA	12.22	39	KINSHASA	CONGO	5.89
13	KARACHI	PAKISTAN	12.20	40	RIYADH	SAUDI ARABIA	5.76
14	LAGOS	NIGERIA	11.70	41	SANTIAGO	CHILE	5.70
15	RIO DE JANEIRO	BRAZIL	11.62	42	MIAMI	USA	5.48
16	OSAKA, KOBE	JAPAN	11.32	43	BELO HORIZONTE	BRAZIL	5.45
17	CAIRO	EGYPT	11.29	44	PHILADELPHIA	USA	5.36
18	BEIJING	CHINA	10.85	45	ST PETERSBURG	RUSSIA	5.35
19	MOSCOW	RUSSIA	10.82	46	AHMADABAD	INDIA	5.34
20	METRO MANILA	PHILIPPINES	10.80	47	MADRID	SPAIN	5.17
21	ISTANBUL	TURKEY	10.00	48	TORONTO	CANADA	5.16
22	PARIS	FRANCE	9.89	49	HO CHI MINH CITY	VIETNAM	5.10
23	SEOUL	SOUTH KOREA	9.52	50	CHONGQING	CHINA	5.06
24	TIANJIN	CHINA	9.39	51	SHENYANG	CHINA	4.94
25	CHICAGO	USA	8.80	52	DALLAS, FORT WORTH	USA	4.72
26	LIMA	PERU	8.35	53	PUNE (POONA)	INDIA	4.67
27	BOGOTÁ	COLOMBIA	7.80	54	KHARTOUM	SUDAN	4.63

Population figures for the world's 100 largest urban areas—central cities and surrounding urban territory combined (2006 figures or estimates).

RANK	CITY/URBAN AREA	COUNTRY	POPULATION IN 2006 (MILLIONS)	RANK	CITY/URBAN AREA	COUNTRY	POPULATION IN 2006 (MILLIONS)
55	SINGAPORE	SINGAPORE	4.47	79	RECIFE	BRAZIL	3.59
56	ATLANTA	USA	4.47	80	MONTERREY	MEXICO	3.58
57	SYDNEY	AUSTRALIA	4.45	81	MONTRÉAL	CANADA	3.53
58	BARCELONA	SPAIN	4.43	82	CHENGDU	CHINA	3.52
59	HOUSTON	USA	4.39	83	PHOENIX, MESA	USA	3.51
60	CHITTAGONG	BANGLADESH	4.37	84	PUSAN	REPUBLIC OF KOREA	3.49
61	BOSTON	USA	4.37				
62	WASHINGTON DC	USA	4.25	85	BRASÍLIA	BRAZIL	3.48
63	HANOI	VIETNAM	4.22	86	JOHANNESBURG	SOUTH AFRICA	3.44
64	YANGON	MYANMAR	4.18	87	KABUL	AFGHANISTAN	3.43
65	BANDUNG	INDONESIA	4.15	88	SALVADOR	BRAZIL	3.41
66	DETROIT	USA	3.99	89	ALGIERS	ALGERIA	3.37
67	JIDDA	SAUDI ARABIA	3.96	90	SAN FRANCISCO, OAKLAND	USA	3.36
68	MILAN	ITALY	3.96				
69	GUADALAJARA	MEXICO	3.95	91	DÜSSELDORF, ESSEN	GERMANY	3.35
70	SURAT	INDIA	3.90	92	FORTALEZA	BRAZIL	3.35
71	GUANGZHOU	CHINA	3.88	93	MEDELLÍN	COLOMBIA	3.33
72	PÔRTO ALEGRE	BRAZIL	3.86	94	BERLIN	GERMANY	3.33
73	CASABLANCA	MOROCCO	3.83	95	PYONGYANG	NORTH KOREA	3.33
74	ALEXANDRIA	EGYPT	3.81	96	CARACAS	VENEZUELA	3.30
75	FRANKFURT, WIESBADEN	GERMANY	3.73	97	XIAN	CHINA	3.28
				98	ATHENS	GREECE	3.25
76	MELBOURNE	AUSTRALIA	3.71	99	EAST RAND (EKURHULENI)	SOUTH AFRICA	3.23
77	ANKARA	TURKEY	3.69				
78	ABIDJAN	CÔTE D'IVOIRE	3.62	100	CAPE TOWN	SOUTH AFRICA	3.21

Credit: City Mayors (www.citymayors.com). This table provides population figures for cities and their surrounding urban areas; in some cases, several cities of similar status and their suburbs make up an urban area. The 2006 population figures are based on censuses carried out between 2000 and 2005 and are adjusted for average annual population changes.

severe threats to the world's food supplies already imperiled by rapidly growing demand, volatile markets, and shortages rarely seen before in urban areas. Global oil reserves dwindle, even as energy demand by world cities soars. Severe water supply and quality issues loom on all continents. Motorized traffic, while enhancing mobility for millions, monopolizes urban space and degrades the daily life space of billions of city dwellers.

energy demand

traffic

Fast-expanding slums in the rising cities of Asia, Africa, and Latin America—forcing many people to live in horrific conditions, deprived of durable housing or safe water supplies or sanitation—raise deep moral, environmental sustainability and health issues. And the human torrent seems unquenchable: In a report on the future economy of India, Goldman Sachs projects that 31 villagers will continue to arrive in an Indian city every minute over the next 43 years—700 million people in all.

fast-expanding slums

While the numbers are difficult to measure, it is clear that hundreds of millions now live in slums and that in many places conditions are deteriorating. As Michael Cohen, a former World Bank official who is now the director of the New School of International Affairs, notes, "When I hear of how many may live in slums, it's unimaginable, a terrible problem. More than half the GDP of countries comes from cities, so it is not a big leap to say the future of the world depends on what happens in the cities of the developing world, whether the issue is social and political conflict, food, energy, or practically any other."

Children at the Jowii primary school in Kibera, Africa's largest slum, Nairobi, Kenya

Some claim that cities have defused the population bomb: In most world regions, women in cities have one fewer children than those in rural areas. Levels of women's education are sometimes an even more powerful predictor of lower fertility rates—and cities offer far more educational opportunities than rural areas.

Joel Cohen, head of the Laboratory of Populations at Rockefeller University and Columbia University, told his fellow panelists at one Summit session that the world would have to build one city of 1 million people *every five days* for the next 42 years to accommodate the massive rural-to-city migration and the natural population increase that follows. "Is this," Cohen asked, "feasible—physically, environmentally, financially, socially?"

Cohen noted that if fertility rates could be reduced by an average of 0.50 fewer children per woman, the population rise to 2050 would be a comparatively more manageable 7.7 billion. Others have calculated that if global fertility averages could be reduced radically (they are currently 2.5 children per woman, ranging from 7.8 in Niger to 1.3 or less in countries including Japan, Italy, Spain, Singapore, Russia, and Poland), world population might level off and ultimately drop by several billion in the next 150 years. But, population experts note, there's little hope for long-term population stabilization or decline in the absence of stepped-up availability of reproductive health services, as well as broad gains in the status, rights, and opportunities of women.

A CLOSER LOOK

For now and most likely for the remainder of the 21st century, the massive global population increases—flowing with amazing speed and velocity in high measure into the cities of the developing world—seem all but sure to continue. As overwhelming as this rural-to-urban migration tsunami appears, however, the movement from countryside is hardly a new phenomenon. It has been a worldwide push-pull phenomenon for several centuries: pushed by mechanized agriculture reducing the demand for field hands, pulled by the factories and offices of the city providing the lure of better-paid jobs. Whether 19th century Manchester, 20th century Detroit, or 21st century Lima, São Paulo, Karachi, or Dhaka, the trend has strong parallel roots. "Cities are full of poor people because cities attract poor residents, not because cities make people poor," notes Harvard University economics professor Edward Glaeser.

Urban areas, however, need not be synonymous with centers of poverty. A quarter century ago, 600 million Chinese—two-thirds of that nation's population—were living in extreme poverty (on $1 a day or less); today fewer than 180 million—or 13 percent of China's 1.3 billion—are that poor.

the globe's wealth builders

Cities have always been the globe's wealth builders. "That's what they do," *Whole Earth Catalogue* creator Stewart Brand argues. Consider slum areas across the Global South, he suggests: what looks like chaos, deprivation, and nightmarish conditions is often a heartening, exciting picture of human ambition and ingenuity as well. For example, to the outsider's

Gathering before a free Central Park concert, New York, U.S.A.

A street vendor displays shoes for sale, Conakry, Guinea

The World and Its Cities: Defining Terms

THE CITIES OF THE WORLD, large and small, are the focus of this book. Subgroups range from "megacities" or "metacities," defined as having 10 million inhabitants or more, through medium and smaller-sized cities, to areas called "suburban" in North America or "peri-urban" in much of the developing world. Suburban or peri-urban areas are included because they function organically as part of their city (or metropolitan) regions.

In essence, modern cities and their local sister communities fit a modern redefinition of historic city states, which the authors developed in the 1990s to reflect realities of modern urban settlement. Used throughout this book, the terms "citistate," "metropolitan," and "urban," along with "Global North" and "Global South," are worth examining:

Citistate. This is a region consisting of one or more historic central cities surrounded by cities and towns that have a shared identification; function as a single zone for trade, commerce, and communication; and are characterized by social, economic, and environmental interdependence. Citistates are similar to city states of antiquity (e.g., Athens, Rome, Carthage) or medieval times (e.g., the Hanseatic League), except that modern citistates engage in instant electronic communication and capital transfer, and are the chief recipients of world population growth.

Metropolitan. The technical definition of U.S. metropolitan areas (from the U.S. Office of Management and Budget and used broadly, including by the Brookings Institution) is the area surrounding a densely populated core—typically a city of at least 50,000 people. There are 361 such Metropolitan Statistical Areas in the United States. Brookings analysis focuses primarily on the 100 largest U.S. metropolitan areas, which in 2005 had populations of roughly 500,000 people or more.

Urban. While officially designated metropolitan areas (or functional citistates) are fairly easily identified within individual counties, the global definitional challenge is greater. In reality, global analyses of what is urban or not represent baskets of apples, pears, mangos, and more. Why? Each country sets its own definition. And even within countries, definitions are elastic: In 1991, for example, Uganda simply doubled the population threshold for urban areas, from 1,000 to 2,000.

U.N. figures clearly indicate a fast-paced global urbanization trend—with the urban population of the Global South rising 73 percent between 2005 and 2030 (to 3.9 billion) and a 13 percent increase (to 1 billion) in the Global North. Yet it is fair to say that ambiguity swirls around these figures because definitions of what is urban are so varied. The U.N. estimate of a tipping point, more than half the world's population becoming urban in 2008, has likely been so widely accepted because of lack of any authoritative alternative.

Another complication is that a high proportion of urban development is occurring outside established city boundaries. Estimates put Thailand's real urbanization at close to 50 percent, not the official 30 percent, China's at close to 60 percent instead of the official 43 percent, and India's at approximately 40 percent, not the official 29 percent. If these alternative estimates are correct, world population is probably substantially more urban than the U.N. figures indicate. No matter what the numbers are, however, the fact remains that the world is rapidly growing more urban than ever before.

The Global North and Global South. This book employs the division of the world as "Global North" or "Global South," a rough distinction between the more developed countries of North America, Europe, and Japan and the less developed countries of Africa, Asia, Central America, and South America.

The U.N. Millennium Development Goals

THE MOST AMBITIOUS TARGETS for mankind ever officially adopted, the Millennium Development Goals (MDG) were approved by 189 nations and signed by 147 heads of state and governments during the United Nations Millennium Summit in 2000:

Goal 1: Eradicate extreme poverty and hunger
Goal 2: Achieve universal primary education
Goal 3: Promote gender equality and empower women
Goal 4: Reduce child mortality
Goal 5: Improve maternal health
Goal 6: Combat HIV/AIDS, malaria, and other diseases
Goal 7: Ensure environmental sustainability
Goal 8: Develop a Global Partnership for Development

By 2007, halfway to the 2015 target year for most of the goals, significant but uneven progress was being reported:

The proportion of people living in extreme poverty and hunger fell by nearly a third, but remained at roughly 41 percent in sub-Saharan Africa and 30 percent in Southern Asia.

Most economies were failing to provide employment opportunities for their youth.

Warming of the planet, now unequivocal, climbed from 23 metric tons in 1990 to 29 billion metric tons in 2004, raising massive threats to low-lying cities, arid regions, and other areas.

One of the MDG targets (relevant to the communication capabilities of cities around the world) was to make new information technologies more available worldwide. Internet use, by 2005, was growing briskly in virtually all regions of the globe. But while the number of Internet users per 100 people was up to 53 from 43 in developed world regions between 2002 and 2005, it had risen from just one to three in sub-Saharan Africa, two to five in Southern Asia, eight to 15 in Latin America. Cell phone use, by contrast, has expanded more rapidly; Africa's mobile telephony growth rate is the fastest of any world region—up to 192.5 million cellular subscribers in 2006.

eye, city slums can appear to be human cesspools of dire poverty, and in many respects conditions *are* truly nightmarish. But take a closer look, Brand says, and "you can also find people getting out of poverty as fast as they can, working as street vendors, artisans...Slum dwellers are today's dominant builders and designers. Everyone works. Kids usually can get an education in cities. And starvation, a huge issue in the countryside, is pretty rare."

Mumbai—which includes Dharavi, with some 600,000 residents making it the largest slum in all of Asia—may seem crushed by the burden of poverty. But an informal economy hums: on a Mumbai street one may find, in close proximity, a food stall, Internet cafe, bar, gadget shop, grocer, hairdresser, public phone, school, and public transit stop, along with many residents talking on their cell phones.

Global Urban Summit participants agreed that impatient local authorities must resist the urge to simply demolish and disperse slum settlements and force their residents either to flee or be housed in sterile government-financed projects. While income differences may be immense, they are just one measure of the vitality of urban communities. It is true, notes veteran urbanist Janice Perlman (founder of the Mega-Cities Project, which linked formal and informal sector leaders to exchange ideas among major world cities), that "nearly every 'First World' city contains within it neighborhoods reflecting a 'Third World' city of high infant mortality, malnutrition, homelessness, joblessness, and low life expectancy. And nearly

Mega-Cities Project

every so-called 'Third World' city in the developing world contains within it a world of high finance, high technology, and high fashion."

But unexpected progress *is* possible, she adds: "If cities are to be used as laboratories for urban innovation, they can harvest ideas to be exchanged from the Global North to the Global South as well as from the Global South to the Global North—and, let's be clear, South to South and North to North as well."

HARVESTING IDEAS FOR PACKED CITIES

North–South commonality

One major North–South commonality is self-organization by very low-income people anxious to better their lot by creating beachheads of greater self-sufficiency. It was the self-help impulse following the failed federal urban renewal era that sparked creation of community-development corporations in the United States beginning in the 1960s—a critical turning point for many urban neighborhoods. Now this spirit is mirrored in a wave of organizations such as Shack/Slum Dwellers International (SDI), small groups of developing-world people, often women, pooling their modest assets to upgrade their homes, secure titles to the land their houses sit on, build a latrine block, and start a school. Hundreds of thousands of slum dwellers in 26 countries—from Manila to Cape Town, Mumbai to São Paulo—have been mobilized.

Shack/Slum Dwellers International

In the SDI model, explains Jockin Arputham, the veteran leader of the National Slum Dwellers Federation of India, slum dwellers sit right across the table from local government

A busy floating market, Bangkok, Thailand

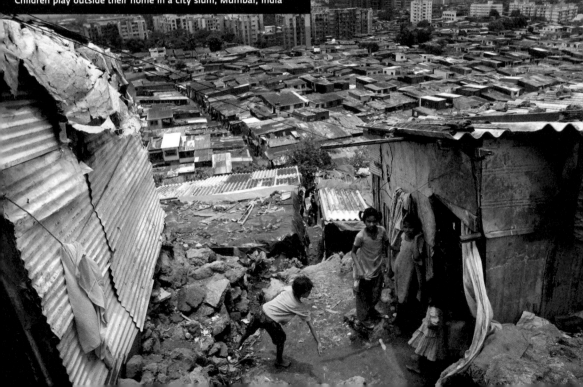

Children play outside their home in a city slum, Mumbai, India

authorities, designing projects and negotiating how they will be financed and carried out. It is a far cry, he suggested, from aid programs conceived elsewhere and then imposed by the United Nations or World Bank.

For all its success, however, SDI's network has yet to fully leverage community social capital for development. Fervid debates took place at the Global Urban Summit on ways to build so-called meta-finance institutions that can provide slum dwellers with investable instruments for housing and infrastructure, financed through links all the way up to mainstream international capital markets. The parallel to the role played in recent decades by so-called intermediary institutions providing housing finance in the United States (the Local Initiatives Support Corporation and the Enterprise Foundation, now Enterprise Community Partners) was compelling.

In late 2007, based in large part on discussions begun at the Rockefeller Foundation Global Urban Summit earlier that year, the Bill & Melinda Gates Foundation announced a $10 million operational and development grant to Slum Dwellers International. The highly flexible funding may even permit SDI chapters to play off the government in one city or nation against another in a search for land, housing, or infrastructure concessions.

Such breakthroughs, realistically, are small chips in the prevailing wall of general indifference of many elites and indifferent middle classes to the cruel circumstances that slum populations face. In the words of Global Urban Summit panelist

Pietro Garau, past chief of research for UN-HABITAT, these

isolated good practices

new approaches are "isolated good practices in the panorama of the big numbers," pointing to the need for serious local government commitment: "If you don't have a body politic at the local level, committed to the right actions, you will not go far."

Yet in direct North–South connections, and programs linking classes in cities, there is at least hope to break down a measure of privileged peoples' feelings that slum dwellers are totally apart from them, close to another species. The Global Urban Summit sessions made it clear to the participants, even those from privileged U.S. cities, that residents of Global South slums are, as one American noted, "more like us than we think." They struggle, as must all families, with crises of health, adolescence, mobility to jobs. They start businesses, schools, and houses of worship.

Susan Pasternak of the University of São Paulo reported that over the past 25 years some South American slums have registered big gains in water and sewer and electric connections, with residents acquiring stoves, radios, refrigerators, even computers and some cars.

And slum youth have dreams easy to identify with. As Asian researcher Arif Hasan told of interviewing young people from low-income families in Karachi, Pakistan, "Every boy wants a motor bike, a cell phone and a girl sitting on the bike behind him. Every girl wants a job so she can have more independence, a cell phone, and a boy on whose motor bike she can ride."

Rising Tides: 21st Century Urbanism

Rakesh Mohan

Deputy Governor, Reserve Bank of India, Mumbai; plenary speaker

AS A MAJORITY OF THE WORLD BECOMES URBAN, policymakers must begin to recognize cities as the fulcrum of world development. Rising tides lift all boats, so all income groups, not just the wealthy, can benefit from the advancement of cities. Institutions such as the United Nations, the World Bank, national governments, and NGOs can no longer mainly target rural economies to mitigate poverty. They must focus on policies that not only accept the inevitability of urban growth but also work to make cities more efficient and equitable.

In many places around the world, urban growth has increased people's access to water, education, and health services, among other benefits. With today's globalized economy marked by free trade and virtually standardized prices of traded products, no particular city or country has much inherent advantage over another. So how well all citizens of countries fare socially and economically will increasingly depend on the efficiency and resources of these cities: their financial institutions and universities, their ability to trade goods, and their capacity to construct improved roads, rails, ports, and airports.

Just a few decades ago, European and U.S. policymakers never imagined that Asia could be the economic competitor it is today. The continent has transformed itself by becoming increasingly urban and increasingly efficient. In Japan, for instance, a heavy concentration of people and economic activity has grown in and around coastal cities. Major infrastructure improvements sparked development of the Tokyo–Nagasaki urban growth corridor, where 60 percent of the nation's residents now live. South Korea has also invested heavily in its principal growth corridor, home to 70 percent of the country's population. Recent decades have seen a surge of economic activity in urban concentrations in Taiwan, Singapore, Hong Kong, and Kuala Lumpur. Today, China is focusing its growth on coastal cities (with the exception of Beijing). The economic growth in all of these Asian cities has demonstrated the value of efficiency, which is facilitated by population concentration and access to trade.

41

Along with quality infrastructure, education is critical to enabling the world's cities to become more efficient. Producing and selling an automobile, for instance, is far more complex than simply transforming a hunk of steel; it involves expertise in design, engineering, and marketing. Recognizing the major role that knowledge plays in urban economies, welfare, and competitiveness, major Asian cities have formed partnerships with universities.

While children in many cities have become literate, the new challenge is providing sufficient vocational education, beginning in secondary school, so that more people are not only literate but are also employable. Technical education has become imperative for successful cities. New models must be created to develop skilled workers, such as Germany's technical education/apprenticeship system. In these late 20th century public–private partnerships, local and state governments coordinated technical training with corporations.

Too often overlooked, quality of life is equally important to a city's current and future vitality and can appeal to people in all socio-economic groups. With overall cleanliness, open spaces, green features, and pedestrian areas, for example, cities can boost their economies in part by attracting "rootless" affluent professionals who can choose to relocate wherever they wish. Well-maintained parks, plazas, widened sidewalks, and improved public transit systems, however, don't just attract the privileged; they can also serve as great equalizers, used by rich and poor residents alike.

With the poorest cities expected to grow the fastest in the coming decades, the world faces a major challenge: How can these critical facilities and urban infrastructure be financed? One answer is innovative partnerships that encourage impoverished people to pool assets. Above all, however, quality urban planning is key. So how do we make urban planning and management sexy occupations? If we could generate funding for new, high-quality planning schools across the globe, we could persuade more talented young people to choose careers in urban planning instead of derivatives.

Urbanization and Economic Growth: Necessary Twin Phenomena?

Was it not remarkable that Rakesh Mohan, in his keynote address to the Global Urban Summit, described cities as the primary economic engines of our time—the sources of creativity, dynamism, and true economic growth in this century?

Mohan is a high official of the Reserve Bank of India. And it is well known that the world's central bankers rarely talk of urbanization. Usually they view national economic stability through a lens of growth rates, inflation, currency, and investments. So how could Mohan have seemingly wandered off the reservation, focusing on *cities*?

The answer is that he is not alone. Mohan's views are spreading rapidly in the developing nations that once saw their future in their rural areas and now increasingly recognize how critical cities are to overall growth and national economic health.

Startling evidence was provided in a paper presented in 2008 to the Commission on Growth and Development, an independent international group headed by Nobel Prize Laureate Michael Spence and sponsored by the Hewlett Foundation along with the governments of Australia, the Netherlands, Sweden, and the United Kingdom, as well as the World Bank.

The paper's author was one of the world's most powerful economic actors—Zhou Xiaochuan, governor of the People's Bank of China. Zhou noted that up to the mid-1990s, the Chinese central government had "resisted urbanization because the authorities thought its pace was too rapid." But, Zhou reported, the Chinese government, recognizing the dynamics of growth inherent in cities, has "reversed policy," responding to "the key role of urbanization" in the transformation of the nation's economy.

The Commission on Growth and Development to which Zhou submitted his observations—and of which he is a member—consists of 21 well-known practitioners from government, business, and the economic policy field from around the world. Their major report, issued in May 2008 after 21 months of deliberation, considered the array of factors that promote growth in developing countries. A primary finding: poverty cannot be reduced in isolation from economic growth—indeed full economic growth *depends on* urbanization. Developing countries must accelerate their rates of growth significantly for their incomes to start catching up with those of industrialized nations, and for the world to achieve a better balance in the distribution of wealth and opportunity.

"The Growth Report," Spence concluded, "kills off once and for all the misguided notion that you can lift people out of poverty in the absence of growth. Growth can spare people en masse from poverty and drudgery. And with India needing to grow at a fast pace for another 13 to 15 years to catch up to where China is today, and China having another 600 million people in agriculture yet to move into more productive employment in urban areas, growth will lift many more people out of poverty in the coming decades."

Many factors do affect economic growth in developing nations. The commission enumerated a substantial list—for example, understanding growth will require leadership, stamina, transparency and support of the population; a nation must be open to engagement with the global economy if it hopes to import knowledge and technology, access markets, and develop its export sector; and it is important to value equity—sharing the benefits of globalization with all classes of society, and dealing with issues of gender inclusiveness.

Housing was noted as a special challenge, as the commission concurred with Zhou's findings that rent controls or restrictions on the use of land "distort private decisions" and "rapidly become very costly." The commission also reflected Zhou's concern that "land is the most valuable asset in urban settings, and how it is allocated, and the mechanisms for allocation, determine how urbanization takes place."

The value of urbanization was underscored in the findings—and not only because of the "agglomeration" theories of the economic power, cited by Mohan, of interaction among multiple corporations, specialized industries, intellectual brain power, and innovation virtually unique to cities. The commission noted that it is "extremely rare" for any nation to achieve per capita incomes over $10,000 (in purchasing power parity terms) before half the population lives in cities.

It is true that a rush to the cities involves downsides—many fast-growth Global South cities, the commission observed, "are disfigured by squalor and bereft of public services." Providing necessary infrastructure early and adequately, and creating stocks of housing provide huge challenges for city governments, challenges they typically lack revenue to address well, making central governments assistance critical.

But is preference for rural areas a feasible alternative? Hardly, the commission concluded. There may be strong reasons for nations to invest in agriculture, which has real economic payoff in today's world markets. But, the panel concluded, "As a way to slow the growth of cities, rural investment is likely to disappoint … No country has ever caught up with the advanced economies through farming alone."

NORTH–SOUTH COMMONALITIES

The big challenge that emerged at the Global Urban Summit was how best to combine insights, strategies, and communications between the Global South and the Global North to enable cities across the globe to have a better chance to achieve prosperity, sustainability, and opportunity. Participants examined new and broadened solutions, along with specific activities of the urban research/practitioner community, ranging from Internet to direct global meetings. While economic and environmental concerns were at the forefront of all the discussions, considerations of equity for various social and economic classes was a major undercurrent throughout the Summit.

Distrust in local authorities, national governments, or professionals in general was at issue. But the *reasons* behind this prevalent distrust were clearly also concerns: simple lack of capacity in many city governments, many localities' support for their elite and apparent lack of commitment to poorer citizens, and both the suspicion and the reality of corruption.

lack of capacity

corruption

Some Global South panelists asserted that the wealthiest in their societies would never concede the privileges they enjoy in today's cities, that we live in a world of indifference, that greater equity could only be achieved through hard "us versus them" political and social conflict. During the Summit's U.S.-focused sessions, there was clear impatience with wealthy individuals and corporations tending only to the growth and security of their own income—the spread, in both the Global North and South, of gated communities and "walling off."

Global North or South, there was clear agreement that equity, opportunity, and the common welfare are inextricably linked—that the potential of improving incomes, education, and environmental standards for even the most troubled groups would, in the long run, provide the optimum benefits for poor and rich alike. The implied formula: More equity equals more opportunity and quality of life for all classes.

Clear strategies emerged during the Summit: Encourage open and candid dialogue between income groups. Build middleclass values by encouraging a socioeconomic mix of people in urban neighborhoods. Tap and develop hidden talents of the poor. Make breathable air and drinkable water a universal right. Create agendas to permit all classes to withstand new century storms worsened by global warming. And don't count on "higher powers"—national governments, specifically, to impose solutions.

Participation is clearly a central element: Unless people believe they are heard, respected, and allowed the chance to participate, they will remain suspicious and resentful of others who "want to help"—a problem most acute in working with low-income communities. This suggests that in any urban initiative, from finance to collecting data to constructing new communities, professionals must listen hard and consistently to the people on the ground who will be affected—ordinary citizens, government workers, private businesses, and NGOs. Tapping new ideas from all realms, creatively partnering, leveraging assets, and building relationships of trust and respect may take time, but they are critical to success.

NETWORKS, A KEY

interdisciplinary approaches

Broad networks—interdisciplinary approaches—are a key to breakthroughs in complex urban problems that resist single-arrow solutions. Health care is not just a medical visit, for example; it means reaching out to women as caregivers, to public health officials, social workers, nutritionists, and mental health personnel, building resistance, discovering "upstream solutions," as well as curing diseases. Likewise, efforts to upgrade slums require broad networks focused on every issue from housing and sanitation to employment opportunities, food markets, and public safety.

Use of data and research tools—from simple neighborhood surveys to increasingly sophisticated GIS (geographic information systems databases) analysis to the kind of satellite monitoring of cities' growing urban footprint is essential. But there is a caution: the tools may be only marginally useful unless the research findings are shared with local governments, integrated across disciplines, and made easily accessible to practitioners and neighborhood representatives. Complex megacities may find real benefits in the new monitoring technologies. Even more dramatic, these 21st century tools may provide make-or-break opportunities (and opportunities to avoid others' mistakes) for the fast-growing smaller cities of the Global South. But in both cases it is effective

South–South networks

networking, especially South–South networks, that is likely to make the critical difference. And the networking can't just be within cities; it must be deepened through frequent

A street barber cuts hair in his "yard," Shanghai, China

Children of the Rocinha favela use a computer at an Internet center established by the rights group Viva Rio, Rio de Janerio, Brazil

global communications exchanges that help ideas spread rapidly to stakeholders.

GROWING GLOBAL LEADERSHIP

Summit participants made frequent reference to U.N. efforts to mobilize national governments to prevent climate disaster; to U.N. Millennium Goals for improving slum conditions; to community-building projects of the World Bank and its sister global finance organizations; and to imaginative efforts by national governments, foundations, and NGOs. All, it was generally agreed, are welcome and necessary, a partial base for 21st century survival, recovery and constructive advance. The participants heard with sympathy the case made by Anna Tibaijuka, UN-HABITAT executive director, for greater U.N. and global attention to the plight of slum dwellers in Global South cities. "Even in the World Bank and the U.N.," she said, "we continually have to combat the mind-set that marginalizes urban issues. But the good news is that slum dwellers are gaining ground in economic recognition for themselves."

national governments

In various forms, a companion idea began to take shape: Is it *also* possible, in this global age, to tap the minds and skills of leaders, activists, academics, and innovators in great cities across the world? Create a global city dialogue of front-line policies, planning, construction, and social action? Explore ways of challenging "same old" approaches, debate alternatives, and mobilize unappreciated human, fiscal, and environmental resources?

Global Cities' Many New Challenges

GLOBALIZATION IS SPELLING AN AGE of competition among world cities. National governments are able to offer their industries less tariff and trade protection. New technologies and efficiencies easily threaten established economies. The scramble for corporate headquarters and activities, research facilities, and manufacturing is often intense. Onetime monopolies may be broken by aggressive business interests in cities halfway around the world.

But trade ties and strategic alliances with other metropolises—some in other hemispheres—may be as vital as competition alone. And many world cities, notes former World Bank official Tim Campbell, are beginning to recognize that they often have more in common with each other than with their national systems. In 80 countries, for example, the process of decentralization is devolving decision-making and some various degrees of added spending powers to localities.

"Of all the global trends on the planet," notes Campbell, "none is more intriguing—more disorganized, yet promising; more unruly, yet filled with creative potential—than the rise of the world's major cities."

Becoming greener—finding inventive ways to save energy and deal with the effects of climate change—is a big part of the challenge. Others are satisfying investors' searches for security and adequate infrastructure and planning well enough to temper the growth of slums while creating parks and attractive downtown areas and lessening the fear of crime—keys to drawing and holding the new century's creative, yet footloose, professional workers.

On the economic front, there is the enticing goal for Global South cities to reverse their traditional dependence on the North and pioneer new technologies: cutting-edge mobile telephone networks avoiding expensive hard-line infrastructure; distributed energy generation; solar and bio-gas to replace the burning of fossil fuels; mobile banking and remittances via cell phone. Global businesses will also be obliged to pay more attention to the Global South market. As the BBC's Business Web site asks, "Would you run a business and ignore 5 billion customers?"

And there's a practical challenge for cities: understanding that in a dramatically shrunken world, their ability to prosper requires close collaboration with surrounding communities. Such cities as Seoul, Stuttgart, and Seattle have illustrated the economic power of full metropolitan

strategies. Now is the time, insists U.S. community economic development strategist Anne Habiby, for systems of "360 degree economics,"
strategically combining the capital and talent of broad metropolitan
regions, and "going local to go global," leveraging a region's foreign-born
nationals to build transnational alliances with international economies.

To build cities that are prosperous, sustainable, *and* inclusive, the mayors and other city officials across the world will need to play a major role in such contact, conversations, and debates. But the capacity of city officials is just one element of this challenge. The fullest talent of the urban world must be engaged in this global debate about critical choices and new directions. Elected and appointed officials, university thinkers, foundations, slum dwellers, bankers, and entrepreneurs bridging continents, disciplines, bureaucracies, and professions—*all* the creative and concerned voices of this urban century will need to be heard, all skills mined.

global urban commons

The time may be ripe, in short, to create a *global urban commons*—face-to-face and Internet conversations to stimulate a worldwide set of new and superior practices, to discover the best mankind can achieve, to forge a global citizenship focused in and on the cities where the human race increasingly gathers.

Notwithstanding the staggering challenges that 21st century cities face, great fonts of knowledge, skills, and both local and global networks do exist and are poised to be tapped. If the world's cities seize these opportunities, they will have more than a fighting chance of succeeding; ignore them and blind forces ranging from climate change to hunger to social conflict may set this urban century on a destructive course. At the Rockefeller Foundation's Global Urban Summit, there was a clear sense of urgency: While the window of opportunity for creative alliances and new strategies may now be open, there is no time to lose.

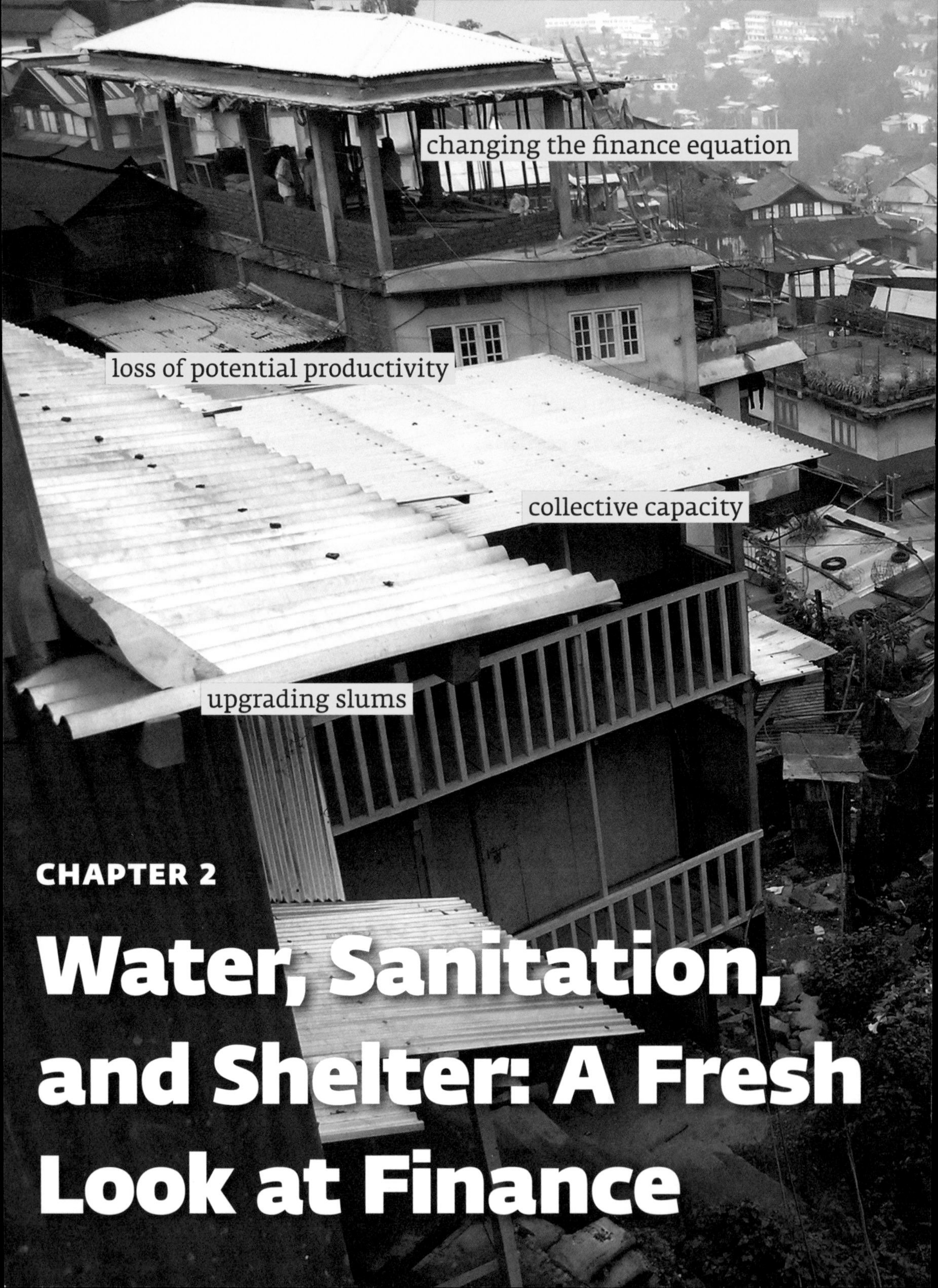

changing the finance equation

loss of potential productivity

collective capacity

upgrading slums

CHAPTER 2

Water, Sanitation, and Shelter: A Fresh Look at Finance

sanitation engineering

inadequate sanitation

innovative financing methods

capital markets

stressful environment

not a crisis for the poor alone

Kohima, India

FOR HUNDREDS OF MILLIONS OF PEOPLE around the world, access to toilets is a luxury and obtaining water for drinking and cooking is an arduous chore. The good news is, as World Bank president Robert Zoellick noted in 2007, global economic forces have lifted some 300 million of the poorest citizens of the world out of extreme poverty since 1990. As he quickly added, however, those forces have left a billion behind. But that billion is just the number of people living in the most primitive conditions on the planet. As much as half the world's population, about 3 billion, subsists on less than $2 (U.S.) a day.

A new look at the role of finance could help increase access to clean water, sanitation, and decent shelter for many. Much heralded for its success in assisting individuals in starting small enterprises, microfinance has also become an effective tool in improving housing with modest investments. Similar approaches taken to larger scale and using the collective assets of organized communities also hold potential for closing the gap on access to water and sanitation.

Over the previous century, the world's leading donor organizations focused on the poor in rural areas. Today, however, with the rural poor migrating to metropolitan areas in vast numbers and with the majority of the world's population now living in urban settings, the new planetary challenge is how to make cities livable for all people. "Many in the world might say, 'Poverty is sad—but the poor will always be with us,' and move on to the next problem," notes Mila Friere, senior adviser to the World Bank's Sustainable Development Network. "However, this is not a crisis for the poor alone. Carrying the economic burden of large concentrations of urban poor will be an expensive mistake for all of us. Conversely, stemming the trends that contribute to urban poverty can bring enormous benefits for *everyone*—in better health, less damage to the environment, better political stability, and higher economic productivity in the most fragile parts of the world."

not a crisis for the poor alone

enormous benefits for *everyone*

Friere's statement, early in the discussions of the Rockefeller Foundation Global Urban Summit at Bellagio, set the tone for this extended dialogue: First it was a remarkable comment coming from a leader of an organization that has long focused mostly on rural, not urban, challenges; second, her forthrightness underscored both the threat from inattention and the rich opportunities in taking action to meet the basic needs of the urban poor of the Global South.

The threat is serious. If the world allows a majority of the earth's increased population to be stuck in squalid conditions, deprived of basic necessities, and cut off from reasonable access to mainstream jobs, what outcome is possible other than a huge loss of potential productivity, at best, and rampant social and political instability and environmental disasters, at worst?

loss of potential productivity

It is important to understand that making necessary change need not be about giving handouts. All over the developing world, examples are emerging of poor people who are channeling their assets and aspirations into improving their living conditions by pooling local savings and showing powerful social cohesion to thwart the forces blighting their communities. But until this commitment among poor people is connected to larger sources of capital than today's meager communal savings, all efforts to mobilize their communities could be wasted.

microfinance

In order for microfinance and similar approaches to significantly improve access to shelter, water, and sanitation, however, mind-sets must change. People who control the flow of capital—from political leaders to banking officials—must recognize that change cannot be only top down. Financing the basic necessities for the least well-off communities must start with intensely local initiatives. The next step is where the finance community enters: making more adaptive credit formulas—not *more lax* credit formulas, simply *nimbler*.

innovative financing methods

Not only are the poor not helpless, but assisting them in financing their basic needs can be a profitable venture for investors. Innovative financing methods, ripe for greater awareness and support, are poised to be taken to scale. And with economic challenges so severe and widespread, taking these new finance models to breathtaking scale is critical.

THE CHALLENGE: ENORMOUS AND STILL GROWING

Across the globe, the trend toward urban living shows no signs of a slowdown. According to U.N. estimates, more than 90 percent of the unprecedented urban growth projected by 2030 will occur in cities in the developing world, the Global South. In Asia and Africa, where nearly 40 percent of people now reside in urban areas, a majority will live in cities by 2030.

Asia already has the largest total number of urban residents, while Africa is the fastest growing. By 2030, the world will have more than 2,000 urban regions with populations more than 1 million apiece.

As people flock to cities for a better life, urban infrastructure and government cannot cope. Already hundreds of millions inhabit what officials politely call informal settlements known as slums by those who live in them. The world's slum population is growing at a rate of 25 million a year. Half the burgeoning urban population of Asia, Africa, and Latin America live in these areas, where families are squeezed into small spaces with dirt floors, sheltered by scrap siding and makeshift roofs. Many women must take a long, perilous journey for a single bucket of water. Limited or no access to toilets results in streams of raw sewage along narrow dirt paths between shanties; in fact, UN-HABITAT estimates that up to 2.5 billion people do not have convenient access to toilets, even in urbanized areas.

Despite these squalid conditions, people continue to arrive in cities. "If the world is urbanizing," says Rakesh Mohan of the Reserve Bank of India, "it's because people think it's a good idea. And they are right: In general, despite the slums, despite the very poor state of many parts of cities, we find reductions in poverty and a continuous increase in access to services—electricity, water, health across the board. Even Mumbai pavement dwellers have access to municipal schools." Yet these families pay a heavy price in their housing quality.

Real Parque favela near Morumbi, one of the city's important financial districts, São Paulo, Brazil

Slum residents collect their belongings after deadly monsoon rains, Karachi, Pakistan

They can only afford shelter in what is usually an illegal settlement, located on the least valuable land—often on a steep hillside or a floodplain, or in an industrial waste zone where few people would choose to live voluntarily.

This type of stressful environment defines life for many in Dhaka, the capital of Bangladesh, where large slum areas rest on a floodplain rife with factory waste water. In this city, 3.4 million people (out of the total population of 13 million) live in some 5,000 slum settlements. Sixty percent of Nairobi's citizens are packed into more than 130 slums squeezed into spaces that take up only 5 percent of the land. In Mumbai, home to Dharavi, the largest slum in the world, half the city's 11 million people live in slums, which are growing 11 times faster than the city as a whole. A hundred thousand or more of these people live without addresses—in the streets, alongside rail tracks, in trash dumps. And unlike the Mumbai pavement dwellers Mohan mentioned, sometimes children from Dharavi and other slums find that schools refuse to accept them. Officially, these residents do not exist.

In amazing contrast, what also defines life in most slums is entrepreneurial hustle—people doing what they can with what they have. A mostly informal economy, even in a massively deprived slum such as Dharavi, creates locally made goods and services that are sold outside the slum. Many of the small enterprises, such as those making textiles or selling recycled goods, are actually registered businesses. And many inhabitants migrate every day to work as gardeners, nannies, construction workers, or drivers for steady, if low, wages. Many more work in the slum as seamstresses, carpenters, masons, and shopkeepers.

Not all the urban poor, of course, live in slums, and not all slum dwellers are equally poor. Indeed, in many of the *favelas* (slums) of Rio de Janeiro, the basics of electricity and water have become stable, along with a robust local economy. Drug lords may constitute the strongest local governance, but life is a far cry from the hardships of Kibera, Nairobi, where human feces in plastic bags thrown from windows and doors have given rise to its reputation for "flying toilets."

no legal entitlement to secure tenures

Often with no legal entitlement to secure tenures, slum dwellers are evicted and must find other informal dwellings. This is sometimes because, whether inspired by civic reform or land speculation, cities bent on improvement slate slum areas for redevelopment. Recent proposals in Mumbai, for instance, suggest that new mixed-income apartments (sometimes viewed by slum dwellers as destructive to their existing communities), or even golf courses or a cricket stadium, would constitute a better use of land.

BACK TO BASICS

The core problem is that sanitation, safe water supplies, and decent shelter are not connected to the world's abundant sources of capital. Although links to creative small-scale financing structures do exist, a persistent gap lies between small-scale and larger capital flows. At the Global Urban

the world's abundant sources of capital

Nairobi's Kibera

KIBERA — with a population somewhere between 400,000 and 600,000 and just one of some 200 slums in Nairobi, Kenya — illustrates the challenge of helping a community afford water, sanitation, and shelter. Nearly 1,200 people are crammed into each hectare; this means that a family of five has about nine square meters of space.

Most housing consists of tin shacks with mud walls. Pit latrines stand in for normal sanitation and each is shared by some 75 people. Aromas of open-air food preparation blend with the odor of human waste as plastic bags filled with feces litter dirt paths. Even if children were recognized as legal residents, sufficient space for them does not exist in schools they could reach. Ideas about upgrading are met with skepticism, with most people suspicious of being "upgraded" to homelessness.

Why does anyone stay? The lure of urban employment, even in the informal sector (such as street peddling), is strong for people whose earlier lives were mired in rural poverty. And where else would they live? Even basic and often substandard tenement housing costs nearly $100 (U.S.) a month, close to a whole month's income for many families. Kibera housing may be illegal, but the rent is only $12 a month.

Yet, as Kenyan Rasna Warah wrote for the WorldWatch Institute's 2007 *State of the World* book, this misery is mixed with "immense opportunity and enterprise…where dreams of escaping poverty are first nurtured."

Mumbai: City of Contrasts

ALREADY HOME TO MORE THAN 11 million people, Mumbai, India, is on its way to becoming the largest city in the world. Nearly half of its people live in slums, however, the largest of which is Dharavi, with a population of about 1 million. Unlike slums that crawl up hillsides at the edges of cities, this one is located in a planner's ideal spot for urban development: right between two principal train lines serving suburbanites' access to jobs, adjacent to Mumbai's new corporate center development, and close to an international airport. Dharavi's residents contribute much to Mumbai's robust economy. Many have mainstream jobs but cannot afford to live in the nicer parts of the city where Manhattan-like prices prevail, leaving an average of some 3,000 central Mumbai housing units vacant at any given time. Others toil as vegetable vendors, construction laborers, factory workers, and domestics—at wages that many would not accept.

Inside this slum, a thriving informal economy generates what is estimated to be about $650 (U.S.) million a year in sales and exportable products. Slum dwellers excel in handcrafts, from creating leather goods and garments to pottery-making. Though many homes have electricity, boasting color televisions, DVD players, and stoves, rain turns dirt paths to slippery mud and the landscape is littered with trash and uncollected garbage.

Because Dharavi is centrally located, there are recurring efforts to redevelop the land. One such recent plan would displace 300,000 people on the promise of on-site relocation into very modest formalized tenement housing—but only for those families who can prove they took up residence in the slum prior to 1995. Dharavi residents, fearful of ending up displaced without being relocated and of having nowhere to restart local businesses, are resisting, demanding a meaningful voice in the redevelopment process.

Mumbai, already the commercial and cultural capital of India, continues its aspirational march toward becoming to India what Shanghai is to China. The city and the state of Maharashtra have committed some $9 billion to improve infrastructure where slum dwellers live. The documented need, however, is at least $60 billion.

Summit, participants explored ways to bridge this gap. That a major first step had already been taken, many noted, was apparent simply by looking around the room. Here in one place, all tackling the challenges of improving access to water, sanitation, and housing, was an unusually broad cross section of international experts: academic researchers and consultants from the field, NGO representatives and government officials, slum-based community organizers and, in especially large numbers, financiers. Summing up the feelings of many, David Smith, founder of the Affordable Housing Institute, remarked how pleased he was that the Summit had "succeeded in bringing all the tribes together for a whole week."

These experts agreed that it is critical to intervene *before* slum dwelling becomes a permanent norm for urban living around the world. While they were eager to move from defining the problem to discussing potential innovations in financing the work that needs to be done, they began by sharing their basic analyses of the problems involved in providing water, sanitation, and shelter to the urban poor.

WATER WOES

There are only two certainties in the debate over water in cities of the developing world: one is that no one lives without water; the other is that there is no definitive count of how many people have difficulty accessing it today. Estimates, derived mostly from sampling with questionnaires, suggest that up to half the urban populations in Asia and Africa,

Children walk on the water pipeline that runs through one of the city's biggest slums, Mumbai, India

struggle for water

and a third of those in Latin America, struggle for water. Some predictions indicate that there will simply not be enough water for the basic needs of these cities, owing to population increases, persistent pollution, and water that is wasted because of inadequate management.

Poor people in slums do of course find water. But it varies considerably in quality and often costs 10 to 20 times more than conventionally piped water. It is usually women in these settlements who are responsible for fetching water, which they must haul in metal or plastic containers as large as they can carry. Not only is this repetitive task arduous, but it can also be dangerous. "Even if you don't care about women going 14 hours a day without a bathroom or risking rape by going out for water at night, you should care about the economic implications," said civil engineer Barbara Evans, pointing to all the time and energy wasted every day by so many people in the recurring search for a life necessity taken for granted by so many others in the world.

When the United Nations' Millennium Development Goals (MDGs) were adopted in 2000, the focus came squarely on water, which was identified along with sanitation as the key driver for lifting people out of the deepest poverty. Launched in 2003 at the Third World Water Forum held in Japan, the influential "Camdessus Report" pointed to the paltry share of national or even local budgets aimed at providing water and called for a doubling of capital flows for water. All sources totaled, though, show that the share of spending remains in the single digits.

How can this be, given how critical access to water is? Some experts believe that donor organizations are still making the transition from an emphasis on rural poverty to the mounting challenges of the urban poor. But scarce resources also reflect a crowded set of municipal priorities, caught in a maelstrom of financing needs. The result: Government fails to make water access important and the formal market cannot profitably serve the very poor without government support. Neither sector seems able or willing to pay to avert the gathering urban storm feeding off this neglect.

Even as most banks come closer to providing financing for housing, "water and sanitation are not equal priorities, often not eligible at all," Ravinath Goonesekera, former mayor of Moratuwa, Sri Lanka, pointed out, lamenting the private sector's general reluctance to pursue financing for water and sanitation projects. Where financing capacity exists, it largely comes from governments and large development banks.

This failure for water to be ranked as key is cruelly exacerbated by local governments' inclination to ignore the existence of these poor settlements, said economist and urban planner Elliott Sclar. Sclar, director of the Center for Sustainable Urban Development at Columbia University, recalls traveling to large Latin American cities and finding that official maps had "grayed out" the slums. In Bangladesh, when a group of NGOs set out to connect a settlement in Dhaka to water points, the water authority took the position that service was simply not possible tenure rights for residents who could not demonstrate any tenure rights.

No one suggests that solutions are simple, but the practices of many large state-protected water authorities appear to be part of the problem. On the outskirts of Lima, Peru, large water towers are emblazoned with slogans such as "Water is Health—Care for It." Yet a million of the city's 8 million people struggle to get daily water, and Sedapal, the state monopoly water company, presides over a distribution system that leaks 40 percent of the flowing water. Internet access is easier than tapping a share of water. To be fair, wasteful leakage is a widespread international problem, whether the water authority is public or private, large or small.

wasteful leakage

Anna Tibaijuka, executive director of UN-HABITAT, pointed out that often it is the local government authority that presents the biggest barrier to getting water to the poor. "How can you deliver water and sanitation," she asked, "when you find that not only is 60 percent of the water being wasted but this high cost is unaccounted for?" Nonetheless, Tibaijuka added, there is a growing Water and Sanitation Trust Fund at work with some $70 million in capital, connected to $1 billion in follow-up investment with the Asian Development Bank and $540 million with the African Development Bank.

Very poor, landlocked Burkina Faso in western Africa has a leading International Institute for Water and Environmental Engineering at its University in Ouagadougou. Though there are numerous water and environmental engineering programs based within African universities, this is a rare free-standing institute, training desperately needed engineers. Burkina Faso

training desperately needed engineers

Regaining Dignity:
Partnerships with the Poor

Anna Kajumulo Tibaijuka

Undersecretary-General and Executive Director, UN-HABITAT; plenary speaker

MY JOB WITH THE UNITED NATIONS is to advocate for the urban poor across the world—a group growing rapidly in number, but still marginal for policy makers. Although to be poor in the countryside is hard, at least life can be lived there despite the difficulty. But to be poor in such growing Global South cities as Nairobi and Cape Town is to lose one's dignity as well.

Yet the process of urbanization is irreversible. Policies intended to send people back countryside have not worked anywhere. From record-breaking city populations of 1 million, the world has proceeded to megacities of 10 million or more and now faces the emergence of "metacities" of 20 million or more.

Poor women—often the first to stretch the limits of urban expansion as they move to cities seeking scarce work and housing—pose a special challenge, one which the UN-HABITAT foundation is currently targeting. Overcrowding is endemic. Slum dwellers are often there because they want to be close to central business districts and their employment possibilities. Try to move the poor out of the center of town and you'll meet resistance because, with their limited access to transportation, proximity is critical for them.

Access to basic water supplies and sanitation is another major issue. Too many cities disregard their basic responsibilities, often allowing most of their pumped water to be wasted. In many countries poor people, frequently obliged to buy potable water from vendors, easily pay 10 to 20 times more per liter than their wealthier neighbors. Because of this, they consume much less water, with malnutrition and disease an all-too-common consequence. Too many municipalities provide services to exclusive suburbs near city centers, while making no provisions for the poor.

For too long, the urban poor have been obliged to work hard while earning little because institutions—bureaucratic systems, harassment, municipalities that allow houses to be built in vulnerable places—disregard their legitimate needs and aspirations. We must begin to view the urban poor as an asset. We must find innovative ways to form partnerships with the private sector, use international capital to leverage domestic savings of hard-working poor people, and recognize that combined economic potential.

Even in the World Bank and the United Nations, we continually have to combat the mind-set that marginalizes urban issues. But the good news is that slum dwellers are gaining ground in getting economic recognition.

also has a sophisticated public–private partnership in place to improve access to water, but it runs into both financial and cultural barriers. Field researchers report that people resist paying for clean water and say they prefer the taste of the water they know, even though it is neither safe nor convenient.

Cost certainly is an issue. Burkina Faso illustrates at least one dimension of the African problem. Its government spends a little more than $13 million a year on water resources (and about $4 million more on sanitation). To meet its share of the MDGs for 2015, that figure would need to be $116 million. In the Global South, 10 million more people gained access to clean water between 1900 and 2004, but over the same period, the absolute number of people in dire need grew by an additional 60 million, a clear sign that the world is losing this race against time.

So what does providing water cost? In a briefing paper provided to panelists, Catarina Fonseca, of the International Water and Sanitation Centre in the Netherlands, cited a recent study that yielded a range of estimates, depending on the type of water provision and the geographic location of the proposed distribution system. Generally the cost for getting water to each household site ranged from $100 to $214 (or twice that if the system were built where no water provision existed before). Costs were a lot lower, according to the Global Water Partnership, if the provision was limited to a standpipe convenient for people to use as a communal source. Those costs, if shared by benefiting households, were $33 to

gained access to clean water

73

$69 per household with annual operating costs of only $8, versus $32 for the household connection.

SANITATION, A SIMILAR STORY

Although the developed world has grown accustomed to private indoor toilets over the past century, for some 2.6 billion of our fellow human beings—both urban and rural—this now routine accommodation remains only a remote possibility. A majority of cities in the developing world have no sewer systems. A 2006 U.N. Human Development report provides this range of cost estimates for various sanitation approaches:

no sewer systems

(U.S. dollars)

A COMMUNAL TOILET OR LATRINE (COST PER PERSON)	$ 12–40
A BASIC SANITARY LATRINE	$ 10–50
AN IMPROVED LATRINE OR IN-HOME POUR-FLUSH TOILET	$ 40–260
A COMMUNITY-MANAGED NETWORK OF SEWER PIPES	$ 40–300
A FLUSH TOILET CONNECTED TO SEWER OR SEPTIC	$ 400–1,500

Consultants in the field have in fact long been intrigued by the possibility of a community network, through which local citizens participate in setting up and managing a system of sewer pipes. They tell and retell the story of the 1980 Orangi Pilot Project, in Karachi, Pakistan, an early experiment in which good quality sewers were installed, serving each house. Those benefiting took responsibility for planning, financing, overseeing construction, and managing the care of the internal pipe system that connected to the government's drains. Costs were a fifth of what the official agency would have charged.

That network now serves hundreds of thousands of people, noted Gordon McGranahan and David Satterthwaite, both affiliated with the London-based International Institute for Environment and Development, in the Worldwatch Institute's 2007 *State of the World*. Attempts to replicate the Orangi results, however, have seen mixed outcomes.

Studies conducted by the United Nations estimated that creating a formal sewer connection would cost from $24 to $260 per person served, per year. An installation as sophisticated as a septic tank would cost $799 a year for every person who benefited. That makes pit latrines a more practical solution for most settlements. Without any running water but enclosed and presumably safe and sanitary, these latrines cost between $11 and $54 per person per year. Since some of this cost is paid to the slum dwellers themselves for running and cleaning their latrines, this process recycles money back into the local economy.

Even at the latrine level, however, cost remains a major barrier, along with the inertia born of entrenched habits developed while living without toilet facilities. Diarrhea, hookworms, and skin boils are a consequence of the absence of toilets as fecal matter seeps into the soil and streams, noted Ravi Singh, of Hasanpur, India, in a September 2007 *Los Angeles Times* article. Though Singh holds no official position, he has become a self-appointed guardian of better sanitation habits. Some 700,000 Indians die each year of diarrhea, most of them under the age of five, according to a 2002 report by the World Health

Organization. Yet, Singh said, when latrines are installed, the long-standing habit of defecating outdoors dies hard. Coping mechanisms developed in the face of the persistent inaccessibility of sanitary, safe, and convenient facilities are not easily relinquished. Singh's solution: shame. He uses a whistle and, at night, a flashlight. Progress may be slow in places where the practice of defecating and urinating outdoors in public is not yet taboo. But without the provision of adequate facilities, no progress is possible at all.

Hundreds of millions of people suffer from disease related to unclean water or lack of sanitation, and U.N. studies catalog a million or more children who die every year as a direct result of inadequate water and sanitation. The death rate of children under the age of 5 is already ten times higher in the developing world's cities than in cities of the developed world; in the worst urban conditions, 15 percent of children die before their fifth birthday. Regardless of whether cost or custom is the main barrier, the conditions in which too many people live are simply unacceptable.

SHELTER: FROM SHACKS TO HOUSES

Already an enormous problem around the world, the lack of adequate shelter worsens every year with rapid population increases. Although new housing is continually built, the formal housing market does not stretch to the most shelter-vulnerable. Filling the void are the many irregular, informal settlements in cities, where the birth rates remain high and

informal
settlements

Shanty town children beat the heat by bathing in the polluted waters of the Wawa River, just south of Manila, Baccor, Philippines

A mobile water vehicle provides drinking water for residents of a local slum, Hyderbad, India

rural migration continues unabated. Here a house is an incremental investment. It starts as one room; over months and years, another is built on. As rooms are added, more families are housed in the same dwelling. When the house reaches three or four rooms, one of the families has often become landlord to two or three others.

These shacks are often improved: When people are able, they add real floors over the dirt and durable walls and roofs, install a basic kitchen, and, if water is available, a tap and a toilet. But these costs are many multiples of residents' incomes, and there is no functioning long-term formalized mortgage market for slums. This is not because these potential customers are uninterested in financing their homes, but because of financial obstacles. (Of course, ownership is not the only option, and often not the best one. But renting can be just as costly.) If the

no written title   landlord has no written title, if the structure is not formally registered, if the building does not meet code, a lender has no hard collateral. If the borrower has no formal income, is paid in cash, or perhaps has no birth certificate, there is no payment record to create a credit history. Add to these challenges the very small size of loans and formal lenders often just give up because the loans they can make still seem too costly for the poor to repay. So the urban poor build their homes one wall at a time, cement block by cement block.

Meanwhile, even as it is hard to expand supply, slum dwellers have minimal income available to pay for housing. The result: families crowded into extraordinarily tight spaces, often only a single room for every function and every person. And, absent some serious intervention, why would anyone expect this pattern to change? As Affordable Housing Institute founder David Smith put it, "Slums are economically rational. They always come into being in rapidly urbanizing environments—*unless* people do something to change the economics."

Slum living means loss of privacy and dignity. It also means constant health threats as anyone's disease becomes everyone's problem. Sleep quality suffers, so daily productivity is limited. In communities with open sewers, contaminated water, and exposure to industrial waste, public health declines.

Those U.N. Millennium Development Goals so proudly adopted in 2000 include one that commits the world to improving the lives of 100 million people who live under these conditions—by 2015. Compared to the size of the problem, the goal was not considered very ambitious. Analysts now argue over whether this limited goal has been largely realized, as communities and governments and donor organizations have worked diligently on assistance. One Global Urban Summit panel suggested keeping the emphasis on the core of the goal, to improve the lives of 100 million slum dwellers, but noted that we must also get serious about alternatives to new slum formation— a challenge that relies on better systems of finance.

MAKING THE POOR PROFITABLE

Governments, investment communities, and donor organizations must learn from small-scale experience and adapt finance

Rays of Light

THE CHALLENGES OF URBAN POVERTY in the Global South are so massive that there is a natural temptation to despair and suggest the problem is just too big, with any possible interventions too little or too late.

But defeatism may be as unnecessary as it is ill-advised. There *is* evidence that governments enlisting the appropriate partners can slow, if not reverse, the trends toward urban slums.

Brazil, Mexico, South Africa, Thailand, and Tunisia stand out for their commitments to upgrading service provision to slums, according to UN-HABITAT. Smaller countries, such as Ghana and Morocco, have also stepped up their action programs. In sub-Saharan Africa, Burkina Faso, Senegal, and Tanzania have reformed policies governing land and housing. Morocco has publicly declared its intention to be slum-free ("*Villes sans bidonvilles*") by 2010, and is backing this promise up with a bold program of social housing construction.

All such programs, of course, depend on good governance: respect for the rule of law, reasonable transparency, and accountability. The upgrading of the *favela* Bairro in Rio de Janeiro is entirely traceable to the institutional structures now built up for efficient service delivery, according to the UN-HABITAT report on the *State of the World's Cities*.

Critical to all necessary advances are government leaders who care about the success of their *entire* societies.

practices to address the difficult circumstances of the urban poor. The first step on the path of progress is acknowledging the assets of these communities: the resourcefulness of the people, their aspirations for improvement, and, yes, even their savings rates, which tend to be proportionately higher than rates for the middle and upper classes. The industrious and organized poor in these communities are fully capable of participating in for-profit financial structures.

As UN-HABITAT executive director Anna Tibaijuka said, housing studies in places such as the slums of Nairobi show that some 80 percent of residents are renting, often at high rates. Still, individuals and, even more important, the collective community, have assets—most notably the enterprise, drive, and intelligence of the slum dwellers themselves.

As World Bank Sustainable Development Network senior adviser Mila Friere noted, "We are emerging from an era of trying things that did not work well—interventions that were top-down, hierarchical, bureaucratic, the kinds of processes that the middle and upper classes are accustomed to navigating." Gradually replacing this mentality is an appreciation of the social and knowledge capital inherent in the collective assets of a community—however poor its citizens may be. "This is a new thought for some in the finance world," said Bruce Cameron of the Overseas Private Investment Corporation. The social cohesion of a community, he said, becomes "the first line of collateral and in turn leverages some 'free' money [donor capital], which starts up the ladder toward serious market capital."

collective assets of a community

Changing
the finance
equation

Changing the finance equation by starting with community organizing has not yet caught on among financial institutions, where, as Joel Bolnick, director of the Community Organisation Resource Center, in Cape Town, South Africa, explained, "If you say 'community organizing' or 'political capital,' they hear 'confrontation' and 'ideological activism.' What they miss is the power of monetizing the social capital of the community." When 5,000 families put their collective savings on the table, they demonstrate not only some economic equity but also community organization and political activism. They become a body large and capable enough to sit across the table from government and the private sector. The result can be a real transaction.

Rose Molokoane, a grassroots activist on the board of Shack/Slum Dwellers International, is involved in housing and tenure issues in many international cities. Referring to poor citizens and banking institutions, she admitted, "Well, it's

don't trust
each other

true that we don't trust each other. We go to banking institutions who say we cannot get loans by pooling our resources." Affordable Housing Institute's David Smith added that the problem is compounded by all "the Stone Age financial forms" that remain the currency of real estate transactions all over the world, with down payments, amortization schedules, and reams of paperwork for every detail. Or, in the words of Alfredo Stein, a veteran urban development specialist in Latin America and Africa, "It's men in dark suits behind desks requiring forms and avoiding risks."

COMMUNITY COHESION AS CAPITAL

So how is this culture changed? One starts, argued Stein, with changing the culture of financing institutions to respect the assets the poor have, especially their ability to save and make their payments. "When they are screening for a loan," he said, "they should pay attention to whether it is a woman applying because they are the best payers and that should earn points, and they should look at the whole household, the collective income."

Mary Mathenge, the chief executive officer of Kenya's National Cooperative Housing Union, said this is a matter of "making the communities themselves responsible." Smith agreed but, like Stein, emphasized that credit should also turn on *individual* reputation. Rather than rely on some computer-generated rating, he suggested, ask people in the community, "What do you think about Pablo?"

SHELTER FINANCING SOLUTIONS

Mortgage finance. The standard financing approach is not impossible to use, but is difficult for the poor in most of the developing world. Many cities lack formal registration systems for titles, even if the poor can demonstrate the rights of ownership. Besides, mortgages are rarely issued to people whose incomes do not come from the formal employment sector. In her extensive briefing to the Global South assembly, Diana Mitlin, an economist with the International Institute for Environment and Development

A couple walks by a slum in Tijuana, Mexico

Evidence of slum clearance in the shadow of middle-class housing, Abuja, Nigeria

and the University of Manchester, emphasized the proportional size of the *informal* economy in Africa (41 percent), Latin America (42 percent), and Asia (26 percent). Plus, as Mitlin added, low-income residents typically do not finance an entire house. In the developed world, a house is a finished product before it is occupied; in the Global South, the house is occupied long before it is ever finished. The incremental improvements residents make are largely thanks to their savings. In India, she said, more than 80 percent of housing finance comes from family savings and nonformal sources of credit. A study of 53 households in a favela in Rio de Janeiro found none using a bank for housing; 60 percent were using savings. In Angola less than 2 percent of housing investments came from banks.

thanks to their savings

Panelists generally agreed that up to now mortgages play a very small role in financing shelter for the urban poor, but, as a strategy, it shows up on every list in the hope that more imaginative approaches will emerge to better serve people with limited resources.

Social housing. Some Global South nations are exploring direct government provision of "social housing," a system of subsidies and direct government construction, development, or ownership. This is used in Chile, Costa Rica, Brazil, Argentina, Singapore, and South Africa (as well as in a variety of forms throughout Europe). It resembles what is usually called "public housing" in the United States. The subsidies require some compulsory savings on the part of benefiting communities, but so far are targeted mostly to building entire homes rather than making incremental improvements.

Community funds. Here the approach, which emerged from a pilot in the Philippines, emphasizes a savings and loan system that sets up funds for collective investments in acquiring land, constructing basic infrastructure, and building or improving houses. The idea goes beyond mere finance: It seeks to build strong bonds within the community. The members depend on each other for success and can together create significant leverage in dealing with governments.

Microfinance. A relative newcomer showing considerable promise, microfinance is evolving from its roots as enterprise loans to become a more robust strategy for helping the poorest citizens improve their housing situation. The reason: it works. Where an enterprise microfinance loan might be $500 for five months, a housing microfinance loan might be $2,500 for 18 months. Even though housing microfinance loans are larger in amount and longer in tenure, their default rates are still phenomenally low. The clear indication is that poor people who have proven to be good at saving are also reliable at repaying loans.

The iconic example (just as Pakistan's Orangi sewer project was for sanitation) is the experience of the Grameen Bank, which started in Bangladesh and whose founder, Muhammad Yunus, was honored with a 2006 Nobel Peace Prize. Grameen Bank now has more than 2,000 branches in some 65,000 different villages. Of the nearly $6 billion it has leant, the loan recovery rate is a solid 98 percent. What banker would fail to love that?

loan recovery rate

Grameen has always taken a social capital approach, requiring borrowers to apply as a small group of people, using their moral guarantee as the underlying collateral. One or two of the group may initially benefit; the prospects for the others depend on the reliability of performing on the loan.

Emerging especially in Asia and Latin America, micro-finance loans fit the need because they can finance adding rooms, upgrading the materials used for floors, walls, or roofs, or adding kitchens and toilets. Though microfinance is some-times deployed to add basic infrastructure for water supply, extending it to the water and sanitation challenge goes slowly.

Usually there is an NGO playing a key catalytic role. The panelists heard an accounting of work in Nicaragua, where more than 12,000 households saw their homes improved through microlending of about $800 each. These loans leveraged improvements from local governments and made connections with financial intermediaries more likely.

homes improved

A STRATEGY FOR SCALE

Any plan for scaling up the most promising approaches has to begin with the capacity question: Where can the requisite monies be found? Trying to settle that early in the discussion, Barbara Hewson, managing director of NewLine Capital Partners, rushed to the front of the room to write on the board and declare that "no one should say that the barrier is insufficient capital." She then proceeded to post on the board the rough numbers—all the discretionary global capital, by categories. "At any given time," she said, "it's more than a $100 trillion." Having worked both at Lehman Brothers and JPMorgan Chase, Hewson is experienced in capital markets. Yet, skeptics said, while there may be capital, it is inaccessible to the global urban poor, who are not recognized as a profitable base of customers. Further, because there will never be sufficient capital from donor organizations alone, or even from responsible governments, the private sector must be induced to play a role as financier, even as government is the source of subsidy and donor organizations provide seed capital to create new entities and financial paradigms.

How much would it cost to take upgrading slums to scale? Since estimates vary, the 2005 Task Force on Improving the Lives of Slum Dwellers, coordinated by Sclar and assisted by Gabriella Carolini, an international development fellow at Columbia University, analyzed the leading research on costs and projected a total of $66.5 billion from 2005 to 2020. The task force assumed this would cover purchase of land, housing upgrades, necessary infrastructure, community facilities as well as some programs to build more community capacity. That figure rounds out to $42 per beneficiary per year over the target period.

The task force report, entitled *A Home in the City,* went on to lay out a scheme for finance. If 30 percent of the investment needed could be recovered through small loans and 10 percent were generated by the residents themselves, this would leave $39.9 billion to be raised from donor organizations and governments—or about $2.5 billion a year.

capital markets

upgrading slums

If, as the task force report suggests, middle-income developing nations could handle the upgrading in their cities without the external subsidies, then the numbers become even more manageable. The donor organizations' share would be $1.4 billion a year, while governments in these developing nations would provide $2.3 billion.

upgrading is feasible

So for about $600 per person in today's slums, upgrading is feasible. But skeptics quickly point to the further challenge of bad governance in a number of developing countries. And worse than merely bad governance, corruption within government persists as a corrosive deterrent to the level of investment needed to finance basic necessities for the poorest citizens.

Although there are formidable barriers to improving the lot of even 100 million people now in slum settlements, a strategy for success is apparent and feasible. And the price of failure is high—for everyone. To overcome both scarcity of capital and skepticism from the financial world, the persistent execution of a sound strategy is key. From the first round of discussions at the Global Urban Summit, here are the essential elements of an effective strategy:

Start with the communities. Organize the demand for change. Let this organized demand create the change in supply policy.

Shack/Slum Dwellers International (SDI) is a prime example of this approach. Founded in 1996, this organization has demonstrated the potential of taking the demand principle to scale. SDI has its roots organizing in India during the 1980s.

It was then that an NGO, Society for the Promotion of Area Resource Centers (SPARC), teamed with a women's network called Mahila Milan, to set up a process for communities to take responsibility for managing money, mostly made available by the state, for the community upgrading process. These groups demonstrated that saving just a rupee a day (about two U.S. cents) adds up to collective capacity not just for emergencies but to finance community improvements. These funds were used to leverage more financing, and the communities assumed responsibility to assure that loans would be repaid by the individuals who benefited.

collective capacity

SDI has now organized savings programs that assist some 6 million members in 14 countries. In 11 other countries, SDI is helping to organize savings groups and building federations for families living in slums. It has also been instrumental in securing land rights for 125,000 families and creating nearly 80,000 new housing units. This has led to SDI's formation of Urban Poor Funds, which take advantage of any available grants or subsidies to offer households lower rates of interest than the formal sector does. The payments per household are typically lower than the rent they were previously paying. These transactions not only support improvement in housing but they build leverage in securing tenure rights to the land and in persuading local authorities to improve the delivery of safe, reliable water and sanitation services.

organized savings programs

Another important benefit is that groups gain critical sophistication in managing finance at the community level and

at the community level

Golden Eggs:
Harnessing the Promise of Shadow Cities

Sheela Patel

Co-founder, SPARC
(the Society for
Promotion of Area
Resource Centres),
Mumbai, India

POVERTY, CLIMATE CHANGE, AND URBANIZATION are the most crucial issues for this century. This triad was brought together at the Rockefeller Foundation Global Urban Summit in 2007. For representatives from Slum/Shack Dwellers International (SDI) who attended the Summit, some very important lessons emerged for moving forward. First, there is huge potential in disparate groups of people interested in a particular set of issues meeting as equals in a neutral environment to explore possibilities—learning to understand each other's points of view with patience and examining new ways to address old unsolved problems. Second, we must recognize the power of local and global connectivity to turn a vertical hierarchical structure into a circle; today, global and local entities are so closely linked that they are both critical to developing scalable solutions. Third, with much of this century's development drama taking place in urban areas, we must build new skill sets to engage each other to transform what appears to be crises into potential opportunities.

SDI, including all its affiliates in Asia and Africa, has found that it is not only national governments that have ignored the implications of an urbanizing world, but also foundations and bilateral and multilateral agencies. So it is with these perspectives in mind that we discuss what is required for investments in practical terms, such as institutional capacity building, research in options, strengthening civil society to participate or even lead the process, and terms under which finance should be provided. Even as I write these words, however, the doom and gloom scenario-setting, especially related to poverty, climate change, and urbanization, almost blocks exploration of what human creativity and ingenuity can produce as responses.

In most countries in Asia and Africa, rural areas bring in the majority of votes for national parties and crucial leadership elected for national and provincial governments comes from rural areas. In many of these countries today, most of the dissent faced by national governments is from urban areas. This means that urban issues often take a back seat on political agendas, behind other development issues. Almost all political parties find their overall experience historically in rural development. When governments receive international support, most of this too has a rural focus. When private foundations seek to align with existing priority setting by national governments, they join this process as well. This further delays any urban agenda setting.

Meanwhile, cities and towns become geese that lay golden eggs. Global and national trading services, institutions, and enterprises set in cities produce taxes, wealth, and political donations that are welcomed. But impoverished shadow cities—the informal areas that usually include 15 to 50 percent of all residents—are ignored. In many cases, this is because, with aggregate data reviewed on basic amenities, civic services, or health outcomes, urban populations seem better off overall than rural populations. Rarely is the data disaggregated. When it is, the serious problems facing the poorest half of the urban population become evident.

Since governments and international agencies have ignored urban problems for so long, challenges due to urban poverty, environmental degradation, and other allied conditions often seem insurmountable. Now, when governments and international agencies are suddenly pushed to consider these neglected issues, they sometimes take outdated or inappropriate urban policies off the shelf. Other times they look to examples they have read about or seen in another nation. In India, for instance, the newly set up delimitation exercise is redrawing constituencies based on population. Since urban agglomerations have increased considerably in India in the last ten years, this will now give urban areas more representation. It will be useful to examine the implications this has for development investments.

Market-driven forces can certainly aid urban areas. While some markets emerge and scale up naturally, however, many others have to be produced. Clearly market-based solutions have not magically appeared to produce urban infrastructure or housing or equitable livelihood options for the poor. The persistence of poverty and increasing gaps between the rich and poor in cities is evidence of that. All the ingredients for developing new market possibilities may exist but clearly they need some deep research and experimentation to link demand to supply of resources, embedded in a framework laid by policies that provide incentives for such a strategy. Unfortunately, though, in many parts of the world today, the foundation for such a country-level framework, a stable fiscal environment, is yet to be in place.

learn the advantages of taking vital next steps to connect with higher, more market-oriented sources of continuing capital. In addition, the process itself often significantly improves cohesion within the group, relationships among residents, and pride in the community.

Redefine the relationship between lenders and borrowers. Here David Smith may have captured the shift perfectly:

There are essentially three kinds of money: debt, equity, and subsidy. Debt is what bankers think about. It's regular. I can sit behind my desk and make decisions and minimize risk. Subsidy, on the other hand, comes from governments or grant makers. If I give it to you, you should be grateful and I also want to suggest that you buy vegetables with it. The equity model is fundamentally different. It's how the banks themselves were built. It's my money, my confidence, and I can make it grow. Of course, subsidy can be turned into equity, and that's what counts, as people decide they own this asset and can create more with it.

With that terse analysis, Smith finds the juncture between subsidy and equity and underscores the need to take whatever subsidies that may come and convert them into leverage and longer-term equity. Carrying out this step, however, usually requires some sort of financial intermediary organization.

As to lenders, they need not be consigned, as in Dante's *Divine Comedy*, to a flaming desert in the seventh circle of hell, but they do need to awaken to the moral and civic obligations and the missed opportunities of neglecting the financing needs of poor citizens. Of course there are risks, but most risk, where the lender has the option to seize collateral, lies in extending more credit than a household can reasonably manage (look to the United States experience in 2007 and 2008 when too many households could not handle the payment ladders built into subprime loans).

Are the aspirant poor a bad bet? An August 2007 issue of *The Economist* reported the other side of the credit risk. Professors conducting a study at Yale University and Dartmouth College reviewed some 787 rejections for loans in Cape Town, Port Elizabeth, and Durban, South Africa. To test the prevailing standards of who is worthy of credit, they persuaded the lending authorities to reverse their decision for a random 325 applicants. Most of the loans were short-term, often as little as four months. Interest rates were predictably high. But, as it turned out, so were profits for the lenders. Some would say that because interest rates were high, the poor were exploited. A subsequent review of the randomly selected applicants a year later showed lower hunger rates, poverty rates down by 19 percent, and a greater likelihood of employment. The reason? Though interest rates were high, the loans were small, so the outlay cost was low, and the recipients used the money for essentials, such as finishing a new room or buying a sewing machine.

James Mwangi heads the Equity Bank of Africa and offered Global Urban Summit participants ample testimony to both the viability and profitability of lending to motivated poor citizens. Equity Bank, which is listed on the Nairobi stock exchange, has 1.4 million depositors of whom some 400,000 are urban residents. The average balance is $200. The average

lending to motivated poor citizens

loan is $600. Mwangi declares the risk is no greater than among more advantaged people; that the real collateral lies in the community organizations and their ability to put pressure on people to make their payments.

Mwangi's biggest problem is raising capital without compromising his principles of giving the best breaks to the poor. So far he is sticking with his principles, telling Summit participants, "If someone says, 'Here is $10 million but this is how you must use it,' you should say, 'Keep your money.'" Mwangi could easily attract more capital if his bank were charging higher interest rates, but that would undermine the bank's mission. He said the bank's experience shows that lending to the poor at lower rates is profitable. And as evidence, he cites how other banks in Kenya are rethinking their rates and terms to participate in this growing market. Mwangi knows the hard numbers, but he contends that with all the collective knowledge bearing down on this challenge, "We will make a breakthrough. The future is in our hands."

Accept the logic and inevitability of incremental improvements. A 2006 report by Global Urban Development, written by Donatus Okpala and colleagues, estimated that 70 percent of housing improvements in poor Global South areas occur in progressive stages, not all at once, confirming what panelists said at the Global Urban Summit.

If a community has access to a water tap, or a well, a system of piping can progressively expand to bring a water source closer to households. The number of latrines can increase and be located

FINANCING INFORMAL COMMUNITIES

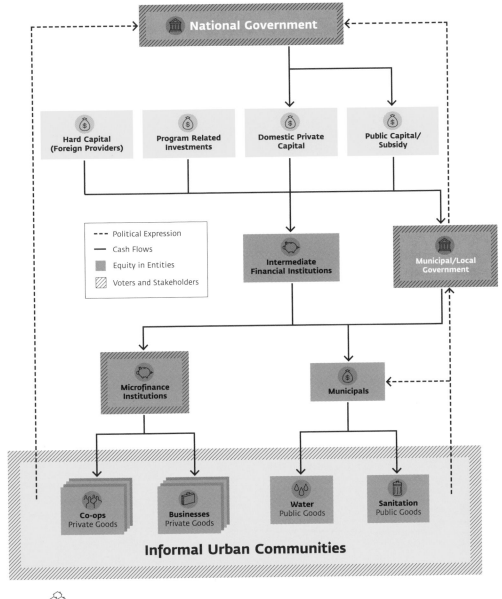

National Government

Hard Capital (Foreign Providers) — Program Related Investments — Domestic Private Capital — Public Capital/Subsidy

- - - Political Expression
— Cash Flows
Equity in Entities
Voters and Stakeholders

Intermediate Financial Institutions — Municipal/Local Government

Microfinance Institutions — Municipals

Co-ops Private Goods — Businesses Private Goods — Water Public Goods — Sanitation Public Goods

Informal Urban Communities

Affordable Housing Institute   Credit: Diagram by Jason Lee

Dilapidated homes bordering an ecologically dead river, Manila, Phillipines

New apartment buildings overlook an impoverished squatter camp in Soweto, Johannesburg, South Africa

for improved safety and convenience. Improving in steady steps makes financing a more realistic strategy for using the collective assets and borrowing power of a community.

Mobilize community assets into larger aggregates. Use the clout from a larger pool of savings and commitments to leverage entrance into higher capital markets. While micro-finance and other small-scale strategies have shown dramatic progress, the key is finding a way to climb the finance ladder up to intermediary finance organizations and then all the way to those major capital markets that Hewson pointed to in her assertion about capital capacity.

a certified success

Microfinance is now a certified success and is gradually extending its reach to housing and infrastructure improve-ments, as communities organize their collective capacity. While microfinance is oriented to individual loans, higher up on the chain of finance there are intermediary organizations with the capital and connections to tap the larger scale sources of capi-tal. The missing link has been between the communities of the urban poor and these intermediary organizations. This is where the concept of *meta*finance emerges. As Lisa Schineller, who is responsible for the Latin American Group of Standard and Poor's, explained, "You leverage off the small savings pool of a group to build up to a community-wide level. That's how you get to larger amounts, longer duration, and more bearable interest rates."

Another vital connection, director of Cape Town's Community Organisation Resource Center Joel Bolnick added, is helping community-based organizations (CBOs) engage with the proliferating community of microfinancing institutions (MFIs). Sometimes, beyond different languages of nations, there are terminological gaps, quipped Sclar. "We say CBOs and we're talking about 'community based organizations.' A banker hears the same acronym and thinks 'collateralized bond obligations,' and a U.S. housing advocate thinks 'Congressional Budget Office.'"

Participants came to new conclusions, based on a more relevant definition of the relationship between borrowers and bankers, and on the new logic of a chain of capital starting with the community. These new relationships, new logic, and new connections require specific action steps. Reporting from one of the groups charged with brainstorming strategies was Sumila Gulyani, World Bank staffer and former director of the Infrastructure and Poverty Action Lab at Columbia University. Gulyani first reminded everyone of essential conditions for

scaling up small successes

scaling up small successes. "You have to rely on the municipality or the state as the unit of action," she said. "You should start with a national framework with a macrofinance conception because local government has constraints ranging from money to mindsets." Some panelists did not agree with this fine point, but wholeheartedly agreed with Gulyani when she said, "Finance may turn out to be a small part of the problem. What we need most is good ideas."

Panelists agreed to a list of strategic levers that could overcome barriers:

- Reliable, community-based, integrated, accessible information from census and GIS (geographic information systems) databases
- Inclusive planning processes that produce real plans
- Capacity building through organizing the demand for improvements
- Outreach through communications and media
- A chain of finance that completes the connections to outside capital

Once the poor are seen not as needy beggars but rather potentially effective partners and profitable customers, it becomes plausible to expand existing capital sources and add new ones. Participants cited the potential for expanding the Urban Poor Funds internationally, adding reimbursable seeding fund operations, coalescing more capital for infrastructure through regional banks, and aggregating housing loan potentials.

There is little question that more imaginative tools and structures are emerging. One example is eBay's MicroPlace. com. Reaping returns of 1 to 4 percent, people use this Web site to invest in lending organizations around the world that make loans to poor traders, farmers, craftspeople, and others to start or expand small businesses. As founder Tracey Pettengill Turner explained, "You get your principal back with your rate of return." Turner was inspired by the Grameen bank experience. Pierre Omidyar, founder of eBay, was already deep into this strategy, having put hundreds of millions of dollars into

imaginative tools and structures

microlending, including Kiva.com, which links individual investors with specific struggling entrepreneurs in the developing world. Kiva has been so successful at attracting capital that it sometimes temporarily runs out of borrowers. The next step, as panelists consistently said, is developing the metafinance capacity.

The new logic behind the power of finance rests on the assumption that success is built on demand and the will and collective capacity of the poorest communities. Essential elements for helping people afford water, sanitation, and shelter are now clear:

- Focus on the full scope of the challenge, not just what seems easiest to finance at the moment. Water, sanitation, and shelter are interdependent. Any missing element drags down the prospects to lift people into full participation in a civil society.
- Mobilize the community to save and pool its assets to leverage its influence and financial access to credit markets.
- Use the network of NGOs as well as bilateral and multilateral donor organizations to fill the gap between the capacity of microfinance to meet the first level of improvements and the supply of capital needed to take these models to serious scale.

Grants may not be necessary, as reports have suggested, in cities and nations with more income or where creative credit enhancements will build the credibility of unconventional borrowers. Still, the scope of the challenge, given the number of slums and the number of people in them, is simply enormous. Nothing less than a major escalation of financing capacity, despite all the optimistic declarations, stands a chance of meeting the minimal MDG goal. Besides, participants agreed, the world should do more than the minimum.

Alfredo Stein, an urban development specialist on Latin America and Africa, reminded the group that there are many institutions hard at work on this challenge. "Just take Central America," he said, "where we think we are reaching about 6 percent of urban families in need. That's a lot of people, but it's still only 6 percent."

And Bolnick, the Community Organisation Resource Center director in Cape Town, warned against the usual practice of taking models that work in the market and pushing them down to make them work for the impoverished. "On the other hand," he said, "if we create a model designed to work for the very poor, it is much easier to scale that up to work for the less poor, where the market can actually support the solution." Diana Mitlin, the International Institute for Environment and Development economist, reminded the group that at least 35 percent of the poor are well beyond the reach of the market.

Where does philanthropy fit into this new equation? As the group was reaching its conclusions, Rockefeller Foundation president Judith Rodin noted, "Remember, philanthropy should be the risk capital, not for projects, but to underwrite the effort that shows how innovations can be scaled up to the need." She said that Rockefeller would use its influence, possibly more than its grants, to persuade others to focus on this challenge. "If it works for the poor," she added, "it can be scaled up for others. But it doesn't work in the other direction."

philanthropy should be the risk capital

CHAPTER 3

Climate Change Resilience: An Urgent Action Agenda

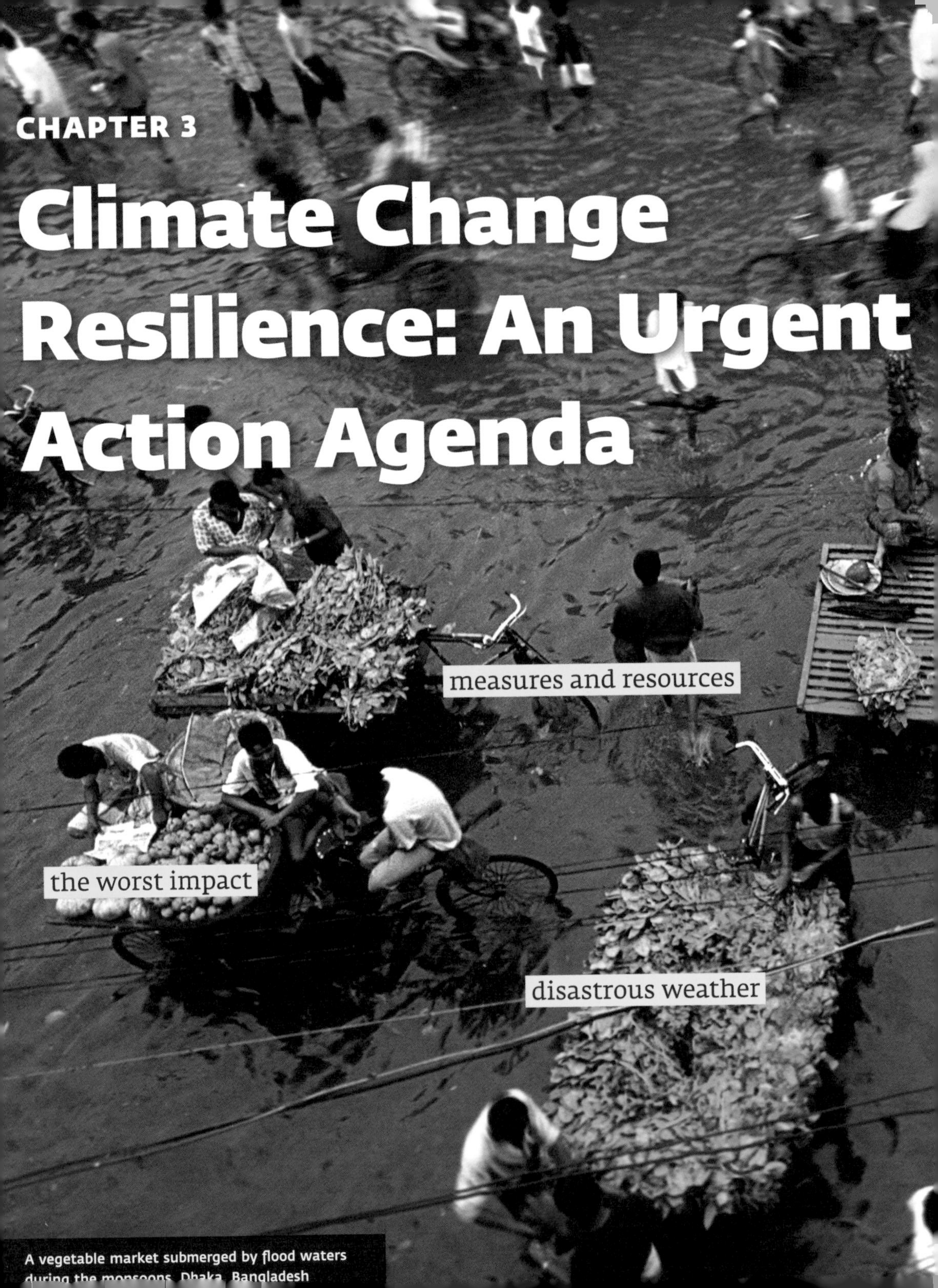

measures and resources

the worst impact

disastrous weather

A vegetable market submerged by flood waters during the monsoons, Dhaka, Bangladesh

finding local allies

carbon-cutting energy investments

talk globally

prepare for weather variability

threat of sea level rises

organized awareness

THE 21ST-CENTURY WEATHER FORECAST IS GRIM. Predictions call for more sudden storm surges and floods. Rising waters imperiling coastal cities around the globe. Broad areas of sustained droughts. Severe ice storms, devastating heat waves. Too much snow in Chicago, too little in the mountains of Austria, savannas disappearing in South Africa, raging fires in Australia, South Asian delta floods too frequent to mention.

Much of the 600 percent growth in low- and middle-sized nations' populations that has occurred over the past 50 years has been in cities, and most of that growth has occurred in geographic areas most vulnerable to climate change. Forty percent of the world's population now live near or on coastlines.

The United Nations forecasts that some 50 million people will become environmental refugees—not at the century's end but by the end of this decade. The immediate gravity of potential climate impacts was dramatized by Global Urban Summit panelist Saleem Huq, founder of the Bangladesh Centre for Advanced Studies, an author of key papers for the International Panel on Climate Change and current head of the Climate Change Group at the International Institute for Environment and Development. Huq declared that "our only chances to cope with global warming challenges lie within the next 20 years—that's our only window." Yet just three months later, Summit speaker and IPCC chair Rajendra Pachauri of India would state baldly: "If there's no action before 2012, that's too late. What we do in the next two to three years will determine our future. *This is the defining moment.*"

environmental refugees

So how is the world to cope?

The major response of Global North cities has been—and is likely to continue to be—mitigation, steps to reduce greenhouse gas emissions. As the debate continues over how rapidly to mitigate the sources, however, a growing number of cities of the North are undertaking aggressive measures to build resilience (or adaptation) to the inevitable effects of climate change that are already on the horizon. Especially for the more vulnerable Global South, this is the central challenge: fortifying the ability of developing countries to bounce back from the dire climate impacts that now seem certain to occur.

aggressive measures to build resilience

Mitigation involves methods of slowing down the buildup of greenhouse gases triggering global warming. Such steps range from individual and business energy conservation tactics to nations engaging economic tools such as cap-and-trade systems and "carbon taxes." For wealthier societies, global warming seems an inconvenience, built on an assumption that the wealth and know-how will be there to build new infrastructure, if need be, for protection.

Meanwhile, the incontrovertible fact is that Global North greenhouse gas emissions, starting with heavy coal burning two centuries ago, compounded by massive oil consumption in the past century, account for all but a small slice of the carbon increase that the scientists confirm is now altering the world's climate. Yet national and personal aspirations for a higher standard of living in once-poor countries have also begun to fuel demand for industrial growth and personal affluence. China, for example, is on the fast track to replace the United States

greenhouse gas emissions

as the number one contributor to greenhouse gas emissions— a trend accelerated not only by added vehicles, but massive industrialization and expanding numbers of coal-fired power plants. The proportion of people in China who own automobiles already approximates the U.S. ratio in the 1920s. In India, personal auto use is soaring; a low-cost auto just came on the market. Both China and India are home to several cities that are highly vulnerable to climate change effects, ranging from droughts to floods.

Looking forward, a preponderance of scientists now see a tipping point beyond which even the most aggressive mitigation would be rendered meaningless by the scale of the environmental impact. For roughly 1 billion of the world's city dwellers who already live in dire physical circumstances of low-quality hous-

mitigation is a distant theory

ing and grossly insufficient public infrastructure, mitigation is a distant theory. For them the only course is to prepare for and rebound from the weather calamities that seem virtually certain to come. Yet for the most part, these cities and urban neighborhoods remain vulnerable.

Already faced with deficient health care systems, overburdened transportation, and many other disadvantages, cities of the Global South also face massive challenges, even with political and public will behind efforts to build resilience. "How can you adapt roads or sewers or storm drains or water pipes that aren't there?" asks David Satterthwaite, senior fellow at the International Institute for Environment and Development.

Northern Lights

EVEN AS THE DEBATE AMONG COUNTRIES over climate change agreements rages on, a growing number of cities in the Global North are undertaking new policies and infrastructure investments designed to adapt to everything from heat waves to floods to water shortages.

Retrofitting flat-roofed buildings with vegetation is now a prominent movement in Basel, Toronto, and Linz, while Chicago leads with a number of public buildings and New York City has an ambitious plan to go beyond just green roofs and retrofit every commercial building for energy efficiency.

In Germany and Belgium new installations to harvest rainwater are being combined with imposition of variable water tariffs, providing significant incentives for reducing water demand. In addition to variable tariffs, Melbourne has instituted permanent restrictions on water use, in anticipation of climate-change induced shortages.

Philadelphia has linked weather forecasting to a Heat-Line and a system both for wide notification of heat crises and for checking on the most vulnerable population. Similar systems are emerging conspicuously in Shanghai and Lisbon. Based on a mapping of its heat-island effects, Tokyo is introducing corridors of greenery to provide ventilation paths to offset some heat effects.

The London Climate Change Partnership has set out to document the best adaptation practices in an effort to see that London emulates the most effective adaptation measures as rapidly as possible.

lack of basic
infrastructure

This lack of basic infrastructure, other Summit panelists noted, easily produces chronic public health deterioration: malnutrition, susceptibility to water and airborne diseases, malaria, diarrhea, and dengue.

The awkward combination of Global North responsibility and Global South exposure to the worst effects of climate change generated ongoing political tension, including a heated discussion after American participants heard Huq and other Global South leaders place blame squarely on the North. Pachauri, whose International Panel on Climate Change would later share the Nobel Peace Prize with Al Gore, was among those who stated that prime responsibility for climate change rests with developed nations. And he added a socioeconomic aspect, evoking memories of New Orleans, "where the worst impacts of hurricane Katrina fell on the poorest of the poor."

the worst
impacts

Yet looking forward, as director of the Center for Sustainable Urban Development at Columbia University and moderator Elliott Sclar stated, "adaptation is the key. If we are going to reverse climate change, we first have to survive long enough to do that."

Sclar also explained the emphasis on the places where the poorest people live. If one improves the conditions for the very poor, the result will be solutions that will work for everyone, he said. Adaptations to climate change that will protect the poor can always be scaled up so that they have broad benefits. But if the approach is to move ahead with the strategies broadly targeted at the entire population, experience shows

broad benefits

A Dangerous Divide:
Combating the Effects of Climate Change

Rajendra K. Pachauri

Chairman, Nobel Prize-winning International Panel on Climate Change; Director-General, the Energy and Resources Institute of India (TERI); plenary speaker

WARMING OF THE CLIMATE SYSTEM is now unequivocal. Global mean temperatures have increased, average sea levels have risen, and snow cover has decreased in the Northern Hemisphere, along with glacier mass and ice caps. Eleven of the last 12 years have been the hottest in recorded history. Compromising coral reefs, tundra, boreal forests, coastlines, marshes, and low-latitude agriculture, the impacts are systemic. This shift in climate can also lead to a range of health problems, from respiratory complications caused by deteriorating air quality to the spread of vector-borne diseases.

Best possible projections indicate a further rise of 1.8 to 4.0 degrees centigrade in this century. The most direct effects will not only be felt in the Arctic and sub-Saharan Africa but particularly in the mega deltas of Asia, such as Dhaka, Calcutta, and Shanghai, as well as in all small islands. While the prime responsibility for climate change lies with developed nations, the poor are those who suffer the most when climate disasters strike—whether in developed or developing countries. Witness Hurricane Katrina in New Orleans.

Across the globe, a dangerous economic divide is widening. In Dhaka, for instance, a city that boasts gleaming shopping malls selling fine silk, 50 percent of the children live below the poverty line. Enormous disparities in income leave poor people relegated to unprotected housing in the most environmentally exposed parts of cities while the privileged increasingly gather in reinforced, gated communities.

For generations, urbanites have distanced themselves from the realities of nature. In the name of urban growth, cowboy economies have glorified the reckless exploitation of anything in one's path. The result has been 150 years of greenhouse gas emissions, despite the many warnings that this path is not sustainable. While we certainly must combat the causes of climate change, we must also increase resilience to the environmental impacts already under way. Especially in delta regions, cities must invest in protective infrastructure, more appropriate zoning and building-design regulation, and better drainage facilities to handle storm surges.

Major changes in lifestyles are also imperative everywhere. From the production of more efficient cars and the systematic reduction of carbon dioxide emissions to the increased use of recycled water and better consumer choices all around, individuals and governments must redefine cultural patterns. Through these efforts, we *can* help mitigate the inevitable effects of climate change.

the disproportionately large plight of the poor is invariably forgotten and left out.

The exposure issue is highlighted by the fact that in 1950 the world had only one "megacity," a place of more than 10 million people—New York. There are now 17 such megacities, with 14 of them along coastlines. Eleven of the 17 are in Asian countries. Current predictions are that by 2015 there will be 20 megacities, many in the developing world, noted Pachauri. He went on to describe an incident in one of those megacities, Mumbai, just before he traveled to the Global Urban Summit: "A week ago we had terrible rains in Mumbai. Within a period of 20 hours we had 553 millimeters (22 inches) of rainfall. The entire city was brought to a halt. The worst affected were naturally the slum dwellers. Because their homes are little shanties that are not built on platforms, they get flooded." After such floods, Pachauri noted, outbreaks of disease are common. The great challenge, he suggested, is to "come to grips with the massive growth that is taking place in the slum populations," finding ways to shield their inhabitants from the fullest and most severe effects of climate change.

most severe
effects of
climate change

Yet the issue, he stressed, is not of building resilience alone, but also the effects of globalization. Pachauri mentioned that more than 70 shopping malls were under construction in India. "What is the design of these shopping malls like?" he asked. His answer: They are virtually identical to those constructed in North America. They are energy guzzlers of the worst kind "and certainly don't use even the traditional knowledge by which we in India have buildings that go back 2,000 years, which, without air conditioning, offered a substantial level of indoor comfort. If we don't use those skills, we've lost them. We just construct boxes and we fit them with air-conditioning equipment."

talk globally

The challenge now, Pachauri continued, "is to talk globally both in terms of mitigation *and* adaptation toward resilience. Construction of good buildings that are relatively climate-proof also represent a measure of mitigation quite apart from the fact that the buildings will be adapting to changes in climate in the future. Because they will be consuming a lot less energy in a conventional sense, they will also be mitigating and reducing the emission of greenhouse gases."

So began a week's exploration of emerging innovations in building climate change resilience. Academic experts, NGO staffers with extensive experience working with nations and cities, local government officials, private-sector representatives such as engineers, and the media participated. More than a dozen nations were represented, with the majority coming from low- and middle-income cities in developing countries.

BARRIERS ALONG THE PATH TO RESILIENCE

Even if most world leaders now agree that climate change

legitimate threat to the world's stability

is a serious, legitimate threat to the world's stability and prosperity, corrective action appears slow. One might easily imagine a rush to align public investment capital around the best adaptive measures known, with a priority on the most vulnerable places. Sadly, this is not yet the case. In fact the resilience agenda, while taking hold in isolated locations, remains blocked on multiple fronts.

Infrastructure that does not exist cannot be improved. The elemental step in any resilience strategy is to strengthen the physical infrastructure: the water pipes, electricity lines, drainage systems, and roads. Perhaps as many as a billion people live in places where infrastructure is so slight or even nonexistent that the idea of improvements is absurd. People are living in shelters cobbled together on hillsides or on floodplains. Sometimes just ordinary heavy rainfalls bring floods to these settlements, damaging fragile structures; waterborne diseases such as diarrhea often follow. In Latin American countries, the most common weather disaster is flooding, which regularly swamps an inadequate infrastructure. Though experts agree it was not caused by climate change, the 2004 tsunami rising out of the Indian Ocean killed 230,000 people and starkly revealed the vulnerability of coastal communities.

disastrous weather

Scarcely a season now passes without some disastrous weather episodes wreaking havoc on communities of the world's poorest peoples. A cyclone hitting the southwest coast of Bangladesh in November 2007 took 3,000 lives and affected over 900,000 families. The devastating tropical cyclone that struck Myanmar (Burma) in May 2008 killed over 85,000 people, left 54,000 missing, and flooded over 1 million acres with salty seawater. So common are lesser though serious storms that they rarely make front page news.

Severe flooding of the Grijalva River leaves a street covered in garbage, Villahermosa, Mexico

In an extensive background paper for Summit discussions, Satterthwaite, the International Institute for Environment and Development senior fellow, collaborated with other experts to explain the goal of building resilience in the tens of thousands of urban centers that are most vulnerable to climate changes. Vulnerability, they noted, has been increasing for decades— indeed across the very decades since an organized awareness in the 1950s led to international commitments of technical assistance to struggling populations. In the 1970s many international agencies committed to "meeting basic needs." Mission failure: today there are more urban dwellers of low- and middle-income nations living in poor quality and overcrowded housing with little or no basic infrastructure than the total 1975 urban population of the Latin America and Caribbean region, Asia, and Africa combined.

organized awareness

The urban poor are disproportionately located in the lowest elevation coastal areas. Gordon McGranahan, director of the Human Settlements program at the International Institute for the Environment and Development, pointed out that these low coastal elevations comprise no more than 2 percent of the world's land, but hold more than 10 percent of the world's population. And those proportions double for low- and middle-income nations.

Satterthwaite, et al., reported that the coastal provinces of China experienced a net in-migration of 17 million people in just the five years between 1995 and 2000. African countries have 37 cities with more than a million people. Half of those cities, including Lagos and Alexandria, are in the low-elevation coastal zone. Much of Mumbai, India, home to the largest slum settlement in the world, is built, essentially, on landfill. The city's low elevation makes it a continuing target for weather disasters.

Shanghai and Dhaka are other examples of large cities in this zone of coastal low elevation. Each of their urban regions has more than 10 million inhabitants. Each has become a robust economic force in its country. Much investment, along with human capital, is at stake in building adaptation measures. But Bangladesh, in particular, has earned the dubious distinction of the world's capital for natural disasters. Today, the Himalayas shed their melting snow, while the entire country, flat and barely above sea level, straddles the largest river delta in the world. Add unusual rainfall, and the country faces a future barely floating above survival. Persistent poverty and corruption, compounding the effects of inadequate infrastructure and poor services, further diminish future prospects.

Competent government is too often the missing piece. Indeed, lack of a fully professional government at the national and local levels explains nearly all the conditions of extreme vulnerability that urban populations face. Bad land-use planning results in the poor being priced out of participation in normal housing markets. The norm in the developed world is that local governments assure rights to property ownership, promote an atmosphere of public safety, and provide basic

human capital

necessities such as water and sanitation services. No such assurance exists where a third of urban humanity resides. Instead, our fellow global citizens live in uncomfortable, even dangerous concentrations without assurance of rights or reliable services. Often there is no drainage system, or if one exists, it is frequently clogged by uncollected garbage or encroaching building structures. In Dhaka, new buildings often result in filling in drains; new road construction frequently blocks an area's natural drainage pattern. When international organizations approve funds for improvements, the money goes to national governments, because that has been their consistent practice. And at that level, many other priorities are arrayed in competition with local investments.

Often public officials complain that they have too many pressing priorities—for example, education and skill gaps, lack of basic medical assistance, or the need to expand job potentials for their residents. Too often, local governments either do not have or choose to ignore information about the looming environmental threat. If the data are not clear, officials cannot grasp the significance of the impending dangers. And even when officials do comprehend the threat, they may see it as so overwhelming that the first response is just to throw up their hands.

Still, having clear data is a critical start. Sclar recalls vividly the time when he asked local government officials in Nairobi about air quality. "Officials told us they didn't need air quality data, because they already knew that air was bad. But

looming environmental threat

clear data is a critical start

Monsoon rains cause death and destruction in the city's slums, Mumbai, India

Rescue team members and volunteers work in the wake of a mudslide, Medellin, Colombia

when we showed them it was 500 times worse than any comparable U.S. cities, things changed," he said.

If local governments acted responsibly, the Global Urban Summit panelists indicated, public policy would not ignore informal settlement patterns or simply prohibit them. Rather, policy would dictate conscious investment in residential alternatives for the population of the lowest income. A practical regulatory framework would be developed. Settling on floodplains would be stopped before it could take hold.

conscious
investment
in residential
alternatives

But the reality is, as panelists said repeatedly, that local governments typically lack both the capacity and the cash to do the "responsible" thing.

Nonetheless, the resilience proposition boils down to basics. The first priority should be to stop doing anything that makes climate change resilience-building even more difficult. Climate change experts call this practice "maladaptation." People in the United States should recognize this immediately from the stories of what the government contemplates in the wake of the Katrina disaster in New Orleans—propping up levees and postponing the restoration of the natural coastline barriers. Ed Blakely, the official now charged with directing the New Orleans recovery, said as much, in condemning the focus on Band-Aids and missing the need for ecological surgery.

maladaptation

It is at this point that the debate unfolds between market-based and more interventionist solutions. Direct government response may seem the most expeditious and can be effective for basic infrastructure. But often government initiatives take inordinate amounts of time or are ill advised (a prime example is the U.S. Army Corps of Engineers' history of building levee and dam structures that create more problems than they solve).

While there is tension about approaches, however, the notion of government interventions versus the market is largely a false dichotomy; all market solutions assume some government capacity to carry out work, so what government can do is always a significant matter. Government, for example, can create market-based incentives. In the New Orleans case, for instance, it could provide regulatory incentives, perhaps a competitive fund, for engineering firms that develop plans to restore the coastal wetlands that historically provided major hurricane buffering. In many Global South locations, government incentives could encourage firms to develop and deploy engineering solutions to shore up weakly constructed buildings in likely storm paths. Incentives could also influence future development in growing regions. Potentially, local government monies could be made available on a matching fund basis with climate resilience-building funds provided by large donor organizations. The underlying point is that critical elements include flexibility of approach, no automatic preference for either public- or private-sector solutions, a clear-eyed view of what produces results, and the use of methods that serve not just powerful private interests, but the basic needs of poor populations as well.

flexibility of approach
public- or private-sector solutions

Other priorities compete for attention and tug at purse strings. Aromar Revi, a leading consultant and founder of TARU, a South Asian research firm, suggested looking at this barrier through the lens of fast-growing India. Over the next 20 years, India will find an additional 220 million added to the 300 million people already living in its cities. The numbers of urban dwellers who are desperately poor are already 70 million and growing. Delhi, Mumbai, and Kolkata (Calcutta) will be among the ten largest cities in the world. Seventy-five smaller cities will grow to more than a million each.

India faces six simultaneous transitions:

- Demographic: growing and also aging
- Geographic: from rural agriculture to urban economies
- Educational: from basic schools to technical and university preparation
- Economic: from local to global economic platforms
- Energy: from oil and coal to gas and renewable sources
- Environmental: from brown to gray to green

Officials feel the pressure, Revi said, to mount each of these challenges, which add up to nothing less than a transformative impact on the entire Indian society. So now the world comes along and says India should shoulder its share of the climate change challenge. According to Revi, "Here's the official position in India: 'You created it, we didn't. So we don't really need to do anything right now. If it comes to it, we'll adapt, but that is way in the future.'"

India is likely a typical case of a country beset by deep poverty amid growing affluence of those with a good education. Climate change has to compete with investments in the economy, in the education of more people, and in institutions and infrastructure. Despite the country's success over the past decade or so, there is still limited mobility potential for most citizens and severe competition for scarce resources. Much of the infrastructure is still substandard, and public services are not improving rapidly.

Revi told participant colleagues that India's push for adaptation must start by finding local allies and forging the right political balance for partnerships, avoiding the top-down approach that is so traditional. Despite daunting obstacles, India must respond: "Mitigation is nice," he said, "but adaptation is mandatory."

Too many professionals in the developed world promote solutions that were conceived in arrogance and born in silos. Building resilience to climate change appears to require considerable customization and scaling to a variety of local situations. There are innovations worth studying and spreading, but Summit panelists agreed that the Western world must get past the notion that it knows what to do and others should simply follow its good advice. Actually, the Global North, with its land consumptive, automobile dependent patterns, doesn't really know what to do, as Satterthwaite put it, "and we have 50 years of disastrous practice to show for it."

Paul Brown, a California engineer, confessed to a kind of epiphany from the Summit discussions. "I now see," he told his colleagues, "that even in the most prosperous part of the world, we're already beginning to retreat from the command-and-

finding local allies

STRATEGIC CLIMATE DRIVERS & RISKS: COASTAL FLOODING, DROUGHT & GLACIAL MELT

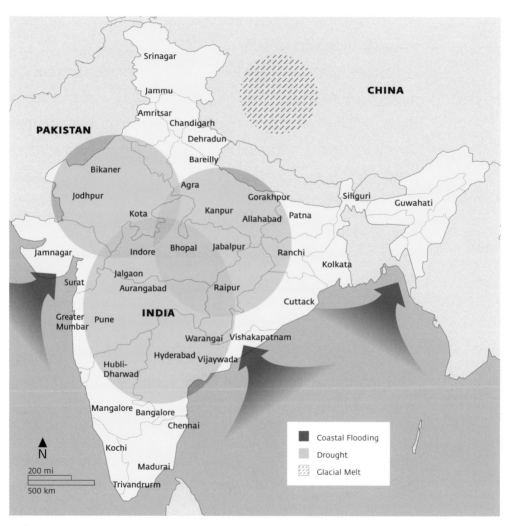

Credit: Aromar Revi, Rockefeller Foundation Global Urban Summit at Bellagio, July 9, 2007

control, large-scale, hands-off system that separated people from nature, urban from rural. We're moving rather toward multijurisdictional, integrated risk-management systems with heavy stakeholder involvement, hands-on, high perceived uncertainty, and heavy reliance on contingency planning."

Brown and others agreed that, in addition to virtually reinventing the processes of engineering good solutions, professionals had to find escape routes from the well-conditioned silos of separated practices. There are water people, energy people, planners, environmentalists, on and on. Each group is looking out for its own, single agenda, with few paying any attention to the crosscutting challenges and to how the whole picture looks. It is no mystery, then, panelists agreed, that proposals are too standard, too limited, and do not seem to fit the problems well. Michael Gelobter, who heads the U.S.-based Redefining Progress organization, pointed out that there are some 70 separate environmental organizations "all locked up in their own bureaucracies and narratives." This is at a time

actions across the boundaries when such extraordinary potential exists for synergistic actions across the boundaries that lie between health, infrastructure, economic development, natural resource preservation, poverty-reduction, and disaster management goals. Any group stuck in a silo will become irrelevant.

Participants pushed for planning that would cross all these boundaries—unleashing a new generation of profes-
local governments and community organizations sionals trained specifically for this coalescing agenda and oriented to work closely with local governments and community

organizations. *New York Times Magazine* writer James Traub suggested calling this new breed a set of "SWAT teams." "That'll make it sound more terrifying," he said, not entirely in jest. (See Chapter 5 for more on training professionals to work in an integrated, cross-disciplinary fashion, particularly on Global South issues.)

SIGNS THAT SUCCESS IS POSSIBLE

It often surprises people who live in wealthy nations just how basic the needs are in the cities of the developing world. In Africa, for example, the density of weather monitoring equipment is eight times less than the world standard. Scarcity of course sometimes leads to innovative responses, such as the massive use of cell phones in Thailand as a basic warning system.

Some resilience-building has been focused on prevention. Satterthwaite, et al., point to both Manizales, Colombia, and Ilo, Peru, where over the past decade NGOs with universities and community-based organizations have worked with local authorities to settle the rapidly growing low income populations into viable areas supported by water, sanitation, electricity, and waste removal. As a result, the poor do not fall victim to illegal developers, ending up in areas prone to landslides or flooding.

But all world nations now facing the climate change threat are challenged to produce more adaptive plans. For those classified as LDC nations (Least Developed Countries), the challenge was set in 1994 by the United Nations Framework

HEALTH RISKS OF GLOBAL WARMING

As temperatures and sea levels rise, so does the jeopardy to human health.

An increase in greenhouse gases triggers environmental changes . . .

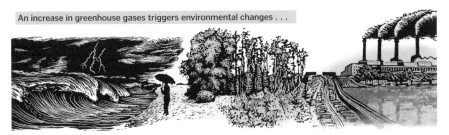

Altered weather and oceans **Shifting ecosystems** **Environmental degradation**

. . . that yield a variety of effects . . .

Heat **Extreme weather and sea-level rise** **Waterborne diseases** **Vector-borne diseases** **Air pollution**

. . . that have numerous consequences for human health:

Heat-related illness and death, especially in the elderly, the very young and the chronically ill.	Crop failure, leading to malnutrition and starvation.	Injury and death from floods, storms and fires.	Health problems of displaced populations, including diarrheal diseases, malnutrition and micronutrient deficiency, and psychological trauma.	Cholera, hepatitis A, leptospirosis, cryptosporidosis, dinoflagellate "red tides," and food and shellfish poisoning, notably from salmonella and vibrio bacteria.	Malaria, dengue, yellow fever, hantavirus pulmonary syndrome, viral encephalitis, chikungunya fever, Rift Valley fever, schistosomiasis, scabies and Lyme disease, among others.	Asthma, allergy and coccidioidomycosis, and chronic lung and heart disease, among others.

Credit: *The Washington Post* 12/17/2007; Patterson Clark; The Lancet, Proceedings of the National Academy of Sciences

SELECTED EXAMPLES OF PLANNED ADAPTATION BY SECTOR

SECTOR	ADAPTATION OPTION/STRATEGY	UNDERLYING POLICY FRAMEWORK	KEY CONSTRAINTS AND OPPORTUNITIES TO IMPLEMENTATION (Roman text= constraints; *italics* = opportunities)
Water	Expanded rainwater harvesting; water storage and conservation techniques; water re-use; desalination; water-use and irrigation efficiency	National water policies and integrated water resources management; water-related hazards management	Financial, human resources and physical barriers; *integrated water resources management; synergies with other sectors*
Agriculture	Adjustment of planting dates and crop variety; crop relocation; improved land management, e.g., erosion control and soil protection through tree planting	R&D policies; institutional reform; land tenure and land reform; training; capacity building; crop insurance; financial incentives, e.g., subsidies and tax credits	Technological and financial constraints; access to new varieties; markets; *longer growing season in higher latitudes; revenues from 'new' products*
Infrastructure/ settlement (including coastal zones)	Relocation; seawalls and storm surge barriers; dune reinforcement; land acquisition and creation of marshlands/wetlands as buffer against sea level rise and flooding; protection of existing natural barriers	Standards and regulations that integrate climate change considerations into design; land-use policies; building codes; insurance	Financial and technological barriers; availability of relocation space; *integrated policies and management; synergies with sustainable development goals*
Human health	Heat-health action plans; emergency medical services; improved climate-sensitive disease surveillance and control; safe water and improved sanitation	Public health policies that recognize climate risk; strengthened health services; regional and international cooperation	Limits to human tolerance (vulnerable groups); knowledge limitations; financial capacity; *upgraded health services; improved quality of life*

SECTOR	ADAPTATION OPTION/STRATEGY	UNDERLYING POLICY FRAMEWORK	KEY CONSTRAINTS AND OPPORTUNITIES TO IMPLEMENTATION (Roman text= constraints; *italics* = opportunities)
Energy	Strengthening of overhead transmission and distribution infrastructure; underground cabling for utilities; energy efficiency; use of renewable sources; reduced dependence on single sources of energy	National energy policies, regulations, and fiscal and financial incentives to encourage use of alternative sources; incorporating climate change in design standards	Access to viable alternatives; financial and technological barriers; acceptance of new technologies; *stimulation of new technologies; use of local resources*
Transport	Ralignment/relocation; design standards and planning for roads, rails, and other infrastructure to cope with warming and drainage	Integrating climate change considerations into national transport policy; investment in R&D for special situations, e.g., permafrost areas	Financial and technological barriers; availability of less vulnerable routes; *improved technologies and integration with key sectors (e.g., energy)*
Tourism	Diversification of tourism attractions and revenues; shifting ski slopes to higher altitudes and glaciers; artificial snow-making	Integrated planning (e.g. carrying capacity; linkages with other sectors); financial incentives, e.g., subsidies and tax credits	Appeal/marketing of new attractions; financial and logistical challenges; potential adverse impact on other sectors (e.g., artificial snow-making may increase energy use); *revenues from 'new' attractions; involvement of wider group of stakeholders*

Note: Other examples from many sectors would include early warning systems.
Credit: Climate Change 2007: Summary for Policymakers of the Synthesis Report of the IPCC Fourth Assessment Report, November 2007

Convention on Climate Change, which originated what is now called National Adaptation Plans of Action (NAPA). One of the panelists, Mozaharul Alam, a researcher at the Bangladesh Centre for Advanced Studies, said that his country, well aware of its geographical vulnerability to flooding, had already organized working groups. Their agendas focus on cyclones, excess salinity, flooding in lowlands, and effects on agriculture, livestock, and fisheries along with food security, and threats to basic industry and the region's infrastructure. (Estimates of Global South agricultural curtailment due to global warming range as high as 40 percent in India, 30 percent in Africa, and 20 percent in Latin America by 2080, according to the Washington-based Center for Global Development. Food supplies on those continents could be in critical shortage, especially as their urban populations rise rapidly.)

The Summit's climate change panelists enjoyed the advantage of having among them the key figure in directing one of the best resilience examples documented to date. Debra Roberts heads the Environmental Management Department of eThekwini Municipality, which has the responsibility for managing Durban, South Africa. The mere existence of a department by that name, headed by a very well-informed public official, distinguishes Durban on the adaptation scene.

best resilience examples

In 2004 Roberts ran a series of seminars on climate change for municipal officials, using materials and insights from a four-month-long program in the United States focused on the science of climate change and its local impacts. Her belief, now well accepted, was that local governments are not likely to do anything about climate change effects unless they see real benefits for their city. That was the first priority, Roberts told the group. What followed was a series of "headlines," elements of a strategy for the city to respond to the threat of climate change. Then officials began incorporating responses into the long-term planning for each department. Roberts's work included reaching out to tribal leaders, who might not otherwise have been included in planning. When she mentioned this to participants, the principle struck a chord of common experience. David Satterthwaite immediately reminded the panel of how often there is talk about building grassroots enthusiasm for difficult issues in developing countries. "I can think of four or five illiterate women who have showed up for climate change projects and turned out to be champions," he said.

building grassroots enthusiasm

Durban's strategy was completed in 2006, identifying actions to be taken and assigning them to the departments of municipal government that seemed to be in the best position to implement change. Durban has a generally thriving economy based on petrochemicals, banking, and automotive production, though unemployment remains stubbornly high. There is a large informal settlement zone just off the coast, where poor shelter structures and overcrowding pose a fragile target for flooding and the waterborne diseases that follow. But an even greater worry to the economy is the threat of sea level rises to the region's industrial zone. Just as concern was crystallizing

threat of sea-level rises

Urban Core Economic
Assets at Risk

Informal Settlements
Subsistence and Vulnerability

Rural Drought Belt

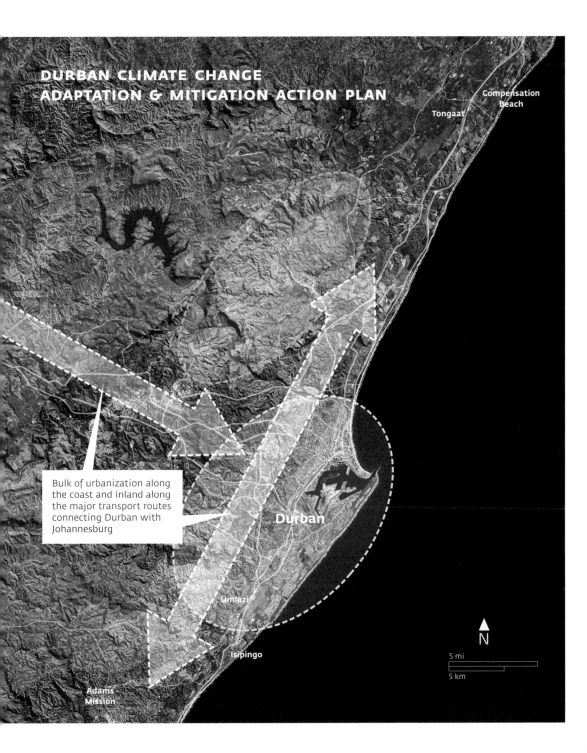

DURBAN CLIMATE CHANGE ADAPTATION & MITIGATION ACTION PLAN

Compensation Beach

Tongaat

Bulk of urbanization along the coast and inland along the major transport routes connecting Durban with Johannesburg

Durban

Umlazi

Isipingo

Adams Mission

N

5 mi
5 km

The Trinity River and its levees near downtown Dallas, Texas, U.S.A.

City officials open cooling centers as temperatures approach 100°F, Chicago, Illinois, U.S.A.

in the minds of officials, several storms in early 2007 roiled the region, inflicting extensive damage to infrastructure.

So Durban's strategy is becoming increasingly specific. Shoreline defense, previously calibrated to no more than a 20-centimeter rise in sea levels, had to be adjusted. Water supply strategies must now incorporate both droughts and excessive rainfall, with a premium on measures that reduce the demand for fresh water. Urban drainage must be improved and new buildings constructed away from risky locations. Catchment basins for runoff must be designed and built, if industrial areas are to be protected. A key step: mapping the risk and targeting the resilience measures by risk levels. Durban is in a leading position to showcase the critical steps, from disaster-coping to proactive preparation for disasters.

mapping the risk

ACHIEVING RESILIENCE: WHAT DOES IT LOOK LIKE?

Maps and data. Participants agreed, based on experience in such places as Cape Town, South Africa, and Karachi, Pakistan, that local hazard mapping is the most effective starting point. A picture of the problems persuades people in the community to participate and becomes the foundation for a new conversation with local government officials. In addition to the best evacuation routes, maps should show where housing, as well as business and industry locations, are imperiled by such threats as predictable rises in water levels. These maps should help generate open local debate on key questions: Where might drinking-water supplies be compromised by sudden salinization or

generate open local debate

contamination from industrial factory waste? Where and how might drainage systems be compromised? How might food supply chains be interrupted? (An awareness of these perils, it was noted, leads both citizens and their local governments to an awareness of second-stage dangers of dehydration and malnutrition, as well as standing water that invites outbreaks of mosquitoes, which carry the deadly malaria and dengue viruses.)

Maps have to be supported with good data, which an interested university team, a community organization, or an NGO staff can often provide. The issue is not just a matter of general vulnerability, but scales of vulnerability: Which areas are in the most danger and why? A simple gap analysis is then possible, showing what measures and resources the communities themselves can apply to the challenge and where outside help will be needed, and in what amounts.

measures and resources

But maps are not reliable, even if done by university teams, if community members themselves are not partners. People who live in these communities know better than anyone else which areas flood more than others during a storm. Once this reality is a part of the mapping, a powerful tool is born.

Community education and participation. Experience also shows that involving key members of the community early in the planning is critical to both acceptance and shared responsibility. Contacting women for participation is especially effective. Some observers say that women, long subjected to patriarchal systems, emerge as effective because they have learned to take on issues jointly. Clearly, women in developing countries show a higher tendency toward collaborative approaches, panelists agreed.

Local governments as critical partners. Nearly no one believes effective adaptation is likely without the active participation of local governments. There are legal issues to negotiate. Any change in infrastructure requires permission and assistance. There are always land-use policies to modify or work around and building codes to satisfy or change. Local authorities must be persuaded of the importance of any resilience projects and be on board to assist in the challenge of rounding up needed external funding.

In Durban, where there was already considerable sensitivity to adequate supplies of water, the prospect of sea level rises and its damage demanded attention. Any good plan would have to reduce water demand as well as protect supply. The city is now improving drainage, increasing the height of shoreline stabilization structures, and adding water retention ponds and wetlands. Just as important, it is changing land-use zones so that no more structures are built in the riskiest areas. City officials are also pursuing systematic education of the population on measures to reduce the human health effects of a flood event.

Panelists believed that in most cases it would not be sufficient to cite climate change as a reason for altering city policy, or spending public resources. Local officials feel too much pressure on too many priorities. The salient conclusion: Building resilience must be linked to development, because development potential is the most consistent driver of local

altering city
policy

Ramshackle houses vulnerable to flooding, Jakarta, Indonesia

politics. This connection might be a key to assuring a flow of funds from the national to the local level.

Risk reduction, not risk elimination. Paul Brown, the California engineer, reminded the group that most engineers think that once a risk has been defined and quantified, the solution is straightforward: eliminate it. But this is simply impossible in building resilience to climate change. As Jo da Silva, a structural engineer with ARUP, said, "It's risk *reduction*." Poor communities will opt automatically for practical, *incremental* improvements.

It is important, panelists agreed, to engage community members in resilience planning early on and to translate data into a form sufficiently comprehensible so that citizens can grasp the issues and government officials can respond appropriately. Training, action, and funding, pointed out Madeleen Helmer, head of the Red Cross/Red Crescent Centre, are the three key steps in helping communities succeed with resilience-building strategies. Larry Vale, professor and head of the urban planning and design department at the Massachusetts Institute of Technology, suggested that promoting city-to-city relationships could be effective. As cities make progress, they should seek out partnerships, helping each other with each increment of success.

Accepting the principle of incremental progress also caused panelists to visit the standards issue. Brown reminded the group that engineers often suggest some flexibility in standards—the idea of making as much immediate progress as

helping
communities
succeed

possible considering the resources available. But flexibility, it was noted, may result in unacceptable legal liability. The unfortunate, not infrequent result can be that no work is done at all. This hurdle must be met and overcome, participants agreed, noting that there will never be enough money to carry out all resilience-building measures at the highest desirable standards.

prepare for weather variability

Urban communities can still do a lot to prepare for weather variability as well as extreme climate events, however. Taking a community-based approach, the coastal town of Cavite City, in the Philippines, put new houses up on stilts, strengthened the structure of existing homes, adopted a plan for evacuating to safer places during emergencies, and accumulated sandbags to use on the shorelines. While those measures certainly have not erased all vulnerability to the effects of climate change, the community has been significantly strengthened.

FUNDING LOCAL RESILIENCE

Mincing no words, Satterthwaite put the sharpest edge on the problem of connecting available grants and loans to the communities where the greatest risks from climate change lie: "The international funding system," he asserted, "is superbly disconnected from the sources of innovations. The World Bank does not fund them. Neither do the bilateral agencies. Almost all the big donors have moved away from supporting local engagement."

This does not mean that funds do not flow; the question is how often they are funneled to local communities and cutting-edge innovations. For example, the International

Fossil Fuel Burning: Who Pays the Bill?

ONE SUMMIT PARTICIPANT after another suggested that major private firms should shoulder some of the adaptation agenda costs. They pointed especially to industries generating literally billions of dollars in profits from the energy consumed from fossil fuels.

Major managers of the world's equity capital seem to be thinking along the same lines. *The Economist* reported in the fall of 2007 that 315 major institutional investors representing more than $40 trillion in investable capital sent letters to 2,400 firms around the world. Under the name of the Carbon Disclosure Project, the letters posed stark questions: How big were the companies' emissions of greenhouse gases, and what were they doing about climate change?

At the same time a group of investors and NGOs petitioned America's stockmarket regulator, the Securities and Exchange Commission, to clarify whether firms were obligated to disclose how climate change affects their future prospects.

Imagine the dilemma for energy firms, most of which have plans for additional coal-fired plants (150 in the United States alone, threatening cumulative emissions that might easily eclipse such mitigation practices as reduced driving or green building construction). Can the energy firms predict their liabilities if radical changes in emission allowances are enacted? A total of 43 resolutions about climate change impacts on investor values were introduced in shareholder meetings in 2007. After Exxon Mobil saw 31 percent of its shareholders demanding that it set targets for emissions cuts, ConocoPhillips almost immediately volunteered to set targets.

As disclosure demands escalate, the pressures on the big energy companies to finance a major part of the globe's growing climate adaptation costs may rise as well.

Institute for Environment and Development reports several sources: a Least Developed Countries Fund (to support NAPA's); a Special Climate Change Fund covering all developing countries; the Adaptation Fund, fueled by a 2 percent levy on projects that channel carbon-cutting energy investments from developed to developing countries; and the Strategic Priority on Adaptation, started with $50 million from the Global Environment Facility's trust funds and aimed at pilot adaptation projects.

carbon-cutting energy investments

There may well be more formal fund arrangements. And certainly there are many bilateral and multilateral funding proposals that would support resilience-building measures.

Summit participants agreed that substantially more funding would be necessary. How much more? Estimates ranged from $50 billion (but "one could spend half that just in New Orleans") to $120 billion a year until at least $1 trillion is reached. Even with the eventual cost unknown, panelists concluded that the priority is getting climate change issues mainstreamed into local (and national) budgets.

getting climate change issues mainstreamed

Yet a big intergovernmental problem remains. Nancy Kete, managing director of the World Resources Institute's Center for Transport and the Environment, challenged the assumption that resilience-building funds can be channeled through national governments. "The cities won't end up with the money," she said. "We need to insist that both public and private funds go directly to where the adaptation projects are"—at the local, rather than the national, level.

Several ideas for potential funding sources were raised: Carol Howe of UNESCO's SWITCH organization quickly volunteered the oil companies—a perfect synchronization of problem causing and solution promoting. "Maybe, since the oil companies are working in most of these countries, extracting the resource directly in many, they could just adopt a country," she said.

solution
promoting

The international banking community was mentioned as another candidate, invested as it ought to be in the long-term social and economic stability of the world. Kete said any push on the banking industry has to communicate clearly the urgency of focusing on the vulnerable urban regions where global population is increasingly concentrated.

Revi pointed out that many cities can handle the finance if they have the will. As Shanghai invests in the new model Pudong city rising up from the marshes, it is generally assumed that it can afford whatever measures are required for it to be a model of urban resilience. And super-rich cities such as Abu Dhabi and Dubai can also cover their bets with resilience-building measures as they erect fancy structures on shallow spits of man-made islands, including many that could be quickly overwhelmed by any serious storm. Singapore is already considering a system of dikes.

a carbon tax

Part of the picture, some panelists asserted, must eventually include a carbon tax, or what some participants called a "global fossil fuel excise tax." Every economist agrees that imposing a tax reduces the incidence of whatever is taxed; a carbon tax would raise costs from use of gasoline and diesel fuel, as well as coal-fired heat or electric energy. The simplicity of the tax would send an unmistakable global economic signal to switch to more sustainable, less CO_2-spawning practices. Much public discussion and negotiation between nations has focused on cap-and-trade mechanisms, but the Global Urban Summit panelists were highly skeptical of the impact such measures would have. They felt, by contrast, that as the immense challenges of climate change resilience become ever more vivid, the circle of attention may turn to the most sweeping mitigation step possible—national and world-wide taxes to dampen mankind's profligate generation of climate-altering carbon emissions.

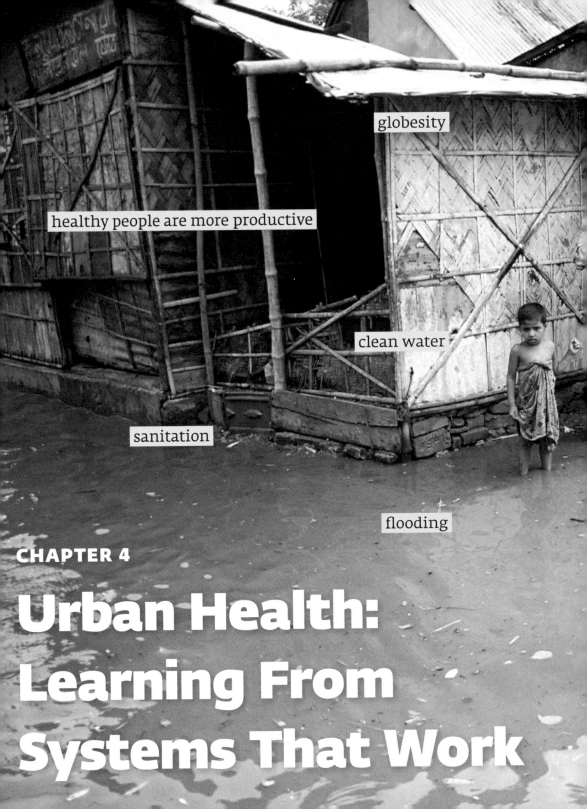

globesity

healthy people are more productive

clean water

sanitation

flooding

CHAPTER 4

Urban Health: Learning From Systems That Work

Floodwaters surround houses, Dhaka, Bangladesh

pandemic preparedness

link between social capital and health

potential for resilience

triple health burden

feed garbage into a giant concrete oven

"IF WE DON'T ACT NOW," warned the former health minister for Mexico, Julio Frenk, addressing the issue of global health, "the divide between rich and poor, North and South, will continue to grow, with serious consequences for economic development."

Frenk's simple but compelling logic struck a theme often repeated in the Summit sessions on Urban Health. Later, Gordon McGranahan, who heads the Human Settlements Group at the London-based International Institute for Environment and Development, would put an even finer point on this logic: "Maximizing health would be far better for the poor than maximizing economic output," he said.

Layers of bureaucracy, sometimes openly corrupt, have clogged financial pipelines and sometimes just gobbled up millions of donor dollars intended for economic development in poor nations, McGranahan told those assembled. Not much of this funding actually results in better lives for the poor. Too often resources never arrive at the local level, where they are desperately needed. A focus on health, McGranahan argued, would be a more effective and powerful alternative for improving the quality of life and economic outlook—for the urban poor. The bottom line is that healthy people are more productive.

healthy people are more productive

These Summit participants came from a wide variety of institutes and agencies organized around global urban health issues, including academia, journalism, philanthropy, and major NGOs such as the World Health Organization (WHO), USAID, and UN-HABITAT.

Health improvement, in its broadest sense, quickly emerged as the connective tissue linking all of the challenges facing the Global South for this century. Health is intricately interwoven with such basic urban challenges as clean water and adequate sanitation. It touches more complex concerns, too, from how urban areas are designed and planned, to managing a globalized economy, to surviving the effects of climate change.

Informal settlements, too often just slums where people live in squalor, may be the epicenter of the world's most critical health problems. Poor sanitation, frequent flooding, open sewers, dumping, people living atop garbage dumps, rapidly spreading diseases, proximity to air pollutants—all these factors lead to poor health outcomes for at least 1 billion people, a profound health and moral issue. The conditions challenge entire metropolises—and the entire world. That's because within hours, a slum bug can spread to cities worldwide, making pandemic preparedness, as one participant put it, "the speedboat for slum research."

The overarching theme of this week-long Summit session was the need to shift the health conversation from the vulnerabilities of the Global South to its potential for resilience, to talk less about its problems and instead figure out how to encourage, nurture, and spread examples of positive interventions. Another crosscutting theme was the call to rely more on social capital, networks, and community-driven approaches to replace top-heavy, donor-driven, bureaucracy-laden projects.

clean water

sanitation

effects of climate change

flooding

air pollutants

pandemic preparedness

potential for resilience

The week's deliberations were formally launched with a forceful presentation by Frenk, who is now a senior fellow with the Bill & Melinda Gates Foundation. In Frenk's estimation, today's poor carry a triple health burden. Many have yet to emerge from persisting health problems such as reproductive diseases, or malaria and dengue. Exacerbated by inadequate living conditions, these maladies persist because health systems fail. And with climate warming welcoming mosquitoes to new locales, more urban communities, such as Nairobi, are likely targets of vector-borne disease.

triple health burden

Added to these are communicable disease patterns, from erstwhile diseases such as tuberculosis to the still-growing threat of HIV/AIDS. And on top of those burdens, globalization's effects show up in rising rates of mental illness and hazards resulting from climate change. Side by side, malnutrition and obesity—called "globesity" by Frenk—also now plague the urban poor across the developing world.

globesity

Yet Frenk also brought a message of optimism and hope. During his ministerial service, Mexico adopted a broad new health initiative, supported by a 93 percent legislative majority. The program's three pillars include incentives to improve personal health, the beginnings of universal access to health care, and innovation such as reliance on social capital and networks rather than just more health centers.

Setting a research-driven framework for the week's discussions was Trudy Harpham, author and researcher with wide experience in the developing world. She began by outlining

Growing out of Poverty:
Revolutionizing Health Care

Julio Frenk

Former Minister of Health for Mexico, currently a senior fellow with the Bill & Melinda Gates Foundation, Seattle, Washington, and President of the Carso Health Institute, Mexico; plenary speaker

WITHOUT HEALTHY POPULATIONS, countries will not grow out of poverty. Some 70 percent of urban dwellers in Africa and 43 percent in Latin America are poor. Living conditions in the cities of these regions can be fertile ground for infectious diseases, malnutrition, injury, and mental illness, often making urban poverty far more oppressive than rural poverty. Mal-development is also common in these urban settings. In contrast to advanced societies, where new problems tend to replace old ones, in mal-developed societies, old and new problems coexist in a complex present fraught with contradictions. Throughout cities in the developing world, traditional public health problems are compounded by new maladies related to globalization, climate change, and detrimental lifestyles.

To persuade finance ministers to support building or revamping health systems, you have to show them that improving the health of citizens can help achieve economic objectives. For example, healthy children perform better academically and healthy people of all ages are more productive. In Mexico we have put a new program into law that embraces successful reforms while making health care universally available as a social right. This program took a three-pronged approach:

1. We launched a new generation of health-promotion and disease-prevention strategies, such as high tobacco taxes to discourage smoking among young people, improved traffic flows to reduce motor vehicle accidents, and strengthened crime prevention policies and other efforts to discourage family and gender violence.

2. We are moving toward universal health insurance. Mexico's segmented health system was tied to employment, overlooking 50 percent of the population. The insurance plan for the self-employed is on target to help cover all of the more than 100 million residents by 2010.

3. We have been innovative in care and delivery. In the past, primary care meant primitive care for poor people. The new concept involves fewer health centers and more networks: sets of agile services

153

recognizing that disease and health concerns are not discrete episodes but conditions that must be addressed throughout life. Utilizing technological advances including information technology, these redesigned services provide coordinated continuity of care for mobile populations.

With the United States and Mexico straddling the busiest border in the world, illegal immigration into the United States does factor into these mobile populations. Keep in mind, however, that the majority of border crossings for health-care reasons are from the United States into Mexico—Americans seeking cheaper drugs and treatments. In this age of globalization, the mobility of populations within and from all countries must be considered in the planning process for improved health systems.

the principal determinants of the health of the urban poor. Harpham reminded the group that the underlying causes of poor health are complex, spanning multiple sectors and multiple levels, extending well beyond just poor access to medical treatment.

DETERMINANTS OF HEALTH

Harpham recalled the Alma Ata Declaration on Primary Care, the visionary agenda that emerged from the International Conference on Primary Care in 1978. Its emphasis on primary care has since been adopted by all members of the WHO. The original Alma Ata vision targeted multiple sector responses. In practice, however, what emerged was selective primary health care. Anything resembling a multi-sector approach was left waiting in the wings.

Multi-sector approaches, Harpham continued, must start with "joined-up" government. Getting government departments with their separate missions, however, to communicate and coordinate invariably becomes a major challenge. A prime example is the Healthy Cities project, popularized in the United States in the 1990s. It asserted that hospitals, clinics, and doctors alone cannot serve human health adequately; that jobs, the environment, social conditions, and treatment of children are just as—if not more—critical to peoples' long-term health; and that all segments of a community need to be engaged in a comprehensive place-based health strategy. Healthy Cities sought to increase local government capacity to improve living

Healthy Cities

conditions and to form partnerships with other communities and community-based organizations. It also stressed creating a network of cities within and across nations to exchange important information and technology.

However, an evaluation of the Healthy Cities program conducted by Harpham and her colleagues in 2001 found limited, though respectable, impact. The initiative did raise awareness in many places; in some cities the program mounted some significant project to improve the environment. But limited political commitment undermined even small successes.

In Europe, Healthy Cities also performed reasonably well in some instances, though it still failed to yield lasting urban health plans. But in the Global South the initiative never took hold at all. The explanation, in retrospect, seems obvious: Most of the participating municipalities had not requested these projects. Instigated by donors, Healthy Cities lacked the legitimacy and energy of a local initiative driven by community demand. Eliya Zulu, deputy director of the African Population and Health Research Center, put it best: "It is critical that the people in the community are actively involved and demand it," he said. "And without government commitment as well, there's not much that can be achieved."

On a positive note, an important change has begun in health research, Harpham reported. Health studies used to focus mostly on the biological, demographic, and behavioral characteristics of individuals. What is now clear is the powerful impact of other factors, most prominently the relationships

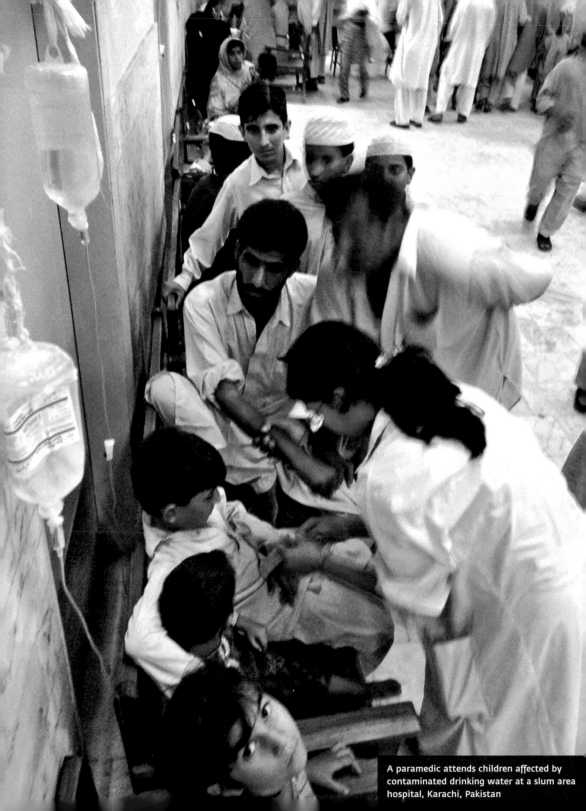

A paramedic attends children affected by contaminated drinking water at a slum area hospital, Karachi, Pakistan

formed by people in a defined place—what is now commonly called "social capital."

No list of determinants of urban health is complete without an exploration of four critical factors that exert a powerful impact on the health of the community:

Poverty. People commonly equate slums with poverty, but poor neighborhoods are not uniformly poor. Some studies even suggest that a tenth of people living in slums have enough income to have more choices about where they live. Conversely the poor can also be found embedded in more moderate-income communities. There are also many people who remain in one place geographically but move in and out of poverty. Since statistical averaging can easily distort reality, strategies to reach all the poor must resist temptations to see communities as homogeneous.

Household income, or livelihood, emerges as the most trusted measure of financial standing. It includes all members and sources and takes into account the relative vulnerabilities of various financial sources. As poverty is shown to be anything but one-dimensional, the argument for multilevel and intersectoral responses grows stronger.

Although urban poverty may not be uniformly well understood, the health consequences of poverty seem quite clear and are among the greatest challenges facing the world today. Poor people are likelier to get sick, less likely to have access to care, and unlikely to receive adequate treatment. The driving lesson in urban health is the velocity of the growth of the urban poor, with Latin America, Africa, and Asia as the major theaters. Some

CURRENT AND PROJECTED NUMBER OF SLUM DWELLERS, BY REGION

REGION	East Asia	Latin America and the Caribbean	North Africa	Oceania	Sub-Saharan Africa	South Central Asia	Southeast Asia	Western Asia	TOTAL
Urban population, 2001 (millions)	533	399	76	2	231	452	203	125	**2,021**
Number of slum dwellers, 2001 (millions)	193.8	127.6	21.4	0.5	166.2	262.4	56.8	41.3	**869.9**
Percent of slum dwellers from urban population, 2001	36.4	32	28.1	25	72	58	28	33.1	**43**
Projected urban population, 2020 (millions)	845.7	543.2	137.2	3.8	452.3	748.8	337.6	194.9	**3,263.4**
Percent of slum dwellers, 2020 (assuming nothing is done)	36.4	32.0	28.1	25.0	72.0	58.0	28.0	33.1	**43.0**
Projected number of slum dwellers, 2020 (millions)	307.5	173.7	38.5	0.9	325.4	434.7	94.4	64.4	**1,439.6**
Increase in number of slum dwellers, 2001–20 (millions)	113.7	46.1	17.2	0.4	159.2	172.3	37.7	23.1	**569.7**
Percent of slum dwellers targeted for upgrading, 2001–20	20.0	8.1	3.0	0.1	27.9	30.2	6.6	4.1	**100**
Number of slum dwellers targeted for upgrading, 2001–20 (millions)	20.0	8.1	3.0	0.1	27.9	30.2	6.6	4.1	**100**
Low-income urban dwellers requiring alternatives, 2005–2020 (millions)	113.7	46.1	17.2	0.5	159.2	172.3	37.7	23.1	**569.7**

Note: Numbers in table may not sum to totals due to rounding
Credit: Adapted from data in UN-HABITAT 2003a, p. 14

60 percent of today's poor live in Asia, and 60 percent of the projected growth in poverty will occur there if current trends persist.

Social Capital. The impact that social dynamics have on community health is gaining wider attention among health researchers. The consequences of social dysfunction are already well understood. For example, when gangs disrupt the safety of communities and street violence is common, residents' health, particularly their mental health, is compromised. But now there is also growing interest in the positive connections between social capital and health. The notion is that health can be improved by strengthening the social networks, inter-personal relationships, and mediating institutions—places of worship, block clubs, etc.—that link people to one another.

link between
social capital
and health

Unfortunately, there are few studies confirming the link between social capital and health in the cities of developing nations. One frequently cited study comes from Cali, Colombia. During the height of that city's drug-related violence, the usual law enforcement and medical interventions were having little effect. Local officials decided to work to strengthen the relation-ships linking young men to each other and to key community institutions. This social model had a dramatic effect and homi-cide rates plummeted.

Physical Environment. The Global South now faces mul-tiple perils of population explosion and climate change on top of an unforgiving plague of poor access to drinking water, basic sanitation, and shelter.

Poor Health Takes Many Forms

IN SUB-SAHARAN AFRICA the dominant threats to health continue to be the living conditions that people in the developed world blithely assume are omnipresent: piped potable water, access to toilets that are safe and sanitary, housing that affords enough space for families and keeps out harsh elements.

In Asia, health problems among the poor are made even worse by high rates of smoking and drug use, respiratory and heart disease being the all-too common consequences. HIV/AIDS remains a major cause of death across the Global South; it is the number one cause in Africa. In India, groups of poor people commonly make their living sorting through trash for its salvage value. Worse, up to 80 percent of the nearly 400,000 known tons of electronics recycled in just the United States ends up in India, China, or Nigeria, where workers use hammers and bare hands to extract metal and glass, exposing themselves to a potentially lethal brew of toxic chemicals.

Poor sanitation alone accounts for a high proportion of the death rates from malaria and diarrhea every year all over the Global South. Many of these deaths are of children. And in addition to both inadequate sanitation and shelter, many people also face the daily specter of violence. Densely packed living conditions set the stage for brutal behavior that causes injuries and death. The likelihood of violence increases further as the raw contrasts between those making a good living and those just scraping by widens—even within the slums themselves. Often cited are the *favelas* of Latin America—also known as *barriadas*, *vecinidades*, or *pueblas jovenes*—where, even when there is decent and stable housing, violence persists as a serious problem. Much of the brutality is rooted in illegal drug trade and the organized gangs that fight for control of these markets. Under these circumstances it is hardly mysterious that fear and anxiety become dominant emotions; mental health suffers, even among those with access to services and steady incomes. Depression and anxiety dominate the list of health challenges.

Where people have no regular access to potable water, it is most often the women who take on the burden of taking a container to some source and bearing it back, sometimes several times a day. The physical burden is one thing, but stories abound of women subjected to theft, even rape, on these journeys of necessity. In many places, women must also endure a silent form of personal violation, such as when public facilities provide toilets for men only. How can people focus on general improvements in community health when fear of attack and personal affronts are daily experiences?

Pedestrians don masks to avoid respiratory problems from air pollution, Hong Kong, China

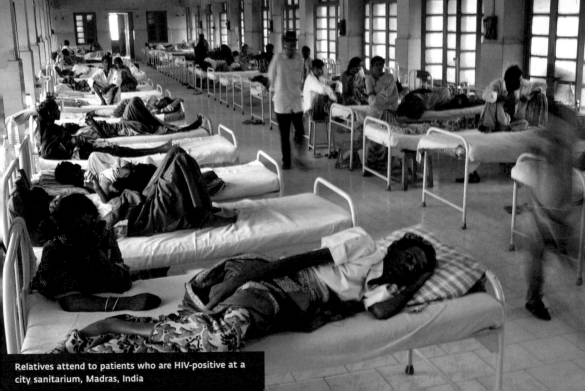

Relatives attend to patients who are HIV-positive at a city sanitarium, Madras, India

Failure to access even the basic conditions of a livable environment—water, sanitation, and adequate shelter—accounts for much of the disease that occurs in the Global South. Some 2.5 billion people lack basic sanitation, and an estimated 1.8 million people die annually from the effects of poor sanitation. Many are children under the age of five. Water and sanitation deficiencies explain nearly all instances of childhood diarrhea. Households that rely on wood and dung to fuel indoor stoves produce air pollution that can lead to asthma, tuberculosis, or any number of infectious diseases. Children and the elderly are especially vulnerable. Dangers now considered rare in the developed world (lead paint poisoning, mold, pest infestations, for instance) add to the peril in the Global South.

Industrial Pollution. Although dramatically reduced in the Global North over the past century, dangerous emissions associated with industrial production continue to take a heavy toll, in illness and early death, in cities of the Global South, Russia, and the Ukraine. A 2007 ranking by the Blacksmith Institute of the world's most polluted cities indicated that virtually all the residents were afflicted by industrially generated chemicals pumped by factories into the atmosphere or water supplies. In Vapid, India, one of the cities listed, mercury in groundwater was found to be 96 times higher than WHO standards.

Health Services. Many heads nodded when one Summit panelist suggested that the medical industry had "hijacked" the health care agenda, even in developing countries. The implication: preventive measures and environment make a greater difference. Even so, the availability of medical treatment matters. Key issues are reasonable access to care, the quality of care, and affordability, Harpham said. In the Global South, the poor often wander from place to place seeking appropriate care.

A core problem persists: A significant proportion of the urban poor in Global South cities live in settlements that are not recognized, not mapped, not even acknowledged. "They're not supposed to be here," said Anthony Kolb, urban health adviser for USAID, so government officials conclude they don't "have to provide any services."

settlements that are not recognized

A study from Delhi, India, cited by Harpham underscores the medical services problems that poor people face. It compared services available to residents in seven rich and poor Delhi neighborhoods. Not surprisingly the providers considered to be the most competent were concentrated in the better neighborhoods. More striking, though, was the ease with which poor people became trapped in no-win propositions. Private providers were found less competent but put forth higher effort to meet the needs of the poor. Public providers, by contrast, were better qualified but scored low on effort. "The poor received low-quality care from the private sector because doctors do not know much and low-quality care from the public sector because doctors do not do much," said plenary speaker Frenk.

LEARNING FROM WHAT WORKS

The time is ripe to make a fundamental shift in focus on health for people of the poor neighborhoods of the Global South. "Instead of talking about the problem," said Harpham, "we need now to focus on what to do. Let us not pretend we need more knowledge." In the past ten years, she added, "Much has been learned about 'determinants' of health and outcomes. If more research is needed, it should be about the interventions, with less focus on vulnerability and more about resilience."

Harpham's implication: what is still uncertain is which interventions pay off. But the clearly promising arenas are social capital and networks. Some participants, however, were not so certain that enough is known to pin down which programs are worth financing. "We all understand the problem, but we still do not have enough information about what works to know what to finance," said Mark Rosenburg, executive director of the Task Force for Child Survival and Development.

Several participants suggested compiling an urban health index that would catalog improvements (and reversals) in the conditions that influence health. Establishing a baseline would enable researchers to track progress, show the positive impact of interventions, and build a case for investment in better population health. Others suggested that an urban health index might even prove to be a relaunching pad for the Healthy Cities movement. "We need a standard platform because we seem to be data-rich," said Ariel Pablos-Mendez, associate professor of medicine and public health at Columbia

urban health index

University who had recently joined the Rockefeller Foundation staff, but the data "are not coming together in a form to be shared with decision makers."

When the data comes together, a likely finding will be that no region succeeds unless the income levels for all its less-well-off citizens rise. A continued press for economic growth, though insufficient by itself and not even likely without also improving health status, would be one of the key strategies, participants agreed—but only if the economic gains are spread throughout the population. "Urban risks go down as income goes up," said Elliott Sclar, director of the Center for Sustainable Urban Development at Columbia University. "There's a consistent correlation between rises in GDP and social indicators."

Interventions do not have to be immediate or comprehensive successes to be significant. Even if successful health interventions are spotty, limited in scope, and not well-documented, participants agreed that potentially promising initiatives should be cross-fertilized. UN-HABITAT has undertaken an ongoing effort to catalog promising projects, although a scan of its list suggests most included are narrowly focused projects, not multi-sector, multilevel efforts. An exception: an initiative in Surat, said in 1995 to be one of India's filthiest cities. Ravaged by epidemic disease in the wake of historic floods, the city was plagued by tons of debris, including the rotting carcasses of animals. A massive cleanup helped restore this coastal city, known for its textiles and as a major center for

Children receive the polio vaccine at school, Lagos, Nigeria

A family of five travels the streets on a scooter, New Delhi, India

cutting and polishing diamonds. By 1997 Surat could boast that it was India's second cleanest city. Strong public participation processes and early-warning public-health systems anchored the turnaround. When another flood came in 2006 Surat's officials and people drew on their experience and cleaned up from the storm before disease could take hold in the population.

In a Summit background paper, David Vlahov of the New York Academy of Medicine and his colleagues described the experience of the Tirol district in Belo-Horizonte, Brazil's third largest metropolitan area. In 2005 the city launched a program of family health centers. Tirol was able to secure services of a doctor, a physician's assistant, a nurse and three outreach workers from the community. The team was assigned to track the health needs of households in a population tract of some 4,000 people. Team members did not wait for people to call. They went to each house, collecting data on every factor, including daily nutrition, drug use, and infectious diseases. Although the initiative is too new to measure its effects, early results are encouraging.

In Calcutta, India, an organization known as Praysam enlisted children of the urban poor to help survey household conditions and promote changes that could improve community health. The initiative began in the mid-1990s in the city's Rishi Aurobindo Colony. The approach has been so powerful that the area is now considered a model slum. Its alleys are clean, and malaria and diarrhea, once dominant conditions, are now rare. The children say (translated from Bengali),

"We bathe daily and try to be neat, or else we will fall sick and our fun will be beat." This health model, mobilizing for better health through neighborhood children, is now spreading to other urban areas of India. Praysam's founder and philosopher-in-chief, Amian Ganguly, participated in the Summit.

Evidence that small-scale interventions can often help improve health conditions emerged from a discussion group led by University of Zimbabwe epidemiology professor Godfrey Woelke. Some of the examples were putting speed bumps on dangerous residential roads in Harare, Zimbabwe; introducing midday meals in a community in India; and making condoms mandatory for West Bengalis who work the sex trade. Small steps build a climate for collaboration while making community health a little better, the group said.

Smoking remains a major source of health problems in the Global South, especially Asia. In Thailand an aggressive

reduce tobacco use

push is under way to reduce tobacco use. Measures include big tax increases, bans on advertising, and prohibitions on smoking in public places. Funds for health promotion in Thailand have gone from $1 million to $44 million, reported Susan Mercado, with WHO in Kobe, Japan.

Another recent and potentially promising example comes from the sprawling slum of Kibera, in Nairobi, where

feed garbage into a giant concrete oven

volunteers now feed garbage into a giant concrete oven. The process not only removes the solid waste that is otherwise scattered, but it also provides a source of heat for bathing and cooking. Volunteers gather rubbish, even going door to door.

Children scavenge for food in a garbage heap, Harare, Zimbabwe

If the experiment proves successful, the *Christian Science Monitor* reported in 2007, the initiative could be replicated with support from NGOs and the United Nations Environment Program, which provided initial capital.

Public health is also improving in Bogotá, Colombia, thanks to the efforts of recent mayors to promote respect for life and civility (fighting the city and country's notorious violence), tame traffic to create safer streets for the broad masses of the population, add new green spaces available to all citizens, start a model bus system on exclusive rights-of-way, and provide improved access to food and health care for poor residents.

safer streets

ENGAGING THE COMMUNITY: THE CRUCIAL FIRST STEP

Community participation, the panelists noted time and again, is the starting point for every successful initiative to improve the health of the urban poor. Genuine involvement of those most affected is essential to build legitimacy. Veterans of the process counsel that engaging residents requires patience; there are walls of suspicion to overcome and relationships of trust take time to build.

One discussion group reported how the University of São Paulo, in an effort to insulate itself from the violence of the surrounding community, started building walls around its facilities. Later, after direct engagement in the community, the university began employing community members. Over time, relationships developed. People in the community could see roles for themselves within the university and university staff had a fresh sense of the wider community assets.

The bottom line is that improved urban health must start with a heavy dose of inclusion: reaching out, listening, mobilizing the most vulnerable population groups. Where exclusion is evident—ignoring areas where poor people have concentrated, for example, or simply not listening to the voices of the poor when plans and decisions are made—reversing course is the best remedy. WHO's Mercado put it plainly: "Participation is the key element in making this more integrative approach work." The best-known large-scale example of taking engagement seriously is Shack/Slum Dwellers International (SDI). At its origin, community members themselves recognized the need to engage and mobilize the community. SDI has become an association of large national federations making common cause around the urban poor— sharing experiences of organizing and problem-solving.

IMPLEMENTATION: GETTING MORE ON BOARD

Community engagement, while indispensable, is just half the battle. Once the community is mobilized and partnerships forged with local governments, it is important that public officials and other institutional authorities understand that urban health needs to be addressed as a multi-sector challenge. Often a catalyst is required, participants said, to persuade officialdom to cross the usual dividing turf lines. Sometimes an event provides the catalyst. Sometimes it is a persistent individual, a champion for the cause. Public officials, once they come together, find that there is much they can do collaboratively that none of them could manage alone. And they learn to see the community leaders as partners. In the Miraflores area of Lima, Peru, for example, an active mayor linked professionals across multiple sectors to improve conditions for the elderly. The mayor believed this would raise the level of living for the whole city.

engage the media

Another approach is active effort to engage the media to help address community health concerns. That strategy has been used to tackle reproductive-health issues in Indonesia, Bangladesh, and the Philippines. One measurable result: an increase in the use of contraceptive devices.

Forging regional networks of like-minded colleagues can also help advance urban health. A prime example is the Asian Infectious Disease Project, involving local officials in New Delhi, Hanoi, Jakarta, Singapore, Taipei, Tokyo, and Yangon.

Although many of the world's major challenges now exist in cities, national governments have much to say about

State of the World Cities

whether there is any progress. In its State of the World Cities 2006 report, the United Nations highlighted Brazil, Egypt, Mexico, South Africa, Thailand, and Tunisia as having made significant progress in upgrading slums and improving services for the urban poor. Other countries, such as Burkina Faso and Tanzania, had demonstrated a strong political commitment—the necessary starting point.

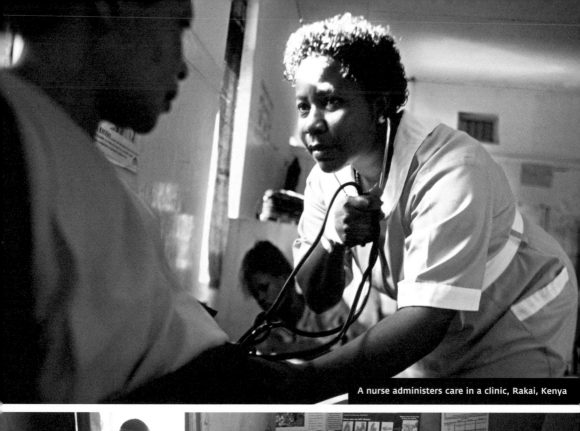

A nurse administers care in a clinic, Rakai, Kenya

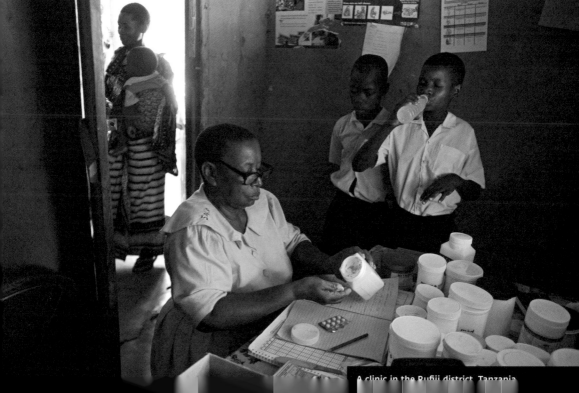

A clinic in the Rufiji district, Tanzania

The U.N. report realistically acknowledges, however, that political commitments must be institutionalized beyond a single administration. The drive for improved health needs to be cemented as a long-term, strategic plank in not just a city's but a country's design for a better future. What would it cost? The United Nations suggests about $1,800 a person served. It also suggests that $1,090 of that could be borne by government, the rest from donor and private capital.

Where national governments do not have a record of commitment to improving health of populations at the local level, financial flows of capital and aid should be specifically framed to ensure that funding reaches the communities where the poorest citizens live.

AN AGENDA FOR ACTION

At the end of a week of hard-hitting discussion and deliberations, the Summit health group reached a strong consensus from multiple discussion groups:

Move from a focus on vulnerabilities to an agenda of resilience. Much has already been learned about the determinants of health. While still measuring the vulnerable conditions of the poor, a next priority should be balancing that effort with at least equal emphasis on solutions and good demonstrations of progress, however small and localized.

Originate every effort within the affected communities. Failure to start with demand from the grassroots crippled the Healthy Cities movement in much of the developing world and limited its impact elsewhere. Authentic (and early) engagement of residents of targeted communities nearly always pays big dividends.

Develop partnerships across levels and sectors. Often, there is great desire to move quickly to get projects under way. But lifting the health of whole communities requires a network of leadership and support that takes time to cultivate. And health departments may not end up leading the charge. Do not ask the WHO to be a community organizer; the agency will not be good at that, said USAID's Kolb. But groups such as the WHO can take a valuable role in setting standards. The aim is to build a culture where narrowly trained professionals can look past their dividing points and imagine and plan for outcomes only a collective force can produce.

Make maps to show the reality. Starting with the community and its residents, collect data, map it, graph it, make tables, and create the most compelling visual and verbal case possible. Make the case clearly for both political leaders and heads of donor organizations. Some cities, participants suggested, could be designated as health observatories, targeted for more systematic mapping, spatial analysis, and tracking of social determinants. Such a project could involve international, national, and local partners, advisory boards, business professionals, and academics to help translate the findings and channel the knowledge. Information gathering is valuable, but the process must emphasize action, added Waleska Caiaffa, associate professor at Brazil's Federal University of Minas Gerais.

Boys travel to work on the locking system of a train, Dhaka, Bangladesh

Orphans eat lunch at the Kibera Community Self Help Program's school, Nairobi, Kenya

Create an urban health index for the cities of the Global South. Rather than listing an index of ills, create a health index cataloging improvements in the conditions that influence health. Establishing a baseline would enable researchers to track progress, show the positive impact of interventions, and build a case for investment in better public health. A widely implemented urban health index would lead to comparisons within cities and across cities. An index would also create a platform on which interventions could be tracked, evaluated, and compared, all vital steps toward replicating and scaling up what works best.

Resurrect, re-brand, and relaunch the Healthy Cities program. The idea behind Healthy Cities was sound; the fault was in its execution. "In too many places," said Marilyn Rice, a regional adviser with the Pan American World Health Organization, "the Healthy Cities program was just a project." It never changed the culture to a multi-sector health orientation. Still, as WHO's Mercado told the group, there have been benefits from the Healthy Cities program, as cities have "learned from each other," particularly from what did not work. Clearly, in too many cities, the silos of separatism survived every effort to create multi-sector partnerships. But, noted Rosenburg of the Task Force for Child Survival and Development, "the transport people are asking the same question as the health people. So maybe if we got these groups together, it's possible we could find important areas of agreement." Mercado cited several examples of progress traceable to Healthy Cities program work:

the health plan created by citizens for themselves in Dar es Salaam, Tanzania; the breakthrough for citizens in Port Alegre, Brazil, to have a say in how public money is spent through the policy known now as "participatory budgeting"; the process that enabled an entire community to coalesce around spaces for walking and cycling in Victoria, Australia.

Design a system of health services that fits the highest priority needs of the urban poor. Improving actual health and medical services is not simply a matter of transporting Western models or the best of the North to the growing cities of the South. Living conditions that facilitate healthier lives is primary. And, of course, what all people of the world share is the desire to have decent access to medical services. We are learning, said Frenk, how easily this becomes segregated. "Unfortunately one of the big distortions for primary health care was to think that it was health care for the poor. It really became not primary health care but primitive health care, and we know very well that services for the poor end up being poor services," he told the Summit assembly.

In sum, health panel participants urged that policy makers and donor organizations recognize the central and catalytic role that health improvement plays in the struggle to assist the urban poor. Better health starts with better living conditions and is a precondition for any financial betterment.

The panel, while respecting the expert knowledge that health professionals and consultants bring, was clear about transforming the typical top-down, donor-driven, bureaucratically organized, standard-delivered, large-scale health system to one that originates with bottom-up, community-driven organizing and priority setting. Experience in the field shows that when local communities get organized, they set priorities that reflect their needs. The result is programs that reflect a variety of approaches, not one standard solution.

To persuade the world to care and invest in strangers who live in places most people have never been to will require a real leap forward in communication, participants agreed. "We need more stories, not just studies," said Brenda Wilson, National Public Radio foreign correspondent, expressing the hope that people will support a health agenda for the urban poor. To do this it is essential to "talk straight," avoiding the usual language of studies and academic conferences.

As to the health professionals, the message is to escape those silos, look at the problem broadly, and cultivate partners in community organizations and NGOs. The Center for Sustainable Urban Development's Sclar found the right tone for a conclusion as he simultaneously set the stage for the Summit's following week: "We need planners and lawyers and public health people, but now we really need people who understand this broader agenda," he said. "We need a new class of urban professionals who know how to move across lines."

slum upgrading

threat of climate change

overcrowding

design for high density

CHAPTER 5

Designing the Inclusive City

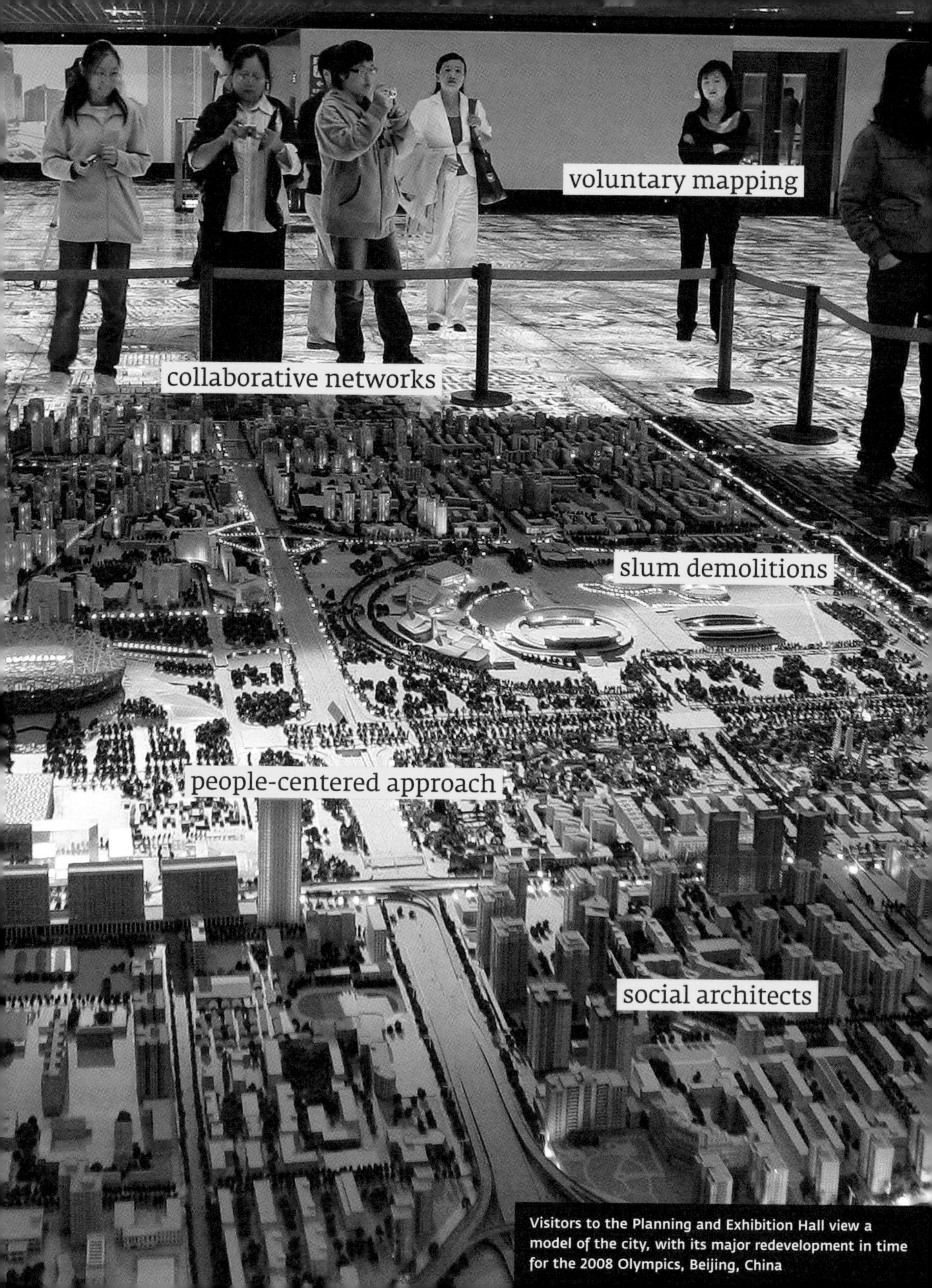

voluntary mapping

collaborative networks

slum demolitions

people-centered approach

social architects

Visitors to the Planning and Exhibition Hall view a
model of the city, with its major redevelopment in time
for the 2008 Olympics, Beijing, China

THE GLOBE FINDS ITSELF IN A FRENZY OF CITY BUILDING, responding to economic growth from Singapore to Dubai and the challenges of living and work space for the added billions of humanity pouring into Global South cities, whether Jakarta, Mumbai, or Lagos, or much smaller, newer urban centers.

But who is doing the planning—and how well is it being done? Are the planners, who should grasp the big picture of urban form, being heeded—and if so, are they prepared with a holistic grasp of city design? Are architects, engineers, landscapers, hydrologists, transportation planners, and land lawyers reading off the same page? Or are the key urban professionals collaborating only by fits and starts, and often when it is too late to make the wisest integrated decisions?

Just as critical: Are city leaders willing to consult not just the economic deal makers and technical experts on city design, but cross-sections of their own citizenry, before leaping to major city-building or city-altering decisions? Unless they do, can there be any hope for truly inclusive cities, places that honor and find a place for people of all economic strata?

A rare assembly of academicians, planners, architects, consultants, economists, local officials, and journalists from some 15 countries spent a full week at the Summit in Bellagio trying to analyze the challenges of 21st century planning. They were joined by a group of young urban professionals associated with the Global Studio program. The more youthful planners assured their older colleagues in no uncertain terms that

silos will not work

the familiar 20th century model of professional silos will not work to cope with the momentous city building challenges of this time. The session leader, Elliott Sclar of the Center for Sustainable Urban Development at Columbia University, articulated the issue early in the discussions: that planners operate in one sphere with their principles and maps, economists think about their models, architects compete for design distinctions—even while the challenges of today's cities cry out for collaborative approaches.

The sessions were also marked by clear resistance to the still-strong notion that cities of the Global South should simply "look North," examining and benefiting from what works in the United States and Europe. Today and tomorrow's paradigm needs new focus, insisted participants in the session, especially those from the Global South. Smart Southern cities will obviously look worldwide for positive models. But increasingly they need to be learning from one another to build capacity for the new century's challenges. The cities of the Global South are the population giants of the 21st century and will be hosts to the majority of the population growth over the next 40 years. They are distinctly different from most Northern metropolises. The future of urban learning needs a brand new focus: "South-to-South," across Africa, Latin America, and Asia, in a rich variety of forums and formats. Paradoxically this can begin to bridge the gap between the North and the South, as it has the potential to lead to more equitable relations and exchanges in the future. There is a lot to be learned on both sides but little will be learned on either if one player consistently dominates.

Underscoring the need for a new paradigm, some participants from developing countries bristled when seasoned and conference-savvy experts from famed Global North institutions jumped into a lead role in discussions, even "speaking for" the Global South representatives who were in the room and knew their own capacity for communication and their clear advantage from experience.

But a clear consensus was reached that Global South universities, professional associations, civil society groups, and local governments need to foster more direct, South-to-South dialogue and exchange of experience and learning. And not just to begin to level the playing field between the North and South but because 1) so many talented Global South urban experts and urban civil society groups are emerging (groups purposefully invited and strongly represented at the Summit) and 2) the destiny of the most rapidly growing cities of the 21st century, almost all of the Global South, lies in their hands.

RACING THE BULLDOZERS

Issues of rapid slum development dominated many of the conversations, inevitably so in the face of estimates that up to 70 percent of residents in the Global South's expanding cities are living in sprawling, unplanned slums. But the challenges of the times, Rockefeller Foundation vice president Darren Walker and others underscored, are broader: to prepare planners and other professionals who are committed to developing and growing cities that provide the best possible environments for

Global Studio Program

CAN THE WORLD'S CITY-BUILDING professionals learn, coalesce, and work more effectively to plan more sustainable metropolises and meet the United Nations' Millennium Development Goals to reduce poverty, disease, and hardship worldwide, with special focus on slums of the fast-developing Global South?

The Global Studio initiative has that precise goal. The project was conceived in 2004 by the Millennium Project's Task Force on Improving the Lives of Slum Dwellers, whose report was called *A Home in the City*. The Millennium Project, headed by Professor Jeffrey Sachs, director of the Earth Institute at Columbia University, was commissioned by then-U.N. Secretary General Kofi Annan to plan world action to achieve the Millennium Development Goals. Founding members of the Global Studio included Anna Rubbo of the University of Sydney, Elliott Sclar and Gabriella Carolini of Columbia University, and Pietro Garau of the University of Rome La Sapienza.

The forums attract professionals involved in city-building, representatives of NGOs, and academics, along with students. Participation in studio field work is by application; accepted students demonstrate not merely preparation in planning and design, but a proclivity toward turning design into action as well as a passion for alleviating poverty.

A lead university in the city where a Global Studio program has been scheduled hosts it; Wits University in Johannesburg, for example, hosted the 2007 program. Prior studios were held in Istanbul (2005) and Vancouver (2006). The program itself consists of forums and site visits, followed by actual field work, with students forming interdisciplinary collaborative teams with community members to identify and execute strategies for community improvement.

Students from both developed and developing countries take part and work together. On the Global South Side, African representation has been especially strong, with young professionals from several countries including Kenya, Nigeria, South Africa, and Uganda.

In the first studio program, in Istanbul, 120 students from 20 countries participated. They started each project with a simple set of questions, such as asking residents of an Istanbul slum what they liked and disliked about where they live, and what physical changes would improve their lives. They also asked questions aimed at understanding the political context of each settlement and looked for signs of grassroots leadership and expressions of vision for a better future.

In Vancouver in 2006, the students focused on a neighborhood with a high percentage of female drug users. These women said they needed guidance to available resources, but also daily access to a safe park in which to gather, rest, and use sanitary restrooms. Students helped them make these improvements, along with a collective petition for engaging their municipal council. In addition to having an impact on these women's lives, the experience generated opportunities for students to share the results of their work in meetings around the world, including a formal presentation to the 2006 United Nations World Urban Forum, also held in Vancouver.

The 2007 class worked in three slums of Johannesburg, including the well-known area called Alexandra, or Alex. Again, students asked simple but revelatory questions. The slum residents said their roofs leaked and their huts were always cold in winter and insufferably hot in summer. Students showed them how to make roofing superior to the makeshift corrugated tin covers using available materials. They found an affordable supply of insulating materials and demonstrated easy techniques of installation. By the second day residents were taking over, doing the work themselves and spreading the know-how from neighbor to neighbor. And that was the point, said Anna Rubbo, a professor of architecture at the University of Sydney.

The stories quickly reminded Arif Hasan, a veteran of the Karachi Orangi Pilot Project, of his own experience establishing a resource center that he considered a "do-tank." Alejandro Aravena, an architect and professor at Chile's Universidad Católica, said that not only was the Global Studio experience indispensable to education, but it can be profitable and "even sexy." Aravena has his own "doing tank," as he called it, under way with Elemental, a partnership with the Chile Oil Company to build extremely low-cost housing.

residents of all economic groups, cities in which all feel welcome and can have a stake.

The critical question: Will planners and their allied professions have both the knowledge to get ahead of slum-leveling bulldozers and the propensity to press for more inclusive cities? Are they ready to urge political decision makers to plan for urbanization rather than ignoring it or trying to stop it? Are they ready to plan inclusive cities?

So far their achievements are limited. Indeed, just months before the Summit the Indian minister of state for urban development, Ajay Maken, issued his Master Plan 2021 for New Delhi, which was guided by three priorities: obliterating the slums (which currently house some 60 percent of the city's 15 million people), taming traffic, and developing a Manhattan-style skyline. High-rises for the slum dwellers are supposed to take the place of their slum shanties; all height restrictions in buildings would be lifted except in a few historical areas.

Early in 2008 the bulldozers were already sending tens of thousands of residents fleeing with their belongings from Mumbai's sprawling Nehru Nagar slum. Up next is the best known slum of all, Dharavi, home to somewhere between 600,000 and 1 million people—and a thriving export economy worth, some say, in the billions of dollars. Dharavi's demolition, if local resistance fails to stop it, will be the most sweeping slum clearance in world history. Decisions of the city's politicians and planners will push most of the displaced families into high-rise concrete buildings, albeit with the promise of toilets and electricity. The Toronto's *Globe and Mail* called Mumbai's moves the imposition of "the discipline of the planner upon the imponderable chaos of the slum" and a fundamental error because slum dwellers are not typically dropouts from mainstream society but rather former rural residents and their descendants, clawing their way into the urban mainstream.

Cities of the developed North carry the painful historical scars of a similar practice of slum clearance a half century back. Government officials destroyed vibrant, even if squalid, inner-city neighborhoods, rupturing their developed social networks and undermining their small businesses. "Progress" took the form of mostly high-rise, sterile housing, of the sort commonly called "public housing" in the United States, "social housing" in Canada, and "council estates" in Britain. In the United States, many of the resulting "projects," such as Cabrini Green in Chicago, became so socially disruptive and crime infested that the federal government was busy tearing them down by the 1990s.

slum demolitions

The motive for some of today's slum demolitions in the Global South is apparently city image and, more important, clearing land—even in areas never before considered desirable—close to center cities for new economic enterprises that enrich city coffers and benefit permitting officials either directly or indirectly. In some cases, however, such as Zimbabwe's Operation Clean Out, the aim was just getting rid of nuisance slums. But strong and growing cadres of planning professionals, aware of alternative ways that cities across the Global South

People contemplate a future vision of New Orleans City Park at the "Newer Orleans—A Shared Space" exhibition at the Netherlands Architecture Institute, Rotterdam, Netherlands

Residents are invited to comment on a scale model of the planned part of the city along the Red River, Hanoi, Vietnam

and worldwide have dealt with problems, would constitute a new presence in many city governments and might make a substantial difference over time.

In slum-clearance debates, for example, trained planners would be far more likely to know and understand actual existing slum upgrading projects that have occurred with some success in such nations as Pakistan, Sri Lanka, Indonesia, and Brazil. Upgrades include many of the infrastructure improvements for slum areas mentioned in other chapters of this book: clean water supply, adequate sanitation, storm drainage, and, in some cases, electricity. Advocates claim new development typically costs ten to 15 times more than upgrading and is a blow to residents' incomes by eliminating most of the ground-level spaces that slum families typically use to develop their broad array of enterprises. High-rises undermine social networks as well as economic life.

If such arguments—fully crafted by the MIT School of Architecture for the World Bank—can be introduced into planning courses worldwide, one can imagine a major impact over time as the planning graduates fan out across the globe (http://web.mit.edu/urbanupgrading/).

That there is an immense need for thousands more professional planners, architects, and other city-development professionals across the Global South is without dispute. The entire continent of Africa, for example, is reported to have just 35,000 architects—roughly 25,000 of whom are in Egypt alone.

slum upgrading

Urban Planning: Envisioning Rio's Future

Joaquim Vieira Ferreira Levy

Secretary of Finance, State of Rio de Janeiro, Brazil; plenary speaker

UNTIL 1960, RIO DE JANEIRO WAS THE CAPITAL OF BRAZIL. Once the capital moved to Brasilia the city was left to its own devices. Also the military clamped down on the local liberal elite until the late 1970s. Unsurprisingly, the state became rife with parochial politics and has served mainly as a springboard for ambitious politicians running for president. So, although from time to time people offered good plans for the city, we had no one to implement them.

Complacency led to the growth of *favelas*, where a quarter of Rio's population lives in poverty with utterly inadequate services. This growth was accommodated with interventions and promises of granting property rights to dwellers, while crime came to dominate social life and public spending sprawled. Businesses fled and fiscal accounts became shaky, despite strong oil revenues.

Today, the new administration, led by a young governor, Sergio Cabral, has challenged tired traditional ways. It was high time to bring fiscal discipline and planning for wealth creation rather than for reproducing unfair situations. Cabral understood that good management can improve service delivery drastically, given his state's $20 billion (U.S.) budget.

Investing in well-planned infrastructure is critical because of its impact on job access for millions of people in a metropolitan area covering more than 2,000 square miles. This strategy includes completing a beltway linking two ports, the airport and sites around the most populated areas. It also calls for refurbishing rail lines and coordinating bus lines so that communities are easily connected to job centers.

The transformation of favelas started with Manguinhos and Alemão, where about 300,000 people live along winding, narrow alleys in a crime-ridden environment. Although Alemão's borders are conveniently close to rail and bus lines, just getting out of the favela takes many residents inordinately long periods of time. It also makes it difficult to staff schools and send in health workers.

The state and federal governments have joined forces in addressing favelas' real needs in terms of urbanization and provision of public services, as well as economic transformation. The state is also strengthening law enforcement all around the metropolitan area, including where vigilante militias have usurped the provision of key public services and drug lords bring additional extortion and brutality. In Alemão, a cable car lift will help connect the most distant parts of the community to bus lanes and the nearby rail station.

Making such changes will not be easy. To succeed, we must build social cohesion around the goals of better housing, enhanced sanitation, and mobility, and the enforcement of property rights and zoning as a way to create jobs, attract more investment, and reward household savings. We need to embrace those urban planning challenges as an integral part of a strategy to effectively include the poorest in the economic fabric of the city. That will make us all stronger.

Is There a Cure for Corrupt Governance?

NO WORLD CITY OR NATION is entirely free from instances of "bought" government, misdeeds by those in power that undermine the very idea of civil society. But what are occasional scandals in some societies can become an endemic cancer in others, barring the paths to education, housing, health, gainful employment, and personal security. Among the greatest victims: new, poor residents of fast-growing cities, most often harmed by the actions of corrupt officials and agencies.

But imagine a new, strong generation of urban professionals running city governments—individuals who have been trained in quality institutions and are inculcated with the values of designing, planning, and managing cities that work for everyone. Could a growing cadre of such professionals be an effective antidote to the long-standing cultural and financial plague of corruption?

And if that's the case, what could donor nations and agencies do to bring about trusted governance and official systems stable enough to manage the cities and nations in need?

In his book entitled *The Bottom Billion: Is There a Way Out of the Bad Governance Trap?* Paul Collier writes, "While poverty is falling for about 80 percent of the world, there is a crisis in some 50 states—the bottom billion—due to a struggle between reformers and corrupt leaders—and the corrupt are winning. Seventy-six percent of the world's bottom billion live in countries that have suffered long periods of bad governance and poor economic policies. Bad governance is often so persistent because not everybody loses—reform is against the interests of the leaders who can get rich, and when reform does finally come, capacity is simply lacking. Aid (at least on its own) will not get countries out of the trap.... Although the reformers have truth on their side, truth is just another special interest, and not a particularly powerful one."

Some observers point to poor public sector salaries—whether for police work or clerking for passport offices—as an explanation for persistent bribery demands made for what should be routine public services. Yet the most egregious examples known seem to come at the hands of already well-heeled officials attempting to become even richer. And big international firms seeking major concessions on mineral or oil rights, or looking to land a major construction contract, often become eager to pay what can be easily framed as "facilitation fees." Indeed, as Collier notes, until 1999 if a French company bribed a public official in a developing country, that expenditure was tax-deductible. Although no Western government would openly embrace bribery as a business strategy, which governments would want to unilaterally take the high ground and see their firms miss out on lucrative contracts?

In 1999 the Organization for Economic Co-operation and Development fostered an agreement among all member states to make practices such as facilitation fees a crime—a step in the right direction, though without much assurance of how vigorously nations will enforce the policy.

Consider the landscape ahead. As the world becomes more serious about building infrastructure to adapt to climate change, and more money flows toward assuring systems of pipes to relay fresh water and take away waste, the opportunities for siphoning off money are enormous. Transparency International, the best-known watchdog organization on corruption, pointed out in its 2005 *Global Corruption Report* how susceptible the construction industry is to corrupt practices: first, comparing prices is difficult because each project is different; second, it is tough to anticipate every eventuality so the door is always open for changes (and new charges). A firm might win a contract with a low bid and then work to fatten up the agreement with changes, working in collusion with benefiting government officials.

A reputation for corrupt governance hinders the world's most vulnerable from receiving aid. Consider one prominent piece of evidence: the last round of the World Bank's loans went to six middle- or upper-income countries, which have less than 5 percent of the world's needy population. There is no question that bad public sector governance, sometimes combined with blatant corruption, impedes the flow of vital capital to nations where the urban poor need help. The World Bank has been heavily criticized for these actions.

Transparency International lists and ranks nations saddled by corruption. Myanmar and Bangladesh may be rated the most serious cases, but the list of problem nations is disturbingly long. At least in today's world, instances of corruption making the international news can cause significant action. So when Nigeria's top corruption investigator was sidelined, it made *The New York Times*. When newspapers hinted of suppression,

Nigerian police arrested a prominent former governor on corruption charges. When the head official investigating corruption for the World Bank found corruption undermining more than $500 million of bank projects in India, it became headline news, as did the official's subsequent resignation. Or when the United Nations itself revealed its investigative unit had uncovered ten cases of fraud in contracts worth more than $600 million, the argument over whether to extend the investigative team's work for another year also hit the newsstands.

As violence broke out in Kenya in late 2007 over charges of election fraud, nearly every article carried a reminder of the nation's decades-long struggle to recover from a long period of mismanagement and corruption under former President Daniel arap Moi. With infrastructure lagging woefully behind population rises, a corrupt gang of contractors doubled or tripled usual contracts, got paid, and sometimes did not even do the work. Kenya's current president, Mwai Kibaki, pledged in his 2002 victory to tackle the issue and appointed a high-level official to clean up the government. Shortly after announcing a finding of a massive fraud inside the government, that official was exiled. In the ensuing months Kibaki would remove two ministers who had been accused of corruption, only to reappoint them.

Kenya's strife is a showcase of how "high levels of poverty expose poor populations to political manipulation," explains Jane Weru, who runs the Pamoja Trust, an NGO working on housing and infrastructure progress with Nairobi slum dwellers. What looks like ethnic conflict, she suggests, is, at its core, politics and economics. All that mixes with long-standing tribal tensions.

Thousands of miles away, Karachi's Arif Hasan would characterize the broader political struggle reported from Kenya: "The looting, arson, and destruction of property that has taken place is not a simple law-and-order situation. It has to be understood that you cannot create small islands of insensitive and arrogant affluence in a sea of increasing poverty and deprivation on the one hand, and a ruthlessly manipulated political and judicial dispensation on the other."

There are hopeful signs. The military regime in Bangladesh seems committed to rooting out long-standing pockets of corruption. It has made believers so far of the Asian Development Bank, which has made a $150 million loan, largely aimed at strengthening the Anti-Corruption Commission. The charismatic new president of Tanzania, Jakaya Kikwete (continuing the struggle initiated by former president Benjamin Mkapa), is said to be committed to change, having already pushed through an anti-corruption bill and ordered an investigation into the dealings of the Bank of Tanzania. Skeptics remain, but bilateral money, led by Britain, is donating aid directly to the nation's budget. Former Mozambique president Joquim Chissano won the cash-rich Mo Ibrahim prize in late 2007 for restoring democracy and good governance.

Still, in too many countries where the planet's poorest reside, critics of corrupt practices are simply waved off, told that this is a necessary if sometimes unsavory part of doing business—just part of the culture. In many of these places, however, a few brave people do try to change the system, but they always find well-financed interests arrayed against them. Parties and politicians commonly reserve significant resources to protect the advantages of being in power.

What nearly every observer decries is the absence of a clear and coordinated global strategy for better governance. The path to a strategy raises an almost-obvious list of questions:

- How much difference can a new generation of urban professionals make? If the management of cities is not merely political, but the product of a team of professionals, can corrupt practices be squeezed out?

- What are the key institutions to establish and protect? Are anti-corruption commissions enough? What else?

- How much effect would systems of participatory budgeting have, as people feel they have a voice in setting the priorities of municipal government? Would bringing grassroots voices into public budgeting actually create transparency in how governments allocate monies, disinfecting the process against corruption and assuring a fairer break for poor neighborhoods?

- Could major aid programs be made conditional on governance change on the integrity or professionalism front? If aid were consciously shifted to the most difficult urban arenas (itself a major change), could aid policies openly accept higher failure rates, spend more resources working with local officials, and show more flexibility in seizing opportunities for reform? As author Paul Collier and others point out, all the policy momentum today runs in the opposite direction; most agencies are risk-averse and they constantly try to drive down administrative costs while focusing on the best "success" photo ops.

- Could nations, or groups of nations such as the European Union, use the regulatory tool for leverage, requiring institutional changes as a condition of approving trade deals, particularly in countries dependent on exporting goods?

- What are the prospects for more international agreements, in which clear and serious political standards set the eligibility for participation, much as the four nations making up Mercosur in Latin America require democratic institutions?

No matter what else is tried, it appears that nothing will endure without establishing, nurturing and protecting institutions and professionals who replace the old customs with a new culture.

Growing armies of planners and their colleagues are also imperative because a high proportion of Global South growth is now projected to go into medium-to-smaller-sized cities and not the megacities that have absorbed such vast numbers of people in recent years (though "absorbed" may be too generous a term given the huge slum population growth in these cities). São Paolo, Mumbai, Mexico City, Manila, Jakarta, Delhi, Lagos—none of these cities shows any evidence of better planning, despite their immense size. And smaller developing-world cities often lack even a minimal number of professional staff to help them make timely and smart decisions, even as increasing waves of new residents start to arrive.

URBAN DESIGN AND PLANNING: GRASPING FOR CONNECTIONS

If the emerging cities of this century are to do more than merely cope with urban problems, the practice of urban planning and design must change. The preparation of urban professionals must burst through the walls that separate academic subjects. Complex partnerships must be forged that include a set of major universities to develop and share knowledge about better theory and successful practices.

That was the strong consensus of the Summit session on planning. The rationale was brilliantly summarized by Joseph Sauve of Canada, one of the participating Global Studio graduate students. Sauve, fresh from field experience in the slums of Johannesburg, said, "You look around and see that the trees are botany, the ground suggests geology, the sky reminds you of geography, and people take you to anthropology and sociology; the systems are all politics and economics. How could you study just one thing and think you are prepared?"

Such changes sound simple and straightforward. They are, however, nothing less than revolutionary—insurgent notions pushing against cultural inertia and institutional resistance. It remains true that in most universities *and* city governments, professionals in each specialty area, from planning to engineering to finance, are off doing "their thing" and all too rarely collaborate. Their work may be interrelated, but it is not often interconnected for maximum effectiveness.

Sclar recalled the previous Summit weeklong sessions: "Our best minds told us that little can be done about water or sanitation or housing or even climate change unless they are connected to the agenda for development." Those are the rules of the real political economy, Sclar explained. "And when we got to the issue of urban population health, it was all about the social and physical determinants of health, with implications way beyond the scope of the health professions alone."

So what's to be done to encourage urban professionals to crawl out of those persistent silos and embrace a broader challenge? A key problem, the participants noted, is that the silos of professional practice—and the damage that follows— are direct echoes of the organizational form of the universities where most professionals receive their preparation. Despite all the talk of inter- and multidisciplinary knowledge, people

Residents and volunteers build 200 new homes in one week in the Freedom Park slum, Cape Town, South Africa

A wrecking ball levels a building in the infamous Cabrini-Green

noted, almost all university activity (and faculty rewards) remains organized by separate disciplines.

Yet any single discipline is insufficient to deal with the deep, emerging challenges of 21st century cities. "The categories simply don't work any more," noted Richard Plunz, himself a professor of architecture as well as director of the Urban Design Lab at Columbia University's Earth Institute. Aravena, the architect in Chile, claims that "too many architects are skilled only at issues that interest other architects, so we end up answering the wrong questions. Slums are overcrowded, yes, but the question is how to design for high density without overcrowding." Peter Ngau, head of the Department of Urban and Regional Planning at the University of Nairobi, added that "students are telling universities that what they are being trained to do is irrelevant."

design for high density without overcrowding

Edgar Pieterse, head of a new network for African cities at the University of Cape Town, said it is a matter of focusing on the "how" issues. "You need to know how the bureaucracy and the state work and how to navigate them, and that does not come from studying political science."

Or as Harrison Fraker, dean of the College of Environmental Design at the University of California, Berkeley, put it, "there is such an incomplete understanding of the real system" and its complex interconnections "that I think we just have to reboot."

And though there is no way to reverse that situation instantly, the planning and design participants agreed that they needed to take action and find ways to start spanning the

spanning the silos

silos so that the next generation is better equipped to address the increasingly complex challenges of rapid urbanization.

Along the way, several added, it is essential to address both the numeric maldistribution and attitude of many professionals within the various urban disciplines. As International Union of Architects president Gaetan Siew explained, Italy has three times the number of architects as all of Africa. "Besides," he said, "most students are motivated to build monuments, be the stars of architecture. That's maybe 3 percent of the work out there. Somehow we have to tell them to be social architects as well."

social architects

That means, in turn, a keen awareness of changing demographics. While design professions practice as though this were still the late 20th century, noted Pieterse, the developing world in particular presents an explosion in the number of young people, with profound implications for cities and the global economy.

Both fuel and food are becoming significantly more expensive, perhaps permanently so. The era of climate change and mounting environmental dangers also challenge planners to be ecologically sensitive, to focus on models of true sustainability, and to work with local residents on such fronts as food self-sufficiency, energy conservation, improved local drainage systems, and adequate local transportation services. How can the ingenuity of slum dwellers' house building be matched with research on safe and conserving building materials? What are possible ways to bring in safe electricity and avoid dangers of

Disrupting the Status Quo:
A New Urban Vision

Enrique Peñalosa

Former Mayor of
Bogotá, Colombia

IF NEW YORK, PARIS, OR LONDON could make half of itself disappear to rebuild anew, quite a few things would be done differently the second time around. Since many cities in developing countries are relatively young, they enjoy a similar opportunity today. Most of what they will become by the year 2050 will be built during the next 40 years. So these youthful cities have a historic opportunity to design themselves based on lessons learned from the successes and failures of their older siblings.

The choices made in the way new urban areas grow in the coming decades will determine to a large extent their quality of life, environmental and social sustainability, and overall competitiveness for centuries. If, for example, land is not reserved now for parks, many generations of children will be less happy and healthy. In the past, first land and then capital determined economic growth. In today's post-industrial society, however, it is highly qualified and creative people who are the most crucial resource for economic development. To attract and retain such people, cities must offer a high quality of life. This includes comfortable, fast and accessible public transportation; wide tree-lined sidewalks; protected bicycle lanes; abundant parks, sports facilities and libraries; and a rich cultural life.

Environmentalism, economic development, and social welfare need not conflict. The same urban policies that can lessen negative effects on the natural environment can be used to enhance social equity and quality of life in general.

Over the last 50 years many cities in developing countries saw their populations increase by more than 1,000 percent, yet little was done to make them any better than preexisting advanced cities. For the most part Latin American cities are undistinguished. They should have featured, for example, New York City–style Central Parks, Amsterdam-esque bicycle ways, and Toronto-like greenways. Yet, this type of planning and development was rare. Instead, 20th century cities were designed around the needs of cars far more than those of people.

When less-developed countries did attempt to emulate urban centers in the more advanced countries, particularly the United States, they replicated elements that did not help them enhance their quality of life by saving oil, avoiding global warming, and creating more competitive cities. It is still difficult for many of the new upper-middle classes in developing countries to understand that when it comes to urban development, the United States model is to be avoided, not followed.

We cannot let these mistakes be repeated. What must be done during the next 50 years is now clear. Policies designed to improve quality of life, social equity, environmental sustainability and economic development are neither particularly costly nor technically complex. Obstacles to creating better cities are actually political, more than economic or technical. Governments shy away from what should be done in order to appease powerful stakeholders, such as speculative landowners and members of upper-income groups who radically oppose any restrictions on the use of their cars.

This conflict of interest between the car-owning middle and upper classes and the car-less lower-income majorities is complex and often goes unacknowledged. When resources that could have gone to schools, housing and parks are poured into high-velocity urban roads instead, the poor are left with the message that this is progress and that, in time, they will benefit from it as much as their better-off neighbors. Yet, this type of car-centered urban development does a disservice to all residents, whether privileged or poor.

Car infrastructure is by far the main competitor for funds that otherwise could be invested in solving the needs of the poor—and, in turn, improving quality of life for all, since everyone benefits when the poorest among us become less poor. Upper-income citizens in developing countries, however, don't use government-provided services such as public education and public health. So they often fail to see the connection between helping those who do and improving their own lives. All they require from government are security and traffic-jam-free roads. These upper-income citizens do not really use their cities much at all: insulated in their cars, they move from one destination to another, from apartment building to office to mall, from supermarket to country club.

For them the city is a threatening, alien space to be bypassed while going from one private place to another.

In an attempt to solve traffic problems, upper-income citizens demand more, bigger and faster roads. But, as cities like Los Angeles clearly demonstrate, increasing road infrastructure only stimulates more and longer trips, making traffic congestion even worse. Like fences, new roads also divide long-standing neighborhoods and, when built as overhead highways, darken city streets, lower real estate values, and often promote crime. They also encourage further development of far-flung low-density suburban gated communities, which draw upper-income residents away from the hearts of cities and increase their dependence on cars and roads. Of course, some roads and highways are necessary. But to help link poorer residents with jobs, schools, and other urban benefits, any large, new urban roads should incorporate exclusive mass transit bus lanes, protected bicycle paths, and broad sidewalks.

It is clearer today than ever before that the only urban mobility solution is public transportation. Time lost in traffic is increasing annually in all North American cities except Vancouver, which has blocked the construction of highways through the city and promoted density and public transport. But convincing people who can afford cars to use public transportation instead requires more than a good public bus system; governments need to impose restrictions and surcharges on car use, such as parking limitations, congestion pricing, fuel taxes, and other charges whose proceeds should go to subsidize better and cheaper public transportation. In forward-looking cities, "transportation policy" translates into "ways to reduce car use." Unfortunately, too many underdeveloped cities are still trying to facilitate it.

All cities must be both community-minded and realistic about the type of public transportation they provide. Higher-income citizens in developing countries prod their governments to build subways, preferably underground, despite not having the slightest intention of ever using them. They simply do not want buses taking away precious road space from their cars. Yet buses are actually the best transport solution in developing country cities. High investment and operating costs make it impossible to build more than a few rail lines, so trains do not move more than 10 percent of the population in any developing country city. Bus rapid-transport systems begun in Curitiba, Brazil, and used in cities such as Bogotá are moving more passengers per kilometer hour than most rail systems do at comparable speeds and at a fraction of the cost. Their required use of exclusive lanes is a given in a democracy, where public good prevails over private interest. But the idea of making concessions for the community as a whole is not so obvious in the unequal societies of developing countries, where more costly rail systems are often chosen over more economical bus rapid transit.

Urban residents everywhere have the right to walk or bike safely. Bicycle use can save up to 20 percent of poorer citizens' income in developing countries, where it is the only form of transport for many. Even in cities as rich as Utrecht in the Netherlands or Copenhagen, nearly half the population uses bicycles for their daily mobility. Safety, however, for these environmentally friendly modes of transportation is severely lacking in many countries, where pedestrians and cyclists are too often killed by motorists. World Bank and multilateral agencies require environmental impact studies for infrastructure projects, yet they finance roads without bicycle lanes or sidewalks. As cities arise and grow, streets, roads, and drainage canals should always be built with walkways and bicycle paths.

Convenient public transportation is an important tool in helping poor people improve their lives by linking them to employment and educational opportunities. Whether known as *tugurios*, *bidonvilles*, or *favelas*, slums are found in most developing country cities. As we strive to create compact, energy-efficient urban centers, we must not only improve and legalize existing slums but we must also avoid the development of new ones. Urban land reform is more critical than rural land reform ever was. Diverse tax systems and other regulatory mechanisms proposed to solve the problem, however, are always blocked or dodged by landowners. If governments acquired, through voluntary sales or the use of eminent domain, large tracts of land adjacent to existing urban areas, the housing needs of poor people could be met in quality urban environments. Every day that goes by without radical government intervention in urban and suburban land use, slums grow. Opportunities are lost to create a healthy city for all residents.

A city is a collective creation that reflects a society's values. There is much in a good city that cannot be left to the private sector: It is not for developers to decide the width of roads, sidewalks or bicycle lanes; how many or how large parks should be; the maximum height of buildings; or whether there should be shops in residential areas. There are, however, many areas in which private investment and management clearly do much better than the public sector. For instance, governments in developing countries should not own and operate machinery such as excavators, dump trucks, or compactors, and even if bus companies are government-owned, the buses themselves should be owned and operated by contractors. Public services such as electricity, piped gas, water, and garbage collection can often be managed more efficiently and at lower cost by private operators.

Although land around cities should not be left to the free market, housing construction should not be controlled by government institutions. Private corporations can build and market houses for the poor under strict time schedules and pricing parameters. Governments can help by providing housing subsidies to buyers in need.

When cities are at their best, they are protective, beautiful, inclusive, and stimulating places. We must learn from older cities as we imagine the futures of today's growing urban centers. Yet we must also create new urban concepts to make cities more respectful of human dignity so that more people around the world can lead happier lives.

exposed wires? Planners and other publicly supported professionals should be positioned to contribute significantly on all such fronts.

ADDED TENSIONS FOR PLANNERS

There is a continuing dilemma: the entire issue of whether elites care at all about conditions of the poorest in a world characterized by widening gaps in income and increasing separation of humanity by economic classes. Pieterse pointed out that nearly 60 percent of African workers labor in some part of the informal economy, "while elites are utterly comfortable living in enclaves." "In Rwanda," he said, "the real world [of decision makers] is about oil. It's definitely not about the 20 percent at the bottom of the economy."

For decades, participants noted, motivated professionals and NGOs have tried to alleviate alarming slum conditions by appealing to the self-interest of the economically privileged in better-run or less socially divisive cities. "What did we find?" asked Pietro Garau, former Habitat officer and now director of the Urban Research Center for Developing Countries at the University of Rome. "After 30 years of trying self-interest, of working through organizations such as the U.N., we have failed miserably. It is not enough."

All too often, it was noted, elites simply dismiss the interests of the poor as they make decisions central to cities' futures. Thus the whole process of designing cities ostensibly to work for everyone does not reach the poorest citizens who most need the kinds of improvement that investments in planning should produce. "In fact," said Getaam Tiwari, an associate professor at the Indian Institute of Technology, "a majority of people in our cities are completely outside the planning process."

Another thought-provoking question: Who knows best which solutions will work best for slum dwellers? As Darren Walker noted, "We have two kinds of tension at work here. One is North versus South, a tension increased by the North's presumed intellectual superiority. The other, though more subtle, is the struggle to balance professional (whether North or South in its provenance) and authentic local knowledge." It is a false debate, participants agreed, but nonetheless real. University professors and representatives of major donor organizations have special knowledge that is relevant. But there is also tremendous "street knowledge" in troubled low-income communities. And the world is even starting to see maps and indigenous enumeration systems devised by slum dwellers themselves. Indeed, Web sites such as Wikimapia and OpenStreetMap are rapidly showing how significant locally gathered voluntary mapping can be to understand both geography and human activity.

voluntary mapping

Arif Hasan, an architect and planner renowned for his work on the Orangi Project and the Urban Resource Center in Karachi, said it was essential, though probably never popular, to get the design process not just extended to but focused on the challenge faced by the poorest 20 percent of urban citizens.

"We probably need better terms," he said, suggesting that the goal should in fact be creating "the inclusive city," in which the needs of the urban poor are taken as seriously as those of existing elites. Sclar said much of the North is easily made nervous by terms that suggest redistribution. "But socially," he said, "Americans do understand mobility."

Whatever the words we use, Hasan continued, "what's necessary now is new organizations and knowledge that together deal directly with conflicting interests. And we must have space for those interactions—this is how you relate to the real political economy."

POSSIBLE SOLUTIONS

So what steps would bolster the global networking, multidisciplinary learning, and development of sensitive planning and project implementation to deal with the most serious new-century problems of new billions of population amid alarming growth of urban slums? Summit participants developed a number of recommendations:

co-labs

Through a cooperative donor effort, establish a network of up to a dozen university-based centers—"co-labs"—with a majority located in the Global South. These centers should be related to a major university but enjoy a necessary degree of independence from academic governance and constraints. This status, participants insisted, is key to overcoming the rigidity and inertia of separated professional preparation and research. Participants were so enthusiastic about the idea

Buildings surrounding Potsdamer Platz, Berlin, Germany

Traditional houses in the shadow of new high-rise apartment blocks, Shanghai, China

Making Two Cities into One: Securing Land Rights

Jane Weru

Executive Director, Pamoja Trust, Nairobi, Kenya

MANY SEE URBAN DEVELOPMENT as chaotic and uncontrolled. As loads of people move out of unsustainable rural settings into unplanned urban communities, they lay to naught the often myopic plans of city governments. Lands that had been set aside for other purposes are invaded and squatted on, as land and housing markets fail these new entrants into our cities. Services such as water and electricity are pilfered, as utility companies fail to recognize these new areas as legitimate human settlements and accordingly provide services to the people who live there. Most of our cities are therefore in reality two cities in one: the first, a formal and orderly city and the other, a higgledy piggledy world where there are more churches than toilets, where children sleep underneath the matrimonial bed because there is just not enough space.

The informal city is also seen as a threat to society and perceived as a seed bed for rebellion and social and political strife. Large numbers of unemployed and discontented youth are harbored here. The youth often gang up and slowly begin to take over their neighborhoods. Through force and extortion they seize control of water, security, and other services. They can at the least provocation mete out violence on their adversaries or for a fee be hired to achieve a political goal.

One needs to look only as far as Kenya to see the writing on the wall. For those who do not take heed of the large numbers who have been stripped of their citizenry through years of exclusion, then civil strife and mayhem awaits them. Addressing land and access to services in our cities is critical. A priest friend of mine who for many years lived in Korogocho often said that the city of Nairobi is built on a mortal sin. That sin is the fact that 55 percent of the residents of this city squat on only 1 percent of the total land area and 6 percent of the total residential area of the city.

Yet one of the most fundamental rights of man is the right to enjoy the quiet and uncontested occupation of a potion of this earth. This too is a fundamental right of citizenship; the right to the quiet enjoyment of space in the land of which one is a citizen. The failure to have any form of security of occupation without the threat of eviction undermines this right.

The urban poor within our cities are without this right. They see themselves as refugees in their own land with no rights to the lands they occupy and no recognition as legitimate citizens of our cities. They say they have sat on their haunches for too long. They say they cannot settle in peace because they are never too sure when they may need to get up and run because an arsonist's match has been used to burn down their homes and get them off the land. With this level of inequality, brutality, and exclusion, little wonder Nairobi blew up the way it did after the contested 2007 elections.

The challenge of providing security of tenure to the urban poor in our cities is daunting. Often layered property rights exist with tenant, structure owners, and registered property owners all laying claim to these lands. The complexity of this situation calls for a multiplicity of strategies. For instance, in Kenya we have sometimes chosen to address the issue of security of tenure without seeking the immediate registration of rights. We have done this through advocating for the setting aside of lands by the Nairobi City Council as special planning areas, for the purposes of upgrading. Once these lands are secured, the identified residents are free to upgrade their homes and settlements with the assurance that they can in time obtain title documents.

A palpable energy exists in most informal settlements and it is in them that the future of a country lies. Among the teeming masses, I see youth with their hopeful enthusiasm, I see the courage and innovation that it takes to survive in these harsh environments. If we could invest more in our people, in educating our youth, in providing basic services, then that energy, that courage, and that resilience could really count for something.

that they named the centers "co-labs": collaborative centers where students would be prepared for new-century challenges in a multidisciplinary way, where professionals would come together to compare practices, where research rooted in realities of the field could be furthered, and where special events could be staged. And they could also develop and nurture partnerships with local governments, NGOs, key community and economic-development organizations, and philanthropies. University of Nairobi's Ngau pointed to a wide array of global networks. "Some work, some don't," he said, and "we should tap the knowledge of what works." Key points of the co-lab idea, as developed in the sessions:

- Dialogue and co-learning. The forums would bring together residents of developing-world cities with developers, financiers, politicians, and other researchers. The media could be invited to observe. The co-labs would provide a communications platform for emphasizing the focus on design and planning dilemmas that affect the potential improvement of urban conditions for the poor.

- Network and capacity building. The co-labs could form a large network, producing a journal, endowing chairs based on criteria of priorities for the urban poor, sponsoring further studio programs for student experience, collaborating on research around priority themes and issues, and leveraging available bilateral funding.

- Student recruitment. These centers could attract the growing number of students, especially graduate students, who tell survey takers (Paul Farmer of the American Planning Association suggested the figure is as high as 80 percent) that they are looking for international experience.

- Applied research. The centers could undertake the largely neglected area of applied research, offering practical solutions to problems in cities ranging from health and housing to energy and infrastructure. Applied research, it is hoped, would catalyze interdisciplinary commitments across anthropology, economics, energy, environment, architecture, and planning. "Centers would be in a prime position to bring in experienced professionals to mix in on research or forums, tapping groups such as Architects (or Engineers) Without Borders," noted Anna Rubbo, the University of Sydney architecture professor who mentored the 2007 participating Global Studio students.

- Credibility and validation. Accreditation process for the centers could occur *wherever it helps* to ensure a cross-disciplinary, real-world oriented approach that includes applied research as well as traditional academic inquiry. As the College of Environmental Design at the University of California's dean Fraker reminded participants, in the North, especially in the United States, accreditation is nearly never seen as supportive of innovation. "If anything," Fraker said, "it tends to dumb down things, a necessary drill to go through." Those familiar with university life in the Global South, however, reported that the accreditation process is seen there as a more meaningful exercise; indeed, it provides a kind of "badge of legitimacy." In the South, accreditation can be a useful lever for trying something different, if a different course gets an official seal of approval. The Council on Higher Education Accreditation (CHEA), it was suggested, could set up criteria and processes for interdisciplinary programs with credentials to match. CHEA, which has recently published a directory of international programs, could set up an interdisciplinary track that would apply to these emerging centers and their university affiliates.

The panelists understood that the central co-lab idea—serious collaboration around a multidisciplinary approach—is a revolutionary notion in today's world of learning. But the harvesting of many ideas from varied sources, it was suggested, provides superior results. One participant recited an oft-told story of a Manila experiment in which groups were divided from most to least homogenous for a problem-solving exercise. The groups that were most familiar with each other (and most alike) worked really fast and competed well—until the level of problems became more complex. Then only the diverse groups seemed to succeed.

"I'm in agreement" with that overall thrust, said Gary Hack, University of Pennsylvania School of Design dean and experienced practitioner in planning in more than 30 cities around the world. "But," he added, "let's not risk the empty-suit syndrome by ignoring the value of specialization." Even generalists, participants agreed, need an area of special knowledge for success in the real marketplace.

Participants speculated that the collaboration centers, once established, would find promise in a variety of approaches. One working group classified the multiple approaches as people-based, place-based, and ether-based networking. Perhaps most of the centers would be rooted in a suitable location—a place-based asset. But some might take a people-centered approach, and emphasize developing professionals across the board and tackling a realistic range of challenges facing the urban poor, using networks across a variety of locations; young professionals could mix with veterans who could share their rich experience at a variety of locations. The third proposal, given the accelerating use of the Internet, was the promising potential in an ether-based approach. The Internet works well for sharing research, collaborating on projects, generating ideas through multiple-participant brainstorming, and sharing results.

people-centered approach

Ngau insisted that the co-labs could be permanent even if mobile—physically, intellectually, world-oriented. Ideally, the group said, they should generate their own income and thus be free of individual university "ownership" (or intellectual domination).

Build a coalition of funders who will then empanel a group to design a collection of the co-lab centers. Composition of the group should be cross-disciplinary and include people with a practical sense of priorities in rapidly expanding urban areas with concentrations of the poor. Such a design group should be asked to suggest the number and variety of centers, up to some practical limit set by funders. It should recommend

STRUCTURE: URBAN INNOVATION CO-LABORATORY

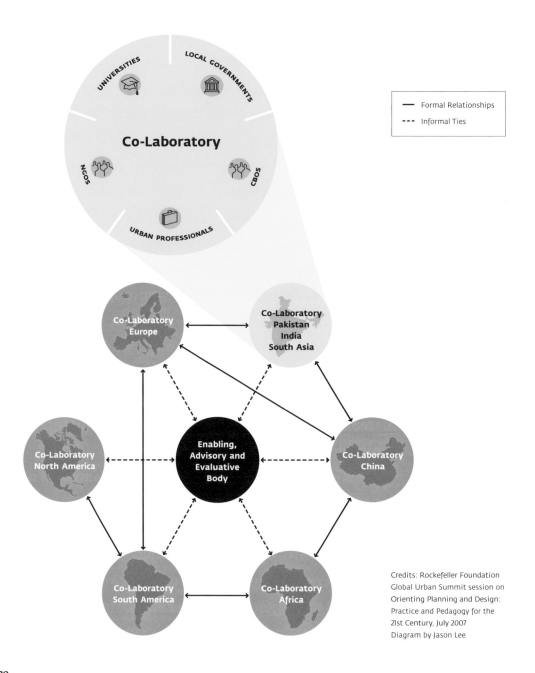

Credits: Rockefeller Foundation
Global Urban Summit session on
Orienting Planning and Design:
Practice and Pedagogy for the
21st Century, July 2007
Diagram by Jason Lee

a strategic geographic balance, not only between North and South, but with a specific goal to generate early and plausible collaborative networks among NGOs, local governments, one or more academic institutions, and indigenous organizations controlled by residents in the least privileged urban areas.

collaborative
networks

The panel would produce a model strategic plan, including a method of sustainable finance, and a governance model that balances a necessary degree of autonomy with a relationship to suitable academic institutions and other affiliations that might strengthen each center's early standing.

Stress that field experience is as important as intellectual study—each informing and challenging the other. Global Studio students, fresh from the 2007 field work in the slums of Johannesburg, provided vivid evidence of the value of integrating experience in urban communities with the study of architecture and planning. Any student whose preparation was isolated in academia and constrained by narrow disciplines would, judging by their testimony, experience a life-changing epiphany from a few weeks of confronting the pressing problems faced daily by the urban poor. Additionally, any student's sense of what constitutes a practical solution would be transformed.

Another idea advanced: if it is considered normal to require physicians to have a period of residency before starting a full professional practice, why should it make any less sense for urban professionals to have real contact with the people and the problems their practice should serve? Both field experience

A Checklist for Slum Improvement

WHAT IS A MODEL CHECKLIST for upgrading the slums in any developing nation? The Cities Alliance, a global coalition of cities and their development partners committed to scaling up successful approaches to poverty reduction, has produced a list of essential steps. Key elements:

- Demonstrate political will.

- Generate both national and local government vision, commitment, and leadership to achieve slum upgrading.

- Set national and city targets.

- Put it in the budget.

- Support slum upgrading as part of core business, nationally and locally.

- Ensure necessary reforms dealing with land tenure and finance.

- Reform closed and opaque land markets, which encourage corruption, patronage and exploitation of the urban poor, as well as constrain capital markets.

- Engage slum dwellers themselves, who have both the ability and the interest in promoting upgrading, and the private sector, which should be engaged as a risk-sharing partner rather than a mere contractor to the public sector,

- Prevent the growth of new slums.

and intellectual study would be greatly enhanced by exposure to a rich mixture of academic disciplines, corresponding to the mixed nature of problems and solutions.

Enfranchise local professional practice. As panelists repeatedly reminded each other, less than 5 percent of the urban world today functions under any kind of planning regimen. In most places even the notion that advance planning and considerations of design and analysis of how things will fit together is completely new. Far too many urban places show little evidence of good planning; worse, in some places, what passes for planning has merely served a narrow group of developers or the whims of officials with their own interests in play.

Since it is not reasonable to expect high-level professional design and planning practices to reach all parts of cities, why not institute varieties of licenses that can be earned by people engaged in all manner of urban planning and implementation work? Planners, architects, and engineers tend to have professional degrees that represent at least a significant measure of education and capacity. But what of organizers of slum dwellers, business-oriented people working on community economic projects, coordinators of street planning and design, and craftspeople who have proven their ability in upgrading physical infrastructure of formal settlements? Recognition as local community planners would bolster their standing, perhaps putting them on a ladder to more professional preparation. Panelists saw this level of service as akin

varieties of licenses

to what people in the United States see in an "extension service," a vocational practice aimed at the most intensely local level.

Challenge the sources of finance. The Rockefeller Foundation's Walker set the stage for considering finance with a sober assessment, in that "there are not at present a lot of donors interested in this." But he also emphasized the potential of leadership. If a major grant maker such as the Rockefeller Foundation can identify other donors who come to share a strategic vision of what can be accomplished, their stand on the cause of the urban poor might shift the ground of public perception. The key objective should be to build a coalition of potential funders, rather than expecting that some foundations will follow others, and then to recognize that even foundations with their considerable resources lack the cumulative fiscal power to match the scale and scope of the challenge.

shift the ground of public perception

Therefore, we should not allow the profit-making private enterprises of the world to escape responsibility, participants said. International Union of Architect's Siew suggested that the large insurance firms that do business internationally already have a serious stake in seeing that urban areas are better planned. Particularly in view of the threat of climate change, these companies would put a premium on prospects for buildings and infrastructure that are built to higher standards and made more reliable. Chile's Aravena suggested that firms operating in most markets still see that they can profit by building a better public image. "We got Home Depot to finance social

threat of climate change

Visitors to the Shanghai Urban Planning Museum view a vast scale model of the city, Shanghai, China

Aerial view of the city of Curitiba, Brazil

housing in Chile," he said, pointing to how much the firm's involvement raised its profile with the public. Farmer of the American Planning Association pointed to commodities firms, which are, he said "just flush with cash these days." Such companies, along with the shipping companies, will do better if people around the world are doing better, ordering things available to be made and sold and shipped.

Summit participants also thought that oil companies should be approached. Their profits are nearly legendary in these times. And they can hardly escape their primary role in the climate-change challenge. All these big economic entities, people said, should be funding targets for effective co-lab centers across the developing world.

Nor should the World Bank be ignored, the panelists noted, suggesting that it might be now primed for more funding. (In December 2007 the Bank announced that after months of negotiation, 45 countries, including such nations as Egypt, China, and Latvia, agreed for the next round of funding to a three-year donation of more than $25 billion, a 42 percent increase toward poverty reduction and sustainability goals.)

The sense of urgency for urban planning and design is rising rapidly, participants noted, in part because of global climate change and its potentially disastrous impact on world cities. But despite the potential ravages of global warming, the challenge to shape more livable and sustainable conditions for the hundreds of millions of people at the bottom rungs of the

potentially disastrous impact on world cities

global opportunity ladder could hardly be more dramatic and compelling than it is now.

On June 22, 2007, the world's mayors, along with a host of other local government leaders, assembled in Rome. Keenly aware that 2007 marks the halfway point between the adoption of the Millennium Development Goals and the target dates they envisioned, mayors said in one collective voice, "We are running out of time."

Yet the harsh fact is that up to now the universities and allied institutions, where the designers and planners of the century's explosively growing cities must be trained, have not been enlisted as meaningful partners in the endeavor to create livable cities for our time. A challenging agenda of institution building, shaped to new century needs, is today's inescapable imperative.

CHAPTER 6

AMERICA 2050: U.S. Strategy for the Next Half Century

strong federal action

limits on spread

fresh opportunity

national growth strategy

mobilize state government

megaregions

national planning framework

the nation's future growth

alternative energy

the linchpin of sustainable development

THE UNITED STATES HAS SURGED past the 300 million population mark without a coherent plan for where and how it will
house, educate, or otherwise prepare for the next 120 million
Americans (both immigrants and children of today's citizens)
the demographers predict by midcentury. Symbolized by such
disasters as the tragic 2007 collapse of a critical interstate highway bridge in Minnesota, the nation's infrastructure gap, now
estimated by the American Society of Civil Engineers at $1.6
trillion, continues to lag.

A glance at a map of economic activity shows a growing
megaregions majority of Americans now live in ten "megaregions"—each
a network of individual metro regions that share intimately
connected economies, environmental systems, and transportation networks. More than 70 percent of the population expansion and 80 percent of the wealth growth of the next decades
is expected to occur in these megaregions. The nation's ports,
key to U.S. participation in the new global economy, are within
them. Most are already experiencing congestion, high-priced
and overcrowded housing, and degraded environmental systems.

There is no U.S. equivalent of the European Union's
focused funding of transportation, telecommunications, and
human capacity-building programs to advance broad geographic
U.S. regional regions. U.S. regional planning and development also lag
planning behind initiatives in countries such as Japan and South Korea,
and clearly behind those in China and India, Asia's rising
tigers each experiencing a phenomenal boom in infrastructure
building. New high-speed train systems, a key to mobility in

megaregions, are blossoming in some 14 nations worldwide. Yet there is not a single U.S. counterpart.

In a century of troublesome and apparently fast-advancing climate change, the United States faces direct threats to its coastal cities from rising sea levels and to its interior from drought-triggering temperature increases. Yet despite a level of CO_2 emissions indisputably the highest of any nation until China's recent surge of industrial activity, it has trailed—not led—the developed world in attempts to effect significant reductions.

U.S. POPULATION, 2000–2050, BY COUNTY

- More than 15% loss
- 5 to 15% loss
- 4.9% loss to 5% gain
- 5.1 to 15% gain
- 15 to 50% gain
- 50 to 100% gain
- Over 100% gain

Credit: Regional Plan Association, based on data from Woods & Poole 2002 and University of Pennsylvania School of Design 2004

Indeed, look where you will and signals abound of a radically altered world challenging the United States:

- Vastly expanded international trade—already up to 26 percent of the nation's GDP, projected to rise to 35 percent by 2020. U.S. firms and workers also face direct, rising competition as lower-wage countries develop competitive scientific, technical and workforce capacity, plus the expanded infrastructure to support the growing sectors.

- A mounting worldwide energy crisis. As demand rises and petroleum reserves diminish, coal's heavy CO_2 emissions hinder its further development, and the United States continues to import more than 60 percent of its oil supply, much of it from politically unstable and increasingly hostile countries.

- The vast amount of U.S. infrastructure—not only roads but also rail lines, airports, seaports, water, and waste disposal systems—that have aged beyond their normal lives or reached capacity limits, with seriously limited or nonexistent plans for modernization.

- A virtual stalemate in U.S. transportation policy even as rising traffic congestion becomes an ever-greater depressant on the U.S. economy (the cost—in lost time, gas, additional car accidents, and pollution—to New York City alone is $4 billion a year).

- Loss of natural landscapes to low-density sprawl and careless land-use decisions.

- Seriously unbalanced growth and economic opportunity

Resentment and Resolve Over Climate Change

DEEP-FELT RESENTMENT from representatives of the Global South. American defensiveness and guilt. A scramble for higher ground. All were thrown into bold relief during a Summit session on climate change with participants from both the Global North and the Global South.

Addressing the Americans present, Saleem Huq, founder of the Bangladesh Centre for Advanced Studies, began the exchange with his comment that "the rest of the world" had been looking for solutions of unabated carbon emissions "for a long time," including an effort to respect Kyoto limits. But, he continued, "You got off the wagon. You need to catch up rapidly. You may be the biggest economy in the world but you cannot do this on your own. You need to rejoin the conversation with the rest of the world."

David Satterthwaite, an economist who has focused heavily on poverty reduction in urban areas of Africa, Asia, and Latin America, noted: "The political system that has to act isn't the one that has to cope with the effects. It's people like the squatters in Dharavi, in Mumbai, whose lives are being destroyed by climate change."

Patricia Romero Lankao, a Mexican scientist and environmental expert, added that the United States' "current paradigm" of inattention to global warming issues is causing serious global repercussions—perils to the coasts, air pollution, heat waves, and danger of wildfires. Another speaker said that the United States is "setting a horrible example."

One American participant later commented, "Do developing countries expect us to repair the whole world?"

On the contrary, Eliot Sclar, director of the Center for Sustainable Urban Development at Columbia University, explained: "The message Americans are hearing is, 'You made this problem, so you need to *help* clean it up.' Americans must figure out how to open communication on this difficult issue."

Regional Plan Association president Robert Yaro noted that the next president should be strongly urged to provide leadership on this issue: "We need to set realistic goals for the U.S., an agenda that can truly be achieved by the next Congress and President."

As PolicyLink founder and CEO Angela Blackwell put it, "There is no question that the United States has contributed to all sorts of suffering and injustice, both internally and externally. When we live in the U.S., take advantage of our lifestyle and passport, we can't pretend we're not part of it. So we need to assume a role of advocacy for change and willingness to criticize our own government."

Another participant added, "We need to work on our own CO_2 emissions—first turn the United States around, then bring along China and India and Europe." Mark Pisano, Executive Director of the South California Association of Governments, said that the Global North and the Global South "shouldn't be split as we go through a global transformation. We've moved into a new century with information, trade, and the environment becoming the framework around which we organize ourselves. We Americans must think of ourselves as world actors, not King of the Mountain. We must deal responsibly with environmental consequences and do it in a transformative way."

between central cities, older suburbs and newer suburbs, magnifying already deep social inequities.

Could the United States begin to focus on a comprehensive, targeted set of national investments in climate, energy independence, equity and jobs? Can the nation's regions and megaregions be mobilized for the new century? Can a vision as powerful as the Civil Rights Movement of the 1960s be developed, spelling out clear steps toward a sustainable future in which all regions and classes have a stake and can readily see new opportunities?

Yes! It is certainly a daunting challenge, but not impossible. That was the consensus of a panel of urban leaders, transportation experts, and observers of American domestic affairs gathered at the Rockefeller Foundation Global Urban Summit to explore steps for clear and dramatic national action. Although the participants saw many obstacles, they agreed on the imperative of a broad and courageous new-century vision.

targeted set of national investments

courageous new-century vision

THE HISTORICAL CONTEXT

No nation in history has ever enjoyed quite the global dominance that the United States exercised in 1945. The country had just triumphed in a vast world war, fought from Europe to the South Pacific. Its GNP was a scarcely credible three-quarters of the GNP of the entire world. Erstwhile enemies, Germany and Japan, would look to it for political reconstruction and economic recovery. American manufacturing and financial power were set to dominate world markets, American military power to remain unparalleled for a half century or more to come.

But the United States did not rest on its oars. Two huge federal undertakings—the GI Bill, opening the doors of higher education to returning veterans, and housing programs assuring remarkably low-interest mortgages on new homes—threw open the doors of economic opportunity for millions. The Great Depression of the 1930s became a mere memory; an expansive middleclass was created.

In the 1950s, President Dwight Eisenhower inaugurated the Interstate Highway System, advertised by its proponents— truthfully—as the greatest public works project in world history. The interstate system provided the capacity for a fivefold increase for U.S. GDP in the half century after 1955. Then, with its 1960s Civil Rights Movement, the nation began amends for its three centuries of slavery and ensuing subjugation of African-American citizens. Congress enacted immigration reforms that reopened the door to large-scale immigration for the first time in many decades, allowing the United States to attract talented and entrepreneurial people from around the world.

Then, it seems, the country began simply to coast. It responded ineffectively to the Arab oil embargo of the 1970s, failing to wean itself from foreign petroleum or to develop alternative energy sources. In the 1980s, it embraced a politics that asserted that the federal government was the problem— not a common enterprise to forge new national futures.

federal undertakings

Interstate Highway System

Civil Rights Movement

talented and entrepreneurial people

Antitax revolts, begun in California in 1978, spread across the continent. Americans' pride and joy became their booming national economy and its cornucopia of consumer benefits. Government's attention went largely to bolstering personal benefits such as Social Security and Medicare. Federal "urban renewal" efforts in depressed inner city neighborhoods stumbled seriously, welfare became a stigma for its recipients, and federal housing subsidies for the poor stagnated at a mere fraction of the tax favors granted middle- and upper middle–class homeowners through the home mortgage deduction.

Washington's inattention, mirrored by many state and local governments, came at a price. By 2005 the American Society of Civil Engineers could report its numbing $1.6 trillion dollar estimate for the cost of basic infrastructure repairs the United States should make by 2010 in fixing outmoded or disintegrating roads, bridges, schools, dams, waterworks, airport, rail, and public transit systems. Delay needed repairs any longer, the group reported, and the country could anticipate longer commutes, unsafe drinking water, delayed flights, and failing dams.

warning went
unheeded

But the warning went unheeded and reliance on foreign oil remained over 60 percent of domestic demand—and growing—even as the United States has stumbled seriously in responding to the global challenge of reducing greenhouse gas emissions.

Concurrently, no vision emerged of how the nation's metropolitan regions, center cities, and growing varieties of new suburbs could work together to bolster efficiency and create long-term, sustainable growth.

THE AMERICA 2050 INITIATIVE

In the face of national inaction and apparent deep complacency, many organizations and groups within the United States have become alarmed. In 2004 the independent Regional Plan Association (RPA)—author of successive New York regional plans since the 1920s—decided to take action. It enlisted a variety of civic groups and academic and business leaders from across the United States to develop a vision and policy directions for the nation's future growth.

the nation's future growth

The initiative, known as America 2050, was a prime focus of the Global Urban Summit. Participants agreed on a central goal:

Create and promote a grand vision of America in 2050—the world our children and grandchildren will inherit—by tackling critical long-term investment issues now, based on three critical E's: a prosperous economy, quality environment, and social equity.

The time for action cannot be postponed, RPA president Robert Yaro contended: "We've used up the capacity the United States built in the first two-thirds of the 20th century, the investments that made America a global powerhouse. We're living off the investments of our parents and grandparents."

What of the argument that national planning is inherently anti-American, foreign to the country's civic and political

DNA? *Not true*, said Yaro and his colleagues. They invited historian Robert Fishman to the Urban Summit to present his research showing how two grand national plans actually laid the groundwork for America's flowering as a world leader in the 20th century. First came the 1808 Gallatin Plan under President Jefferson for western settlement, leading to the Homestead Act under President Lincoln. Second was America's conservationist movement, sparked by President Theodore Roosevelt with this 1908 resource-based economic development national plan, laying the groundwork for the TVA and other expansive federal development ventures in the 1930s, and eventually the interstate highway system.

Gallatin Plan

America's conservationist movement

Fishman's analysis emboldened participants to endorse a broad range of initiatives that a reawakened and revitalized American federal government could and should embrace.

TIME TO PLAN AMBITIOUSLY: NOW!

There is no time for delay, panelists discussing the America 2050 agenda agreed. To match the nation's third-century needs, a National Growth Plan Strategy, with both federal and state–local elements, is critical:

- Strengthen the nation's vast megaregions, constellations of individual metro regions, and centers of the nation's population and economic growth
- Combat climate change: Reduce the United States' carbon footprint 80 percent by 2050, implemented at all levels of American life

- Reform national transportation policies, including the creation of a clearly mapped multimodal network, maintenance of existing systems, and significant CO_2 emission reduction
- Develop bold new conservation policies, both to use land far more efficiently and to preserve critical natural landscapes in an era of rapid population growth, including state–local initiatives and a new National Landscape Survey
- Focus on equity, assuring that new initiatives serve all socio-economic classes in American society, not just established middle- or higher-income groups

We will have a 21st–century America either by plan or by default, participants agreed. The choice should be clear.

An early step could be to urge the President and Congress to establish a Working Group on America 2050, including (at a minimum) the Secretaries of Agriculture, Transportation, Defense, Homeland Security, Interior, Housing and Urban Development, the EPA Administrator, and perhaps several governors and major city mayors. The assignment of this working group would be to develop a strong national planning framework on the scale of grand national plans of earlier centuries.

national
planning
framework

Continuous nonpartisan education of Congress members (especially freshmen) will be essential in the America 2050 dialogue. Outside the beltway, RPA will work with America 2050 partners in key regions across the country to refine the framework and build nationwide support. In early 2008, following the 2007 Summit, the Rockefeller Foundation joined forces

American National Planning: As Old As the Republic

THERE IS A POPULAR MYTH that national planning and federal leadership on how the country grows are somehow un-American. But this is simply wrong. That convincing case was made by University of Michigan historian Robert Fishman as he told the story of two grand "campaigns" of national planning that helped define Americans' very character, and greatest historic advances, as a country.

First came the revolutionary 1808 "Gallatin Plan" by Albert Gallatin, President Thomas Jefferson's Treasury Secretary, outlining the vision of creating a truly democratic society by planned settlement of the continent by citizen–farmers. The plan was to be a carefully mapped section-by-section area beyond the Alleghenies, the whole enabled by a national system of roads and canals. It faced delays due to growing North–South divisions that Jefferson had hoped to prevent. Instead, the initiative switched to the states, including New York state's building of the Erie Canal. But Gallatin's ideas did reach ultimate fulfillment under President Lincoln: the 1862 Homestead Act that awarded 160 free acres of federal land to any family that would claim and farm it. Concurrently enabling settlements, the federal government made major concessions for growth to the 19th century's most powerful technology and corporate holding: the railroads, which seized vast amounts of land as they opened the West to settlement.

Perversely, the railroads became leading players in an economy of extreme speculation consuming whole forests and polluting entire river systems. That led four decades later to President Theodore Roosevelt's clarion call to conserve, push reforestation of damaged watersheds, and promote development in the South and West around the nation's natural resources. A key moment: a 1908 White House conference of the nation's governors to mobilize national support for permanently protected forests and rivers and for great dams to develop electric power for the people.

But when William Howard Taft succeeded Roosevelt, federal initiatives dwindled and responsibility again shifted to states and cities. Private electric utilities were able to thwart most of the early dam proposals. Only the advent of Franklin Roosevelt's New Deal and the dustbowl of the Depression years finally swept away opposition; the Tennessee Valley Authority and similar hydropower, irrigation, and

In 1908, President Theodore Roosevelt hosted the first meeting of the nation's governors at the White House to discuss conserving America's natural resources. Attended by 39 governors and several Cabinet secretaries and Supreme Court justices, this gathering marked the beginning of the National Governors Association (NGA).

navigation projects on the Columbia, Colorado, and other rivers symbolized the radical new federal approach. The view was *national*—a president from New York State pushing a broad program of forest and farmland preservation and rivershed planning that saved the most devastated regions of the country from disaster and set the stage for development of what would become the post-World War II Sunbelt.

Also under FDR, the National Resources Planning Board of the 1930s began preparing for a nationwide system of "superhighways;" the transcontinental system was finally realized in the interstate highway system proposed and enacted into law under President Eisenhower.

Historian Fishman argues that the interstates—"this massive exercise in national planning—gave American capitalism its second wind after the Depression and World War II, and has been the most important initiative in creating the country we know today."

Since the 1970s, initiative in the federal system has passed back to the states. Yet with growing challenges in transportation, energy supply, and sustainability in a carbon-challenged age, a period of renewed federal initiatives may become mandatory. If 1808 and 1908 were the key launch years for the past great plan thrusts, Fishman asked, what might 2008 bring?

Building America's Future

with Building America's Future, a nonpartisan coalition, led by Pennsylvania governor Edward Rendell, California governor Arnold Schwarzenegger, and New York City mayor Michael Bloomberg, focused on elevating the status of infrastructure investment as an issue of national concern.

MEGAREGION STRATEGIES

Participants agreed that the new lens of megaregions is critical to national economic prosperity, sustainability, and quality of

identify the assets

life. It is necessary to identify the assets and clear challenges of each megaregion, then establish agendas of how the federal and state governments can aid and abet their efforts.

Megaregions differ in their self-awareness. The Northeast Corridor and Southern California are among those with the most debates on shared futures. Yet in some megaregions, it is difficult

arouse public awareness

to even arouse public awareness about joint issues and predicaments. A prime example is the exuberantly expanding PAM, or Piedmont Atlantic Megaregion.

Megaregions everywhere, however, share issues

boundary-crossing policies

demanding cohesive, boundary-crossing policies. The Texas Triangle (San Antonio–Houston–Dallas-Fort Worth), for example, needs to collaborate across hundreds of miles on water issues, including protection of such irreplaceable resources as the Edwards Aquifer.

The Great Lakes megaregion, derisively labeled "Frostbelt" in recent years, needs to make a fundamental transition: from the three often-polluting "C" sectors of corn, coal, and cars

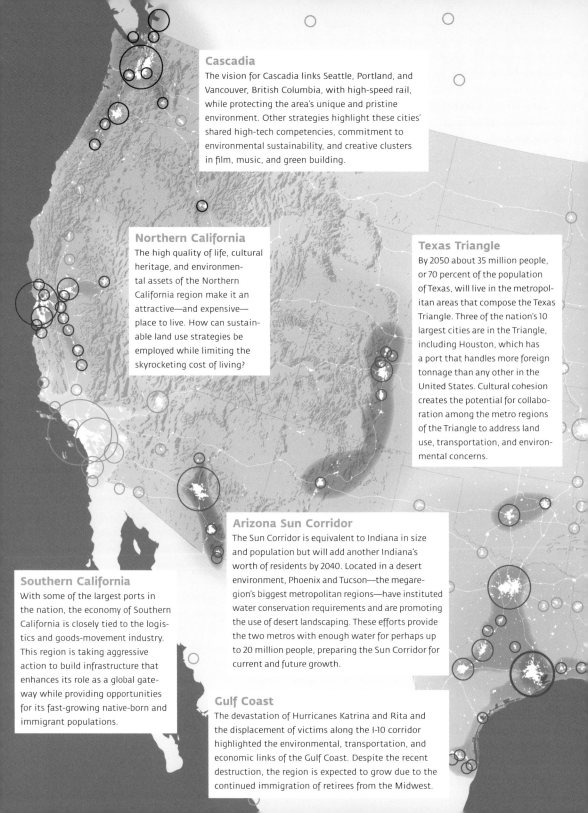

Cascadia
The vision for Cascadia links Seattle, Portland, and Vancouver, British Columbia, with high-speed rail, while protecting the area's unique and pristine environment. Other strategies highlight these cities' shared high-tech competencies, commitment to environmental sustainability, and creative clusters in film, music, and green building.

Northern California
The high quality of life, cultural heritage, and environmental assets of the Northern California region make it an attractive—and expensive—place to live. How can sustainable land use strategies be employed while limiting the skyrocketing cost of living?

Texas Triangle
By 2050 about 35 million people, or 70 percent of the population of Texas, will live in the metropolitan areas that compose the Texas Triangle. Three of the nation's 10 largest cities are in the Triangle, including Houston, which has a port that handles more foreign tonnage than any other in the United States. Cultural cohesion creates the potential for collaboration among the metro regions of the Triangle to address land use, transportation, and environmental concerns.

Arizona Sun Corridor
The Sun Corridor is equivalent to Indiana in size and population but will add another Indiana's worth of residents by 2040. Located in a desert environment, Phoenix and Tucson—the megaregion's biggest metropolitan regions—have instituted water conservation requirements and are promoting the use of desert landscaping. These efforts provide the two metros with enough water for perhaps up to 20 million people, preparing the Sun Corridor for current and future growth.

Southern California
With some of the largest ports in the nation, the economy of Southern California is closely tied to the logistics and goods-movement industry. This region is taking aggressive action to build infrastructure that enhances its role as a global gateway while providing opportunities for its fast-growing native-born and immigrant populations.

Gulf Coast
The devastation of Hurricanes Katrina and Rita and the displacement of victims along the I-10 corridor highlighted the environmental, transportation, and economic links of the Gulf Coast. Despite the recent destruction, the region is expected to grow due to the continued immigration of retirees from the Midwest.

TEN EMERGING MEGAREGIONS

America 2050 has identified at least ten U.S. megaregions: Northeast Corridor, Piedmont Atlantic, Great Lakes, Florida, Gulf Coast, Texas Triangle, Cascadia, Northern California, Southern California, and the Arizona Sun Corridor. Akin to the Global Integration Zones identified by European and Asian planners, all show strong linkages through overlapping suburbs, increased commuting between metro areas, strong transportation connections, and similarities in their industrial clusters.

Northeast

The Northeast is a powerhouse of density and economic output, producing 20 percent of the nation's Gross Domestic Product with 18 percent of the population and only two percent of the nation's land area. Over the next generation, the Northeast will add 18 million new residents. This population growth will demand infrastructure investments and economic growth to accommodate these new residents while preserving quality of life.

Great Lakes

The Great Lakes megaregion is exploring ways to grow its economy in the face of the shrinking role of the manufacturing sector. The region's assets include the environmental resources and amenities of the Great Lakes and a strong research and cultural tradition tied to its leading public universities.

Piedmont Atlantic

The low cost of living and high quality of life in the Southeast are two reasons for this megaregion's booming population, which is anchored by Atlanta but stretches east to Raleigh, North Carolina, and west to Birmingham, Alabama. The region is facing challenges associated with its growing population, such as increased traffic congestion, runaway land consumption, and inadequate infrastructure, which it hopes to address with sustainable solutions.

Metro Area Population

150,000 to 1 million

1–3 million

6 million +

3–6 million

Florida

The Florida megaregion is one of the fastest growing in the nation and possesses a wealth of diversity, with six of every ten new residents in the last decade coming from foreign countries. It is both dense and populous, with the major international city of Miami acting as a gateway to Latin America. Regional strategies to protect the Everglades have preserved the natural heritage of the state.

Source: Regional Plan Association

to new, clean industries associated with reduction of greenhouse gases. The auto sector, under such a scenario, would be encouraged to focus on hybrids, the coal sector on carbon capture and storage, the corn sector on alternative crops and biomass production. More steps, including targeted federal aid, would be pursued to develop an innovation economy, building on the strength of the Midwest's research universities. Major investments would be targeted to new-century-sensitive workforce preparation, and making goods movement at the juncture of the nation's freight railways a much greater priority. "Techbelt" efforts to line up venture capital, already undertaken in such cities as St. Louis, Pittsburgh, and Cleveland, would be widened. (The Brookings Institution, in its 2006 report, *A Vital Center*, called for a federal–state–local compact to revitalize the entire industrial belt, from western Pennsylvania to Missouri.)

new-century-sensitive workforce preparation

The Northern California megaregion, by contrast, is marked by a burgeoning population and severe shortages of affordable housing. The San Francisco Bay metropolitan region is spilling over into the Central Valley, causing serious loss of farmland and extraordinarily long auto commutes—proof that individual metro region approaches are no longer sufficient. Recommendations offered at the Summit included renewed emphasis on environmental protections, clearing local barriers to infill development, consolidating transit services under a single regionwide authority, and incorporating flood hazards into regional planning.

environmental protections

Megaregion initiatives face big hurdles—first public and political muscle, then sources of funding. The Summit panelists had no easy answers to those challenges. But they saw strong opportunities in use of 21st-century electronic tools to visualize and animate choices for growth, stimulate citizen envisioning processes, and employ online voting to reveal and strengthen the public's preferences.

21st-century electronic tools

THE EQUITY CHALLENGE

If environmental, economic development, and housing supply issues can spill across metro lines and require attention on the megaregion scale, what about equity? "Often where you live determines your access to opportunity," said PolicyLink head Angela Blackwell, whether in housing, schooling, employment, or environmental safety. Based on class and race, King County Executive Ron Sims added, "I see an entrenched Two Americas in each of the megaregions." The issue is increasingly important, added Catherine Ross of Georgia Tech's Center for Quality Growth and Regional Development, as we witness immigration spur a fast-evolving "browning of America."

what about equity?

Looking megaregionwide *can* bring fresh opportunity to "left-behind" cities, said RPA president Yaro, noting potentials in the Northeast Corridor megaregion to link economically lagging cities—Baltimore, Newark, and Bridgeport, for example—to the high-powered financial and technology centers of New York, Boston, and Washington. Success is already apparent in Bridgeport, he noted, as it receives a wave of back-office

fresh opportunity

The Piedmont-Atlantic Megaregion

STRETCHING FROM CHARLOTTE TO BIRMINGHAM, Chattanooga to Jacksonville, PAM illustrates the fast convergence of cities and their metro areas with merging geographies and economies. Recent decades have brought massive business, residential growth, and major commercial interaction among PAM's cities. Atlanta and Charlotte are its principal air hubs, the ports of Charleston and Savannah its access points to foreign trade. The fabled prosperity of Atlanta (and now Charlotte as a major center of U.S. banking) continues to draw people—indeed, the region's population is projected to grow by 68 percent by midcentury.

As a major drought starting in 2007 illustrates, however, PAM faces extraordinary water supply challenges, which could seriously limit healthy population growth. Suburban development is usually welcomed with few controls and no impact fees; most development in the Atlanta suburbs still permits septic systems, with potentially serious future water table implications. Environmentally sensitive buffers of green spaces between the cities are crucial, yet regional culture continues to ignore conservation issues.

PAM's most obvious shared problem is traffic congestion (legendary in Atlanta, serious regionwide). As the cities integrate economically, commutes continue to grow longer (even Chattanooga-to-Atlanta daily). High-speed rail could be a significant tool, allowing fast intercity business trips and helping to preserve the urban cores by focusing growth within them instead of sprawl around them. But public transit is weaker here than in any other region of the United States; even the famed Atlanta MARTA system serves only two of metropolitan Atlanta's nine counties.

So is PAM ready to think and act responsively to these regional issues? Should natural leadership come from governors of the region, or mayors of such cities as Atlanta and Charlotte, or from the business sector? Without a more sustainable, carbon-saving, water-planning, and economically efficient PAM, can any U.S. survival goals for the century be realized? Indeed, there is a global stake. If they were a single country, the southeastern states PAM largely dominates (Alabama, Florida, Georgia, North Carolina, South Carolina, Tennessee, and Virginia) would already rank as the world's seventh-biggest CO_2 emitter.

Necessary Roughness:
Sustainable Breakthroughs in Atlanta

Shirley Franklin

Mayor of Atlanta, Georgia, U.S.A.; plenary speaker

ASSERTIVE MANAGEMENT is a large part of my formula for preparing Atlanta—the de facto capital of the new American South—for 21st-century realities. During my first year in office I raised property taxes 50 percent, laid off 12 percent of the work force, and required all employees to take five days of furlough. I proposed tripling the water and sewer rates. Each time I tackled a tough issue, my favorable rating went up. My motto: Tell the truth and do what you say. I had won my first term by only 181 votes. For my second term, I got 91 percent of the vote. We did what was necessary first, no matter how difficult.

Issues of race, class, and personal property versus community benefit are certainly still driving our public policy debate. However, sustainability is one issue that is particularly hard for people in my region to swallow. My city has few sidewalks and the longest commutes of any region. Our public transit system is still largely limited to two of 28 counties. Our wide-open spaces are perfect for SUVs and trucks. So we're tied to our cars—the bigger the better. And even with 5 million people, we're still building all over the region with septic tanks, which only defers the cost. Our region has hit the wall on air quality as well as water quality and runoff. People say our main problem is traffic, but it's really a shortage of water.

It's clear that to turn more attention to sustainability, we need a real cultural shift. When the U.S. Conference of Mayors was debating its Climate Protection Agreement, a fellow Southern mayor said to me, 'We're from the South and we don't believe in this stuff. You can't vote for it.' Well, a growing number of mayors from the Southeast have now joined me in supporting this agreement, but the cultural traditions of the South remain a real constraint in our part of the country.

The good news is that we're already seeing a positive shift in Atlanta. The Beltline and the Peachtree Corridor Redesign are two examples of major improvements on a par with efforts in lead cities across the United States. Originally proposed by a graduate student at Georgia Tech, the

Beltline is a 22-mile rails-to-trails transit and denser development project. The city had to create a special tax district and a zoning overlay and has now raised about $200 million of the long-term $500 million budget for new infrastructure. This project has already stimulated $1 billion in new development.

The Peachtree Corridor project, the start of a 25-year effort to remake Atlanta's legendary main street, was launched jointly by the city and private corporations. A $1.5 million redevelopment plan produced a design that will revive the streetcar and create a tree-lined pedestrian environment that links to MARTA at five points.

I intend to use the last 900 days of my mayoralty identifying the stakeholders of an Atlanta sustainability plan for the next 50 years. The idea is to get people thinking on a broader, more multifaceted scale. For instance, when the city and region consider a second airport, we will measure its potential environmental impacts on the region but also look intensely inward to move from fuel- and energy-guzzling to a more sustainable future. And we need federal regulations and incentives to force us to seek alternatives to our current small-town traditions. After all, if it weren't for a federal judge's order, I might never have become "the sewer mayor."

Skyline at twilight, Atlanta, Georgia, U.S.A.

commerce and new demand for its housing stock as Stamford, 23 miles closer to New York, moves "from a back office to front-office space," becoming a major U.S. financial center. Key to the connection, noted Yaro, is the recent state of Connecticut action to upgrade service and lower fares on its long-troubled Metro North commuter rail service.

Improved rail transportation is vital to new prosperity all along Northeast Corridor, Yaro said—especially upgrading Amtrak and moving toward the types of high-speed rail systems that serve business interests of European and Asian competitor regions so well. The payoff is increased efficiency for the "hot cities" while helping the troubled urban centers get back on their feet—a responsibility, Yaro said, that the U.S. "federal government has walked away from." The European Union, by contrast, has sought since the 1980s to strengthen lagging areas through its Structural and Cohesion Funds, which constitute more than a third of the EU's budget.

Repeated efforts to create a more even economic break for the more disadvantaged classes, in most U.S. regions on most occasions, have failed ever since the 1926 Supreme Court decision in the landmark *Euclid v. Amber* zoning decision, which granted local governments major land-use controls.

limits on density

Interpreted to include setting limits on density and segregating land uses from each other, *Euclid* evolved into a powerful tool—rarely challenged successfully—to protect American middle-class values and property interests. The major post-World War II effect, bolstered by racially discriminatory lending

European Megaregion Success

MODERN-DAY EUROPE has been several steps ahead of the United States in recognizing and acting on regional and megaregion issues. Through its Structural and Cohesion Funds, for example, the European Union systematically targets funds for 1) helping lagging nations and regions bolster their economies and 2) fostering more efficient trans-European transportation networks encompassing all modes (motorways, waterways, rails, and airlines).

The economic resurgence of entire nations—Ireland and Spain, and to a lesser extent Greece, for instance—marked dramatic early success of the funds. But while individual metro areas face serious problems in lack of social cohesion, poverty, unemployment, or criminality, the overall attention of the EU has moved to them more slowly. One early metro success was in helping Manchester, England, through job training and environmental restoration.

Europe's best-known megaregion was originally identified as "the blue banana," a strip of extraordinarily prosperous urbanity stretching from the northwest of London to Milan, gaining its name from the curvature of the band including such cities as Brussels, Amsterdam, Frankfurt, and Zurich. But European urbanists see a dramatically wider network emerging, its arms reaching into northern, eastern, and southern areas. Dutch spatial expert Leo van der Meer nicknames the multiple interlinked regions the "red octopus" for its many directions and tentacles. It would include such new east-west megaregion corridors as 1) Amsterdam/Rotterdam-Ruhr Area-Braunschweig/Goettingen-Berlin-Poznan-Warsaw and 2) Stuttgart-Ulm-Munich-Vienna-Budapest-Belgrade. The north-south axis would be enlarged by connecting central Europe to Hamburg, Copenhagen, and Stockholm.

Discussions are under way about how to strengthen southern Europe by defining a new diagonal megaregion stretching from Lisbon to Milan, including Madrid, Barcelona, and Marseilles. With heavy North African immigration, this diagonal would reflect many of the same cross-border issues of merging Global North and Global South seen in Southern California and its intimate ties, economic and social, through San Diego into Baja California.

Europe's megaregions are prospering together around a continental-scale high-speed rail network financed in part by the EU and its plan to create a trans-European network of modern rails, roads, and intermodal goods-movement systems.

policies and unintended effects of the interstate highway system, was to promote low-density, single-use, auto-dependent communities on the urban fringe. Cities, facing simultaneous "white flight," were hollowed out; some experiencing severe racial disturbances. Those who complained about their communities' plight sometimes heard a negative message from national leadership: "If you don't like where you are, vote with your feet."

create housing opportunities

With rare exceptions, state-led efforts to create housing opportunities for lower-income families in affluent suburbs or enforce land- and resource-conserving growth management rules have stumbled over the issue of local control. Oregon's urban-growth boundaries worked for at least two decades, but efforts in such states as New Jersey, Maryland, and Tennessee tended to expire or lose steam with changes in gubernatorial administrations.

"hands off" policy

Meanwhile the federal government has maintained a scrupulous "hands off" policy—one reason it has been assumed that federal planning is a political impossibility. The only significant exception was the power accorded Metropolitan Planning Organizations (MPOs) to make areawide allocations of a portion of federal transportation dollars, inaugurated in the landmark 1991 Intermodal Surface Transportation Act (ISTEA) and continued in subsequent federal transportation bills. But even backers became skeptical of the ability of the MPOs, dominated by local government elected leaders, to go beyond a polite form of logrolling in their funding allocations. Additionally, central cities, in most MPOs, were severely underrepresented in relation to their actual population.

Some potentially significant shifts have occurred in recent years. Many center cities, notwithstanding the uneven playing field, began a population comeback in the 1990s, in most cases aided by a significant tide of foreign immigration (the "browning" factor of Hispanics, but also Asians in significant numbers). In the New York region, the urban core cities in the 1990s suddenly caught up with the suburbs in growth rate. Numerous factors, in addition to immigration, have been cited, from the increasing lack of affordable suburban housing and baby boomers forsaking crabgrass for urban amenities to the success of a maturing nonprofit community-development sector in providing islands of housing and reviving local neighborhoods to the influx of young professionals attracted to both jobs and homes in revitalized center cities.

Still, stark differences remain in income, education, and savings between successful and fast-growth suburbs on one hand, and the left-behind sections of older cities and aging inner-ring suburbs on the other. A central challenge, as U.S. population rises sharply in this half century, is to break down exclusionary zoning that denies opportunities to working class families, forcing ever-more sprawling development.

Participants explored ways to prevent affluent communities from simply opting out of regional accords and strategies. "Housing is the linchpin of sustainable development," noted Sunne McPeak, formerly Business, Transportation, and

a population comeback

stark differences remain

the linchpin of sustainable development

Housing Agency Secretary in the administration of California's Governor Arnold Schwarzenegger, "along with the three critical E's: a prosperous economy, a quality environment, and social equity." McPeak would require every community, through state law, to develop a five-year plan indicating how it would accommodate its own population increase *including* housing for its service workers (teachers, firefighters, golf course greenskeepers, and the like). A significant portion of a locality's zoning would have to be reserved for higher density development, with the goal of making individual units substantially more affordable. Several California communities are now adopting these principles voluntarily, McPeak indicated, but state law has not yet made the proposed practice mandatory.

Clearly, the goal should be to make all neighborhoods (regardless of their location in a region) stable, healthy, and livable—both to achieve equity *and* to strengthen the entire economy, safety, and quality of life of a region. The tools include housing opportunity, good schools, and transit systems that allow people to connect to jobs wherever they are in a region. They must also include a willingness, early on, to engage new population groups, immigrants, and disadvantaged Americans alike in conversations on community and regional strategies, tapping their energies and making them legitimate partners in the civic process.

The parallel to America 2050's broad national goals is compelling. The core concept is that each community, city, town, or neighborhood, like each region and megaregion,

strengthen the entire economy

should be encouraged and assisted, through a mixture of self-help and outside assistance—*provided at least an even playing field*—to prosper in an extraordinarily challenging century. An entire megaregion must function well, noted PolicyLink's Angela Blackwell, for the entire megaregion to

competitive be competitive. Such an approach and mind-set, combined with imaginative new federal initiatives, succeeded with sensational nation-building results from the Jefferson to the Eisenhower administrations.

Accomplishing as much in the 21st century may be more complex than in earlier times, given the way metropolitan regions and megaregions, where most Americans now live, tend to defy historic city, county, and state boundaries. In addition to urging responsive new federal policies, Global Urban

mobilize state governments Summit participants also pointed to the need to mobilize state governments, with their impressive constitutional powers, to intervene on behalf of their own economically trailing regions. Whatever the level—megaregion, state, single metro region, and city—there was clear consensus that a "winners-all" set of strategies and tools were never more needed.

WHITHER NON-MEGA AMERICA?

Map-drawers of megaregions on a continental scale face an immediate dilemma: What does their targeting of the cen-

big new urban regions tury's big new urban regions say to the vast stretches of the United States that are still overwhelmingly small-city and rurally oriented?

The restored Union Station is a hub of rail, shopping, and cultural activities, Kansas City, Missouri, U.S.A.

Fresh fruit and vegetables at the outdoor Farmer's Market on Union Square, one of more than 30 farmer's markets in the NYC GreenMarket program, New York City, U.S.A.

An early point of attention, Yaro said, should be to the special economies and potentials of urban centers that fall outside of the newly defined megaregions. Examples would include Louisville and Memphis, key hubs, respectively, for United Parcel Service and Federal Express, the United States' two leading just-in-time-delivery entities. Other such leading cities in their respective parts of the United States would be Denver, Kansas City, and Salt Lake City.

Many of those cities, in fact, serve as regional centers for geographically huge parts of the nation. Yaro insisted that just as Presidents Jefferson and Lincoln looked to the great land spaces of the West, and the two Roosevelts focused on large natural spaces for economic regeneration, including roadways and the expansive navigation systems on the Mississippi and Missouri Rivers, America 2050's agenda must be inclusive, working for the entire United States, not just the megaregions. "This is not about feathering the nests of successful places," he said, "but making sure every place can succeed; the notion of fairness must be imbedded in our national DNA."

The Great Plains, for example, could be positioned to become the new Persian Gulf of an alternative-energy world. They are the locus of hundreds of millions of acres of relatively fertile land, ideal for growing environmentally acceptable forms of biofuels. Additionally or alternatively, they could, with wind farms and solar power, be critical producers of extraordinarily promising new alternative-energy sources.

an alternative-energy world

Managing and maintaining those systems would, in turn, provide thousands of new jobs.

The America 2050 ideal is to target ranges of opportunity, from metro and megaregions to broad swaths of the nation—"dancing with the scales" wherever possible—to strengthen the nation for the century. The focus need not be physical facilities alone. One Summit participant suggested a 21st-century version of the 1862 Homestead Act signed by President Lincoln, which laid the groundwork for America's land-grant colleges and universities. A modern version might authorize a new educational network or enrichment program to reach all states and regions, re-democratizing higher education for our time.

the 1862 Homestead Act

CARBON REDUCTION: THE "80 BY 50" GOAL

Summit participants determined that the science of global climate change is so compelling that an immediate and comprehensive national action plan, crossing all layers of government and incorporating corporate and citizen action, is imperative. The goal is to reduce national carbon emissions by 80 percent (from their 2000 levels) by 2050, with clear interim targets for 2020 and 2030 that move the country onto a fast track toward slowing, stopping, then reversing carbon emissions.

Two compelling reasons exist—1) Moral: the world's poor, who live in countries that have not contributed to the greenhouse gas problem, will bear the earliest and most severe

Embracing Science:
Preventing a Diminished Future

Ron Sims

County Executive, King County, Washington, U.S.A.; plenary speaker

WHEN THE UNIVERSITY OF WASHINGTON evaluated King County's prospects for 2050, the results were frightening. With reduced snow pack in the Cascades, the region was headed for wintertime flooding. In other seasons there would not be enough water for either people or fish. If we continued on our current path we would not be able to handle the 300,000 additional people projected to live in King County within a few decades. When faced with this diminished future, we made the decision to embrace science.

As we explored all angles of the climate change issue, we realized that reaching carbon neutrality for the region was our first priority. The repercussions of our *not* doing so could be great not only for us but for the rest of the world. Some experts believe that entire cities—including Alexandria, Mumbai, Shanghai, and Lagos—will be indefensible without a 40 to 60 percent drop in worldwide greenhouse gas emissions. King County is now committed to 80 percent CO_2 reduction by 2050 and we will be implementing a worldwide cap-and-trade system. Requiring clear, measurable results, cap-and-trade is especially promising in developing regions. Africa, for instance, one of the globe's lowest-volume carbon emitters, could (with more transparency) be a huge cap-and-trade beneficiary.

In King County, we also knew, however, that we had to build resilience to the effects of climate change that were already in progress. So the county constructed 300 miles of levees and dissolved all the smaller flood districts, creating one district at the county level to cope with the inevitable deluge. In anticipation of major species changes among trees and animals, the county took steps such as developing new feed systems for salmon. To keep the city dense yet livable, we decided to separate roadways from bikeways, make the public bus fleet much more fuel-efficient, and develop plug-in systems for electric and hybrid cars.

Climate change is now a multi-sector issue. For example, ending sprawling development is not only good for the environment, but improved land use can help prevent obesity, diabetes, and other public health problems: Studies have illustrated the benefits of building pedestrian-friendly cities. So we began efforts to retrofit existing neighborhoods to make them more walkable, a prevention strategy initially targeted at communities at greatest risk (those of people of color and new immigrants). Today walkable neighborhoods are highly popular among all communities in the region.

Considering the connections and interdependencies among disciplines from urban planning to public health and among countries from the United States to Nigeria, combating the negative effects of climate change is a complex challenge that calls for worldwide efforts.

impacts; and 2) Direct: to the extent that global warming advances, the United States itself will be subjected to serious coastal flooding, loss of snow packs, droughts, species loss, and other detrimental effects.

As the world's largest importer of oil and gas, the United States is sending immense sums of money annually to some of the most hostile and unstable regions of the world, undermining the nation's economic vitality and security. Participants concluded that the United States must jump-start the investments critical to a cleaner energy future by legislation that puts a price on carbon—through a carbon tax, a cap-and-trade program, or other vehicle. The country must make a strong commitment to develop renewable energy sources (wind, solar, hydrogen, etc.). It must move rapidly to improve building efficiencies, commit to such renewable energy sources as solar, wind, and geothermal power, and make the transportation sector greener, with biofuels (beyond ethanol) and by producing more fuel-efficient autos. And the United States needs to begin serious planning for resilience to the devastating effects of climate change that, despite current and future mitigation efforts, are already inevitable in vulnerable low-lying coastal communities.

Every single U.S. community—no excuses—must be part of the carbon reduction program.

A research agenda should also focus on 1) future uses of hydrogen, 2) the viability of nuclear technologies based on fission and fusion, 3) the development of carbon capture and

the most hostile and unstable regions

A Lynx train takes commuters downtown, Charlotte, North Carolina, U.S.A.

storage technology for coal-fired power plants, and 4) national models for "green zoning" (land plans that reduce roadway travel through such devices as transit-oriented development).

strong federal action

Strong federal action is required, participants noted, to counter entrenched regional and corporate interests, principally from the coal and automobile sectors, and then assist those industries in adopting new energy technologies and economic opportunities in other sectors. The federal effort should include an executive order requiring a climate action plan for every federal agency and encouraging similar plans at every level of government.

Finally, existing consumer lifestyles, built on high levels of personal consumption that constantly increase energy demand, need to be modified through a broad program of education urging Americans to embrace the old New England adage "Use it up, wear it out, make do, or do without."

TRANSPORTATION

Increased mobility in and around America's megaregions was a major focus of Summit discussions on how national transportation policy should be formulated. Priorities identified included the following:

- Put megaregions and global gateways first in a national transportation investment program. Why? New investments need to be as ambitious in scope as the interstate system, but with much greater focus on intermodal connections, goods movement, rail, and reducing the effects of the sector's air pollution. International trade is expanding rapidly, channeled through key ports and facilities situated in major urban centers. Beyond that, the entire national economy is heavily reliant on efficient movement of people and goods in and between metropolitan regions and megaregions, whether by road or rail, public transportation, airports, or seaports. Current federal transportation policy fails to link these modes in any meaningful way.

- Develop high-speed rail within distinct metropolitan corridors. Late 20th century America was built around the interstate highway system, limited access roads perfect for regions 30 to 60 miles across. But at the scale of megaregions 300 to 500 miles in length, roadway driving times between hubs are excessive. Time getting to and from airports makes air travel inefficient for such distances. Conclusion: the United States has to look to quality 21st-century grade rail service on par with virtually all other mature and rapidly developing world areas.

- Include social and environmental benefits. "Smart" highways, congestion pricing, Intelligent Transportation Systems, and modern rail, America 2050 argues, will not only speed workers, business travelers, and goods between the megaregions' networked cities, but also stimulate idea exchange, expand labor pools, and provide fresh opportunities for workers of today's bypassed areas. Equally critical, natural landscapes and estuaries need to be protected as the green infrastructure that supports clean water, provides

Leading by Example:
Government on Conservation

Earl Blumenauer

Member, House of Representatives (Oregon), U.S.A.; plenary speaker

DURING MY SIX TERMS IN CONGRESS, I have worked with my colleagues to provide federal support for more sustainable communities. We directed $5.5 billion to trails and bike paths around the country, passed the Paul Simon Water for the Poor Act (aimed at making developing countries' access to safe water and sanitation a major goal of U.S. assistance), helped reintroduce streetcars to the U.S. urban fabric, and bolstered our intercity rail system by keeping Amtrak alive.

But more needs to be done. A demographic shock wave is coming in the United States, not just from aging residents but from a population increase from 281 million people in 2000 to 420 million by 2050, doubling the populations of many communities. Yet our housing market is askew: While single-person households increase and baby boomers find fewer buyers for their large homes, we continue to produce a surplus of 20 million McMansions.

It's time for the federal government to catch up with the numerous states, cities, religious institutions, and college campuses that are already working to combat the negative effects of climate change. More than 700 cities have signed the U.S. Conference of Mayors Climate Protection Agreement, underscoring a fresh perspective across the country on responding to global warming. My home town of Portland, Oregon, for example, pledged to reduce its greenhouse gas emissions in 1993 and has since cut them by 1 percent, despite a 17 percent growth in the population.

The federal government must lead by example. Why not rename the General Services Administration the "Green Services Administration" and have it sport a policy that forbids it from buying any building or renting any vehicle that is not green? The Department of Defense is the largest manager of infrastructure in the world (including a half trillion dollars worth of buildings and bridges) and it is the world's single largest energy consumer. Why not decrease its energy appetite, which commanders know is constraining our military effectiveness, and make it another conservation trailblazer? We need to give serious consideration to a federally imposed carbon tax or cap-and-trade system for greenhouse gas emissions.

We must also find new ways to fund badly needed infrastructure investments. If the federal government had simply retained development rights around interstate road entrances, we would have generated enough revenue to pay for the entire system. Today, we could fund essential investments in roads, water, airports, and rail systems by instituting a system like the Base Re-Alignment Commission (BRAC) procedure for military bases: a panel of experts could prioritize a capital budget, which Congress would then accept or reject with a single vote.

Foundations can also play an important role in supporting communities' sustainability efforts. They can help jump-start conservation-related efforts from organizations they already support (in community or mixed-use development, for instance) or they can help leverage investments and focus the media on relevant societal problems and policy choices that otherwise would get little public attention.

The public is ready to take action. Whether it's the growing interest in streetcars, the willingness to fund conservation and open-space initiatives, or the recognition that our children need to be able to walk and bike to school safely, the public is way ahead of officials on the issues that make their communities more livable and sustainable. If we give the public choices that make sense and treat them as partners in the planning process, they are ready and willing to support these conservation and sustainability efforts. Our national security and the future of the planet are at stake.

carbon dioxide "sinks" to reduce greenhouse gas emissions, and supports local agriculture and recreation. One major goal must be reduction of diesel toxicity around major ports.

- Build social equity and environmental and land-use criteria into federal transportation decision-making guidelines. California does this by devolving transportation project decision-making to the MPOs in its regions, which then judge projects against their comprehensive planning framework.

- To provide adequate transportation revenue, Congress should consider either indexing the gas tax to inflation or consider a tax on vehicle miles traveled to ensure a constant revenue stream in the face of greater fuel efficiency, electric cars, and the adoption of biofuels.

Congressional earmarking of transportation projects hampers rational decision-making. Consideration should be given to the Base Re-Alignment Commission (BRAC) method of military base closings, with a single up or down congressional vote, based on recommendations of an independent commission to determine priority national transportation investments. (The BRAC idea was subsequently incorporated in the January 2008 report of the bipartisan National Surface Transportation Policy and Review Commission.)

LANDSCAPE

The America 2050 panel recommended that in the spirit of Theodore Roosevelt, the U.S. Secretary of the Interior should be instructed to conduct a thorough, constantly updated National

CRITICAL LANDSCAPES AND ESTUARIES OF THE NORTHEAST

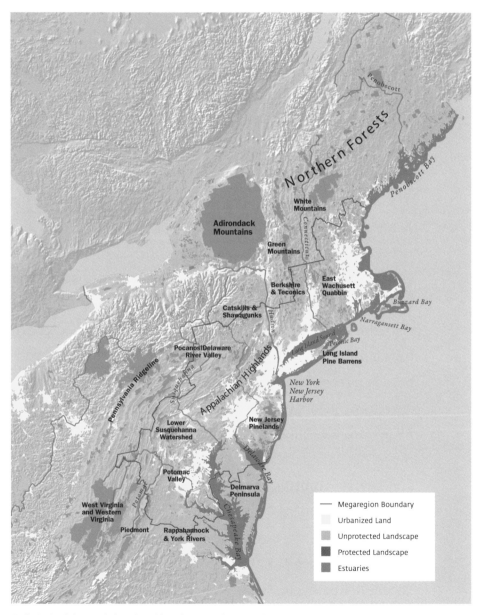

Credit: Regional Plan Association, adapted from the Appalachian Mountain Club

Landscape Survey. Why? The scenic, historic, working land-scapes of America are threatened on multiple fronts, ranging from suburban sprawl, mining, and deforestation to climate change. University of Pennsylvania researchers calculate that if today's rate of urbanization continues, the United States will develop more land in the next four decades than in the past four centuries.

suburban sprawl, mining, and deforestation

In the Eastern United States, vast areas of the Central Appalachians are being destroyed by mountaintop mining for coal, while the great coastal estuaries are threatened by pollution and the spread of low-density subdivisions. In the West, public lands are threatened by strip mining, clear-cutting, and overgrazing. Along the Atlantic, Pacific and Gulf of Mexico coastal areas, barrier beaches and islands and wetlands are threatened by second home development and sea rise. Across the country, national parks suffer from under-maintenance while some of the most productive agricultural lands in or near metropolitan areas are being fragmented by large lot subdivisions.

National Landscape Survey

A National Landscape Survey would identify critical areas to be protected. Examples include geological, hydrological, and ecological areas with important mountain ranges and significant aquifers and recharge zones; areas of high biodiversity; critical wildlife habitats; geneways (pathways for species migration that call out for protection); areas with important cultural, historical, archeological, or visual resources that could be degraded or lost as a result of controlled or incompatible development; resource-protection areas such as regionally or nationally significant farmlands, ranches, forests, and water resources now in the path of rapid development; and finally, natural hazard-protection areas (places prone to fire, floods, hurricanes, avalanches, erosion, or subsidence).

The goal is to establish the National Landscape Survey as a blueprint for protective measures, either by states and localities as a condition for other federal aid, or in federal–state and state–local partnerships. For coastal areas, the survey could identify future storm surge areas and flood zones as sea levels rise. Focusing on the emerging megaregions where open space is most imperiled, the survey might identify, for potential state governments' protection, large (100,000 acre or more) scenic, historic, agricultural and water supply systems. For the Great Plains, the survey might define a potential network of restored prairie ecosystems, integrated into a comprehensive economic development program of business, solar, and wind power generation.

The private sector, including the growing number of businesses that value quality of life in attracting employees in knowledge fields, is also supportive of programs promoting open space and participation in cap-and-trade systems to reduce carbon emissions.

a blueprint for protective measures

cap-and-trade systems

FUTURE STEPS

The urgent America 2050 message, the Summit panelists suggested, could be spread (even relaunched) in a well-planned collaboration in which the Regional Plan Association (which gave birth to the idea) works with other national networks, such as the Urban Land Institute, the Council on Competitiveness, PolicyLink, the American Planning Association, Brookings Metropolitan Policy Program, and National League of Cities, as well as a variety of major business, environmental, religious, and social justice organizations. The reality is, however, Summit participants noted, that major national issue campaigns require millions of dollars and years of effort; the America 2050 agenda will likely be no exception.

National
Growth
Strategy

Yet there was little doubt about the necessity of broad vision and an ambitious target—to bring an America 2050-like agenda to public prominence as quickly as possible, introducing a modern "National Growth Strategy" worthy in spirit of the earlier national development frameworks advanced by President Thomas Jefferson in 1808 and President Theodore Roosevelt in 1908.

CHAPTER 7

U.S. Transportation Challenge: Better Outcomes for Billions Spent

extremely high returns

promoting equity

reaching capacity

lack of accountability

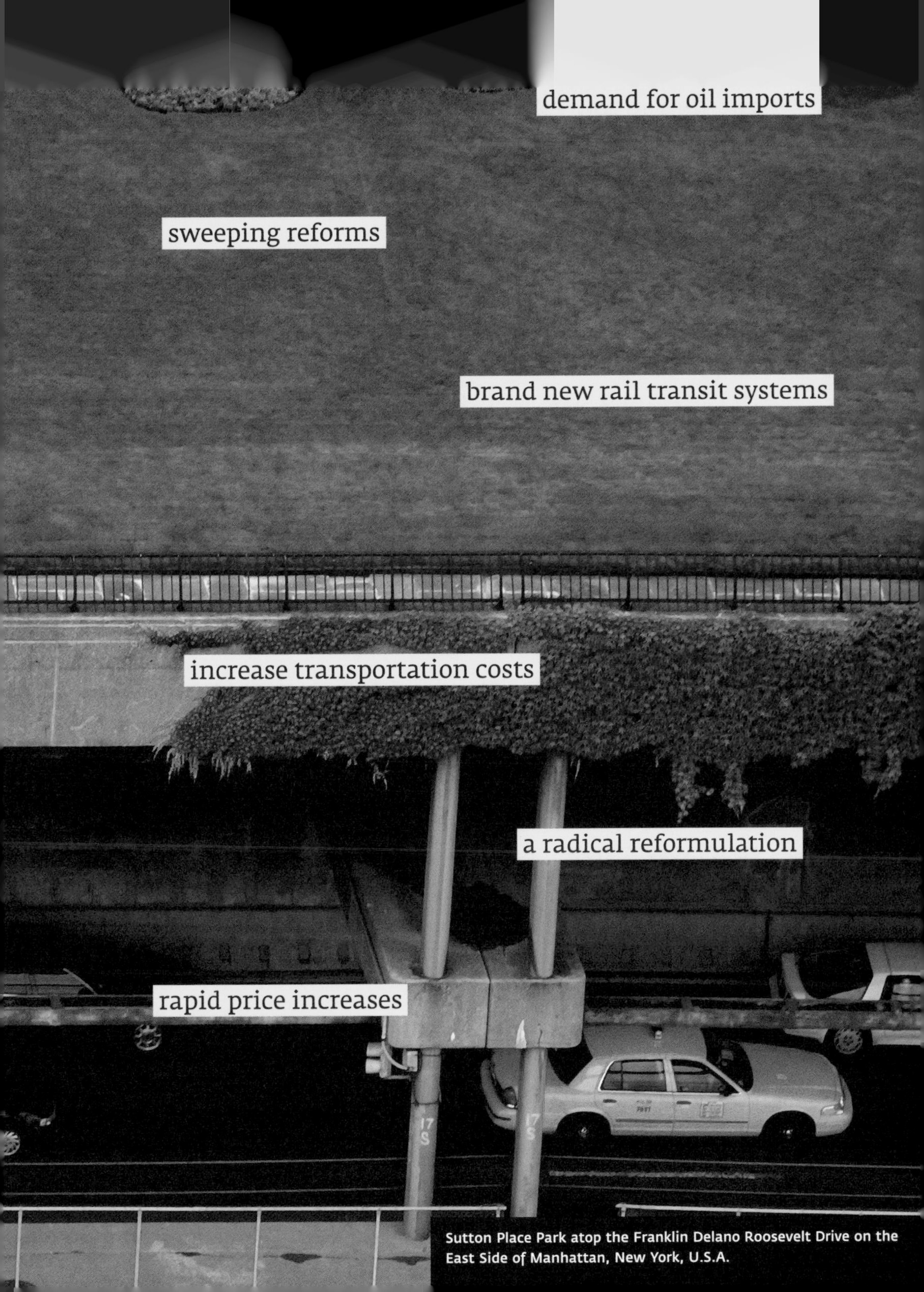

demand for oil imports

sweeping reforms

brand new rail transit systems

increase transportation costs

a radical reformulation

rapid price increases

Sutton Place Park atop the Franklin Delano Roosevelt Drive on the East Side of Manhattan, New York, U.S.A.

THE UNITED STATES' INTERSTATE HIGHWAY SYSTEM, 46,733 miles of multilane highways stretched across a continent, qualifies as the most ambitious network of roadways ever built by humankind. More than 7 million tons of cargo pass through the nation's ports every day, arriving and departing by road and rail.

most ambitious network of roadways

But there are serious—many would say dire—problems. Highways and bridges are deteriorating, with major concentrations of congested roadways. Airports are increasingly overtaxed, partly by short-distance flights that many other nations handle with rail. Ports are becoming clogged with an avalanche of expanded foreign trade.

Much of the U.S. transportation system, built a half century or more ago, is reaching capacity. Particularly in America's metropolitan regions, linchpins of the national economy, traffic tie-ups and ever-lengthening commutes impair citizens' quality of life and business productivity. Globe-imperiling greenhouse-gas emissions from cars and trucks continue to rise. Every year, more than 42,000 Americans are killed and 2.6 million are seriously injured in traffic accidents. Auto emissions and diesel toxicity from truck traffic cause hundreds of thousands of cases of asthma and other life-imperiling conditions each year. Millions of Americans find auto costs, their largest expense outside of basic shelter, consuming ever-larger portions of their household budgets.

reaching capacity

Is the state of affairs in U.S. transportation tolerable? Can significant change be accomplished without sweeping reforms in how federal, state, and local governments fund and manage the nation's transportation system? No, and no, replied the experts in transportation policy, planning, and governance at the Rockefeller Foundation Global Urban Summit. Significant change, they concluded, cannot be accomplished without sweeping reforms in how the federal, state, and local governments fund and manage the nation's transportation system.

sweeping reforms

The group considered and amplified the proposal prepared by Brookings Institution scholars for major reform of national government transportation policy. Participants emphasized the critical role of U.S. metro regions as the organizing principle of the U.S. economy. And although their deliberations took place months before the dramatic world petroleum price increases of 2008, they were already focused on a range of policies designed to reduce fossil fuel consumption by developing rail, public transit, and other forms of transportation for the decades ahead.

critical role of U.S. metro regions

ANATOMY OF A CRISIS

If the United States expects to have a strong transportation system to compete internationally, meet its environmental goals, and support mobility, equity and high quality of life for its citizens, it needs to recognize the multiple alarms now sounding. Along with other participants, Robert Puentes, the Brookings Institution's top transportation expert, outlined the main trouble spots:

Roadway congestion. Road congestion is a significant problem in American cities of all sizes, creating a $78 billion annual drain on the economy—indeed 4.2 billion lost hours and 2.9 billion gallons of wasted fuel, according to the authoritative Texas Transportation Institute. But congestion is worst of all in metro regions, where it has tripled over the past 20 years and had a major negative impact on economies and quality of life.

Sixty-four percent of the nation's roadway congestion is concentrated in the 14 largest urbanized areas (those with 3 million or more people). In those regions the average motorist loses 54 hours a year and wastes 38 gallons of fuel. The economic damage in the New York region alone is close to $4 billion. With suburban expansion, total vehicle miles traveled in urban areas ballooned by 20 percent in the decade prior to the rapid gasoline price increases of 2008.

Virtually all of the nation's global gateways—ports of entry for goods pouring in immense quantities through seaports and airports—are located in metropolitan regions. Major ports such as New York, Miami, San Francisco, Tacoma, Washington, and Portland, Oregon, are already struggling with the massive influx of recent years—a 13 percent increase in trailer trucks alone just in this decade. And there is more to come: Trucks are projected to carry 88 percent of new freight shipments by 2020. Container volume is now predicted to increase 200 percent in the next 20 years, intensifying already-severe port problems. Port traffic intensifies overall local roadway congestion. And with the ports' heavy use of diesel

The Metro Connection

METROPOLITAN FUTURES, quality transportation, the entire U.S. economy in this century—the three are intimately and irrevocably interconnected, Global Urban Summit participants agreed.

In the words of Emil Frankel of Parsons Brinkerhoff, former Connecticut transportation commissioner and assistant U.S. secretary of transportation from 2002 to 2005, "Assuring mobility within America's great metropolitan regions will be key to a growing and competitive national economy. The nation's service- and knowledge-based economy is centered on these major metropolitan regions. Overcoming congestion and constraints to mobility within them is critical to assuring the efficient operation of supply chains and flexibility of labor markets."

Statistics underscore the case: In the past half century, the total population of the United States' metropolitan regions has increased from 85 million to 225 million, a figure expected to rise to roughly 340 million in the next 50 years. More than 83 percent of Americans live in metro regions. The top urbanized 50 areas alone carry 87 percent of daily vehicle miles traveled. Propelled by sharply increased vehicle miles traveled, congestion has essentially doubled in the last 20 years. The Texas Transportation Institute reports that 64 percent of the nation's traffic congestion occurs in the 13 largest urbanized areas alone. And only a third of urban roads are rated in "good" condition, as opposed to more than half in rural areas.

The critical question is how much of the enormous movement of people and goods through our metropolitan regions needs to rely on roads? More freight could clearly be transported by rail, either directly to other major metro areas or to inland intermodal facilities for redistribution to trucks headed for less-dense areas. On the road-passenger side, there are areas where densities are so light that rail transit, in particular, seems impractical. Many such areas could and should be targeted for more concentrated development.

But a clear priority, Brookings' Robert Puentes noted, is to level the playing field between highway and transit projects so that local officials can make sounder investment decisions. Across the nation extraordinarily high numbers of metro areas are bidding for the limited pool of federal transit assistance. Even when they try, they are obliged to run the gauntlet of New Starts funding evaluation, while highway projects are not. An even playing field would presumably make funds more fungible, allowing comparison of benefits, highway versus transit. And it would fix the disparity between the 80 percent federal–local match for roads and the 50 percent match for transit.

Puentes proposes a 25 percent solution in which the federal government would aim to help the top 50 metro areas achieve a balance in which at least 25 percent of workers either use mass transit, bike, or walk to work. Today, only nine of the top 50 metro areas meet that test.

Vehicles jam the highway outside the city, Cedar Rapids, Iowa, U.S.A.

The I-35W bridge over the Mississippi River collapsed during rush hour on August 1, 2007, plunging dozens of cars and their occupants into the water, Minneapolis, Minnesota, U.S.A.

fuel—including arriving ships, terminals, trucks, and trains—local dangers of diesel toxicity are also magnified.

New construction demand. Some degree of continued new highway construction in the United States is certainly necessary, whether to relieve port or airport congestion, ease the bottlenecks around frequently clogged interstate connections, or provide basic road networks for fast-growing areas where development has already occurred. Summaries of investments simply to maintain the current U.S. highway systems for the 2007 to 2017 period are stunning: $2.4 trillion, according to studies for the National Cooperative Highway Research Program, administered by the Transportation Research Board.

A huge gulf exists, however, between a strategy aimed at maintenance and relieving bottlenecks on one hand, and an aggressive new national roadway-building program on the other. The latter could easily add $1 trillion to the total, triggering fast-rising vehicle miles traveled and likely dooming U.S. efforts to reduce greenhouse gas emissions.

A substantial number of extraordinarily expansive projects have been proposed. The most ambitious (though politically contentious) is the Trans-Texas Corridor proposal for 4,000 miles of transportation infrastructure—six lanes for cars, four for trucks, dedicated tracks for high-speed rail, shared rail lines for commuter and freight service, plus a 200-foot-wide strip for utilities. Both tolls and government funds would cover the cost.

Increasingly, officials are looking to tolls (either to fund new roads, add lanes to existing roads, or even gain revenue from existing roads) as a way to avoid taxpayer rage about increased gas taxes. Tolls are also a way of reinforcing a "user pays" philosophy and are convenient, thanks to automated toll collection systems (such as E-ZPass on the East Coast).

popular opposition

State officials have run into a buzz saw of popular opposition to selling off public assets to private (often foreign) investment groups, or explaining why they condemn peoples' homes and farms to build for-profit roads. The 99-year lease of the Chicago Skyway to foreign investors and a parallel deal for the Indiana Toll Road raised public fears of a private concessionaire charging ever-higher tolls for publicly owned roads. Proposals for the sale or long-term lease of the Pennsylvania Turnpike and New Jersey Turnpike, pushed by governors and large investment houses, still have major political support—but opposition as well. There has been less resistance to concession agreements for brand-new toll roads in which the private concessionaire agrees to share toll revenue with the public.

Still unresolved: What justifies major new superroads? Have these plans been assessed versus alternatives including passenger trains, rail freight, and smarter land use? Have proponents considered the phenomenon of "induced travel"—thousands more drivers flooding onto highways initially perceived to be less crowded but that soon fill up with traffic? And does massive road building make sense at all in an era of fast-rising—and probably permanently high—global oil prices?

Arguably adequate roadways *between* metro areas have been provided for through the interstate system; the real challenge is sufficient roadways *within* them to provide reasonable mobility. Yet whole new roadways in existing cities and suburbs would inevitably plow through (and disrupt) existing neighborhoods. Their right-of-way and construction costs would be massive. They would likely trigger new waves of energy-consumptive suburban sprawl and, by virtue of the added vehicle miles traveled that they would encourage, sharply reduce the likelihood of meaningful cutbacks in carbon-dioxide emissions.

A number of state officials, in recent years, have espoused a "Fix It First" position on road infrastructure. But the politics favoring ribbon-cutting on new roadways, even in rural or small town areas where the needs are marginal, remain strong. From 1997 to 2002, spending on new transportation projects rose 41 percent, but on maintenance and services only 27 percent, raising serious questions about future funding sources for basic upkeep of the roadway stock in place.

Rail freight. While no panacea, freight shipment by rail at least relieves the worst congestion pressures created by rising trade in metro centers. But the freight system has its own problems—a shrinkage of operating track from 207,000 miles in 1960 to less than 100,000 miles today. The system is reported to carry 28 percent of the country's ton miles of freight, and 40 percent of intercity ton miles, but it is overstressed as shippers complain of seriously increased trip times.

The contrast to airline, truck, and barge infrastructure, all heavily subsidized by the federal and state governments in recent decades, is striking. Big trucks, the most direct competitors, pay through fees and taxes only 50 to 80 percent of the roadway costs they generate. The railroads, by contrast, receive virtually no government subsidies, despite their own investment of $350 billion in infrastructure and equipment since 1980.

Public transit. Local transit ridership in the United States has been growing in recent years. In 2006, for the first time in a half century (and again in 2007), rides nationwide exceeded 10 billion. During the 2008 energy price rise, rides accelerated again. Many cities, especially in Texas and the West, have added brand new rail transit systems in recent years. From a congestion standpoint, transit has major appeal: its riders *are not* part of the glut of single-passenger cars crowding roadways. And the carbon footprint of transit riders is far below that of car users.

brand new rail transit systems

Transit is far from ubiquitous, however. Just over half of all Americans, and a third of those living in new housing, report that it is available to them. In 54 of the top 100 metros, no rail service exists at all, and bus service is generally low per capita. Only nine of the largest metros have 25 percent or more of their workers commuting by public transit. Job sprawl intensifies the problem, especially among low-income workers. To reach their workplaces they are often forced to buy cars, which consume large portions of their modest incomes. Overall, the working poor spend twice as much of their income on commuting than other workers.

Logically, federal policy would place a priority on transit expansion. But far from it—where federal assistance is offered to new transit projects, the split is only 60 percent federal and 40 percent local or an even 50–50 federal–local division, as opposed to the 80 percent federal, 20 percent local split that highways enjoy. In addition, new transit projects (burgeoning in number in recent years) are subject to intense federal oversight and project selection under the so-called "New Starts" program. Roads and highway projects receive no such rigorous review.

With few exceptions, state governments are missing in action on creation or improvement of public transit systems. One reason is that the constitutions of 30 states explicitly prohibit use of gas tax revenues for any purpose other than road building and maintenance.

Intercity rail. In contrast to virtually all other leading world nations, the United States lacks a world-class rail service connecting its major metropolitan regions. Outside the Northeast Corridor, most major metros lack efficient or reliable service.

The Amtrak system has never had full support of any presidential administration. It lacks a dedicated funding source like the Highway, Transit, or Aviation Trust Funds, and is especially susceptible to Washington's political machinations. The system has had to virtually beg Congress for annual appropriations to avoid shutting down or slashing services. And outside of the Northeast Corridor, it has to negotiate with private rail corporations for use of their tracks.

Road safety. U.S. air and rail systems have safety records relatively comparable to those of other advanced nations. Auto

Traffic on the North Spring Street Bridge, Los Angeles, California, U.S.A.

The Washington Metrorail subway, the country's second-largest rail transit system, Washington, D.C., U.S.A.

Increasing numbers of passengers board Metrolink subway trains at rush hour as gas prices skyrocket in the summer of 2008. Los

and truck crashes in the United States, however, kill some 42,000 people and injure 2.6 million more each year, some inflicted with lifelong paralysis and permanent disability. The toll is not only a serious public health problem but a fiscal one as well: The annual cost, from medical to workplace to travel delay costs, totals some $230 billion.

a serious public-health problem

According to Mark Rosenberg, M.D., former U.S. assistant surgeon general, "If those 42,000 deaths came from air accidents, air traffic would come to a screaming halt. All airports would be closed until we fixed the problem. But because our staggering numbers of road deaths come in ones and twos, they don't get attention. Fatalism is our biggest enemy."

Could a more serious campaign for safer roadways make a difference in the United States? Sweden's Vision Zero effort, for example, has reduced traffic deaths radically by steps such as tough seatbelt and helmet laws, replacing red lights with traffic circles, narrowing urban roadways, adding speed bumps, and limiting in-city speeds to 20 miles an hour. Certainly the United States could do a lot better. While the U.S. death and injury rate is well below that of the developing world, it is substantially higher than that of the European Union and other comparable countries. For example, while U.S. fatalities in 2000 were 15.2 per 100,000 people, they were 9.5 in Australia and Canada, 5.9 in Great Britain, 6.7 in Sweden, and 8.2 in Japan.

Equity factors. Transportation is second only to housing as an ever-increasing expense that American families must face—and it was growing even before the rapid increases of the years since 2000. With rising housing prices near metro centers, young families (at least until the gasoline price surge of 2008) often felt forced into a "drive till you qualify" behavior pattern, intensifying urban sprawl. The bargain was not always as positive as it seemed: for every dollar that a working family saved by moving out of an urban center, it was spending 77 cents more on transportation before petroleum prices began their drastic rise. Even then, once a commute surpassed 12 to 15 miles, the increase in transportation costs usually exceeded the savings the commuter made on housing.

increase in transportation costs

Low-income families are hardest hit by transportation costs. Those who live in urban cores (center cities and older suburbs) often find that they have no acceptable public transit connections to reach entry level jobs in manufacturing, wholesale trade, and the growing malls and superstores now on the metro area periphery. If they are able to obtain autos, their commuting costs (including car insurance) are substantially higher than those of other workers. The net impact is a cut in realized income and severe difficulty in improving their families' standard of living. In some U.S. regions, lower-income families actually spend more on transportation than they do on housing. Transportation, in sum, tends to be strongly regressive in cost.

Can equity be a factor in transportation planning? Yes, and it must be, many Summit participants insisted. "Transportation often leaves poverty concentrated," said Bruce Katz, vice president and director of the Brookings Institution's Metropolitan

Policy Program. "It's a system that can clearly work against the interests of low-income families." As Elliott Sclar, director of the Center for Sustainable Urban Development at Columbia University, noted, "promoting equity—greater real opportunity for low-income families—is not castor oil." To the contrary, it increases poor peoples' productivity and self-reliance and reduces long-term social costs for everyone.

promoting equity

Energy security. Oil fuels 96 percent of the U.S. transportation system. The nation has only 3 percent of the world's known oil reserves. The result is massive dependence on oil imports, up from 17 percent of U.S. demand in 1970 to roughly 60 percent of vastly expanded demand today. With the sharp increases of petroleum prices in recent years, the nation spends and borrows at least $1 billion a day to satisfy its demand for oil imports. The emergence of such nations as China and India as major petroleum importers assures continued rising demand and prices.

demand for oil imports

Foreign affairs experts see serious, growing national security concerns. Canada and Mexico are the two largest exporters of oil to the United States, but major oil imports also come in from countries either unfriendly to the United States, or potentially far less stable, including Saudi Arabia, Venezuela, Nigeria, Algeria, and Iraq.

Any serious cutoff of world energy supplies triggered by terrorist attack, market disruption, or both could pose dire threat to the economy of the nation and its metropolitan regions (whose spread-out, petroleum-dependent economies would be in danger of paralysis). There is already evidence that a portion of the immense U.S. petrodollar exports, especially to pay for

rapid price increases

the rapid price increases of this decade, make their way into the hands of bitterly anti-American terrorists and their allies.

A key U.S. security objective must be to shift its transportation system away from its almost-total petroleum dependence. But how can this be done? Major lifestyle shifts will be required: moving away from big, gas-guzzling SUVs to smaller, more fuel-efficient vehicles, and from overwhelming auto dependence to much greater use of public transit and public policy encouraging more compact, less auto-dependent communities.

The climate-change/land-use nexus. With 5 percent of world population, the United States is responsible for roughly 24 percent of the global greenhouse-gas emissions that threaten dire climate change in the 21st century. The transportation sector, in turn, generates 33 percent of U.S. CO_2 emissions. The CO_2 challenge has overshadowed such environmental challenges as vehicle-generated, ground-level and petrochemical smog because 1) it raises momentous issues of global environmental sustainability and 2) it cannot be controlled by more sophisticated vehicle emission-control systems (such as catalytic converters). With existing technology the only way to reduce CO_2 emissions from vehicles is to burn less gasoline and diesel fuel.

Reduction in fuel burning, in turn, is only possible through 1) increased mile-per-gallon (MPG) efficiency, and

The Port of Miami is among the busiest in the United States, Miami, Florida, U.S.A.

Jet traffic at Newark Airport, Newark, New Jersey, U.S.A.

2) fewer vehicle miles traveled (VMT). U.S. reduction of MPG efficiency has stalled, largely because of the expanded market share of SUVs and light trucks. Even with recently stiffened CAFE (corporate average fuel economy) standards, transportation-related CO_2 emissions in 2030 will be 12 percent above the 2005 level and 40 percent above the 1990 level, according to the Urban Land Institute/Center for Clean Air Policy's *Growing Cooler* report.

What then of VMT? Since 1980, the total number of miles driven by Americans has grown three times faster than the rise in U.S. population, and twice as fast as vehicle registrations. The vast majority of new development has been planned and built on the assumption that people will use cars for virtually all trips. Homes have been built ever further from workplaces; overwhelming majorities of shopping malls, big retail boxes, office parks, and new schools have been constructed at locations only accessible by car. The net result has been more and longer auto trips and a preponderance of people driving alone.

Could the United States develop more compactly? Americans' legendary preference is for communities of single-family homes on spacious lots, the post–World War II American Dream. But surveys show at least a third of consumers would now prefer more compact communities in which homes, town centers, shops, parks, and schools are within walking or biking distance. There is also real impetus, smart-growth advocates argue, to steer away from single-use subdivisions or office parks, focusing instead on attractive mixed-use, walkable

more and longer auto trips

develop more compactly

communities with their own town centers, building offices and stores "up" rather than "out."

In more compact developments, people drive 20 to 40 percent less than those living on the suburban edge with isolated homes and workplaces. The *Growing Cooler* authors calculate that shifting 60 percent of new growth to compact patterns would save 85 million metric tons of CO_2 annually by 2030. If only 60 percent of projected new residential and commercial development is clustered in compact, mixed-use areas, they estimate VMT would be cut back enough to slash transportation-related greenhouse-gas emissions by 7 to 10 percent. And as a by-product of Americans walking and biking more, reductions in obesity and its associated heart disease and diabetes conditions would almost surely follow.

Some good news on VMT may be appearing: a declining growth rate since 2000, with absolute declines reported in 2008.

CARS AND TRUCKS CAUSE 84 PERCENT OF U.S. GREENHOUSE GAS EMISSIONS FROM TRANSPORTATION

🚗	PASSENGER CARS AND LIGHT DUTY TRUCKS	62.5%
🚚	OTHER TRUCKS	21.5%
	TOTAL CARS AND TRUCKS	**84.0%**
🚌	BUSES	0.6%
✈	AIRCRAFT	8.4%
⚓	SHIPS AND BOATS	2.4%
🚆	LOCOMOTIVES	2.7%
	OTHER	1.9%

2006 data, excluding bunker and military vehicles.
Credit: CO_2 Emissions from Fossil Fuel Combustion in Transportation by End Use Sector, Inventory of U.S. Greenhouse Gases and Sinks: 1990–2006 Public Review Draft, Feb. 22, 2008

The reasons, experts are suggesting, reach beyond fast-escalating gasoline prices to some major demographic shifts. Aging baby boomers, like all older people, tend to drive fewer miles. Families without children (a growing share of the population) drive less. The expansion of females entering the work force, and thus likely to add to commuting traffic, has reached its reasonable limits. Public transit appears to be ending decades of losing market share, and there seems to be fresh interest in biking and walking. Still, U.S. VMT patterns are far above averages in other advanced nations, resulting in high exports of dollars to purchase petroleum, and continued high CO_2 emissions.

BROKEN NATIONAL POLICY

Existing federal transportation policy is "dumb, broken, and expensive," Portland, Oregon, metro councilor Robert Liberty said during the Summit. He encountered no dissent. He and other panelists had an extensive list of failures:

Missing goals and accountability. The interstate era, stretching from the 1950s to 1990s, has been called the halcyon years of federal highway planning and construction, the clear goal of an interconnected, continent-wide super-highway system. In the early 1990s, with completion of most of the interstates, Congress began to break with its "highways only" orientation by passage of ISTEA (Intermodal Surface Transportation Efficiency Act), with a new set of goals: "to

a national
intermodal
transportation
system

develop a national intermodal transportation system that moves people and goods in an energy efficient manner."

Marketing Ambitious Reform

THE ROCKEFELLER FOUNDATION Global Urban Summit call was for a dramatic sea change in U.S. transportation policy. But how will it ever occur? Participants wanted to shift *away* from federal transportation decision-making dominated by big-time highway contracting interests, earmarking politicos, auto makers, and oil interests, and road oriented bureaucrats pushing for constant expansion of the asphalt world around us. They were eager to move *toward* a system focused on metropolitan areas and national economic strength, hard-headed cost analysis, emphasis on outcomes, and multimodal solutions.

Or, as a Brookings staff document written during the sessions asserted, the Summit "Transportation Vision is that transportation is a means not an end, must serve national priorities (e.g., economic competitiveness, sustainability, safety, mobility, and access)," and must become a key part of the national discussion.

The first step in helping to realize this new vision, transportation experts suggested, could be to form a constituency *outside* the familiar transportation community. Potential recruits would include 1) business leaders concerned with loss of transportation efficiency in the face of mounting foreign competition; 2) groups focused on national security issues, especially continued high demand for imported oil including shaky Middle East sources; 3) environmentalists anxious to cut back roadway-generated pollution, and to reduce CO_2 emissions; 4) advocates of conserving more land and more sensitively planned communities; and 5) medical and humanitarian groups alarmed about the human carnage on the roads and need for much stronger safety measures. Another suggestion was to reach outside the transportation sphere to target a dozen or so metro areas in which partnerships could be formed with civic and business leaders, with an eye to influence on the political system.

Major interest in new transportation solutions may also appear, panelists believed, in the not unlikely event of a collapse of funding if the Highway Trust Fund runs dry in the near future. Potential backers of major reform in that case, panelists believed, might include such lead public interest groups as the National Governors Association, U.S. Conference of Mayors, and National League of Cities. Major city mayors and county executives might start to ask pointedly, participants suggested, "Why does this system serve us so poorly? And why do we get such a small proportion of transportation money, compared to our population and problems?"

Progressive state officials within the American Society of State Highway and Transportation Officials, Summit participants speculated, may also be interested in a new, more sensitive and objective transportation planning and funding system.

But no one underestimated the difficulty of delivering the message, which is many times more complex than the early 20th century road-building slogan ("Get America out of the mud") or the early interstate pitch ("You'll be able to drive coast to coast without a stoplight").

A powerful new constituency, panelists said, is now critical, ready to stand up against the transportation funding status quo, unflinching in demanding an outcomes-based national transportation system. Without such a new coalition, one participant noted, chances for truly meaningful reform "are chopped liver."

Specific reference was made to confronting "challenges of the global economy, declining productivity growth, energy vulnerability, air pollution, and the need to rebuild the nation's infrastructure." And at least a modest number of transportation funding decisions were to be made by urban regions on their own, through metropolitan planning organizations (MPOs).

But specific national goals have faded in subsequent reauthorizations of the federal transportation program, which now funnels about $50 billion a year to states and localities, mostly for highways but a minority segment for transit. State transportation departments continue to have more expertise in engineering and concrete pouring than urban planning, economic development, or environmental management. States' own project funding formulas, often developed in pre-metropolitan eras, often tilt heavily to rural over urban areas. For example, the booming Denver area boasts more growth, people, and gasoline consumption than any other area of the state, but it gets back only 69 cents in revenues for each $1 of tax revenue. From 1998 to 2003, the share of state transportation dollars allocated to the region actually *declined* from 46 to 28 percent.

The MPOs have also disappointed even their most enthusiastic backers. In many regions they are actually splintered between sections of the metro area, making true regional decision-making virtually impossible. A scattering (Albany, Dallas, Hartford, Minneapolis, San Francisco, Portland, and Seattle, for instance) have improved staff expertise in writing the complex regional transportation plans mandated by federal law. But evaluations of most MPOs indicate serious professional shortcomings. Another problem: In a high percentage, allocation of decision-making MPO board slots, relative to actual population, grossly favors suburban over center city representatives. And in any event, a minuscule percentage of federal transportation dollars actually flow to the MPOs.

grossly favors suburban

Overall, Summit participants found, there is now a huge lack of accountability in the system. Federal support is based on a federal gas tax (18.4 cents a gallon since 1993) earmarked for the national Transportation Trust Fund (which includes separate accounts for roads and transit). But there is virtually no federal oversight or accountability for the road and bridge projects that states or localities actually choose to implement with the funds. The program, noted Thomas Downs, president of the Eno Transportation Foundation, has degenerated into a system in which the federal government collects revenue for the states and sends it back to them. But to the extent the federal government increases its transportation subsidies, the General Accounting Office has found the states frequently reduce transportation outlays from their own revenue base, cutting back sharply on the effective rate of return on the federal investments.

lack of accountability

Congress' role. Failing to identify national transportation goals or priorities, Congress finds itself refereeing transportation money allocation fights between so-called donor and donee states. And the process of congressional earmarking of transportation appropriations for specific projects in members' home states (excesses such as the $398 million project in Alaska that critics labeled "a bridge to nowhere") has served to destroy credibility of the process in the public's mind. In 1987 President Reagan vetoed a transportation reauthorization bill because it included 152 earmarks; in 2005 President Bush signed one with 6,371, costing $27.3 billion.

Federal formulas. Federal transportation allocations to states include no targeting of spending to vital areas. They make no reference to the critical role of metropolitan regions in the national economy. Based on the amount of transportation infrastructure that already exists, they reward additional building and thus set up an insatiable desire to build even more, say critics. They also tend to favor new construction over rehabilitation and maintenance, and make no effort to create economical projects.

One might expect, for example, for Congress to stipulate that funds allocated through the states be deployed for fewer vehicle miles traveled, less greenhouse gas emissions, coordination with land use plans, equitable treatment of various population groups, and a premium on short trip distances and trips made by means other than a single-occupant vehicle. Yet there is not even a hint of such guidelines.

Silos. In the real world of cities and regions, there are extensive, intimate relationships between transportation, housing, economic development, and environmental systems. The federal government, however, appears to operate in silo-like fashion, rarely linking its field activities. In competition for federal transit grants, for instance, no bonus is given to projects that reorient land use and achieve greater densities in housing and commercial development around a project. Investment is often pushed out of high-tax, low-service urban areas and into low-tax, high-service, favored suburban locations. Although metropolitan areas account for most of the nation's economic output and a large majority of all transit use and port and surface freight tonnage, the federal commitment to these areas (either in financial assistance or basic data provision) is spotty and extraordinarily low.

THE EUROPEAN BOMBSHELL

Summit participants raised the idea of a new federal transportation–dollar allocation method, one that would put all investments "through a mode-neutral, multimodal performance screen (a silo buster)," as Shelley Poticha of Reconnecting America proposed. But the trigger for a radical reformulation came with the presentation of Great Britain's recent Eddington Transport Study, which explored the role of transportation in sustaining the United Kingdom's productivity and competitiveness. Faced with fast-rising transportation demand, the British government had asked Sir Rod Eddington, a recently knighted Australian who was once the head of British Airways, to assemble a broad group of experts to define elements of a new transportation approach rooted in principles of economic growth and sustainable development.

a radical reformulation

As Oliver Jones of Britain's Department of Transport explained, the goal was "an economic policy project, not a transport policy project." And its big breakthrough was a determination to gauge and compare actual *outcomes* of any project. In that sense the British formula is agnostic on transportation modes, not predisposed to favor highways, high-speed rail, or any other means of transportation, but rather designed to determine the cost–benefit ratio, the comparable returns on investment, of varied investments the government might make. Cities, key urban corridors, and international gateways were given major consideration because "they're the worst congestion problems, but where our economic future lies," Jones noted.

the cost–benefit ratio

To determine the best types of interventions, the Eddington project created a database of 200 major transportation recommendations made in Britain in the last decade and then calculated the cost–benefit ratio of each. Factors such as fiscal cost, environment, congestion, and foreign trade were included. A major effort was made to consider both the congestion and climate effects of projects. And issues such as safety lanes on motorways were factored in. A national traffic congestion charging scheme was also modeled, with the expectation that it could provide returns of £25 billion a year by 2025.

best types of interventions

The British formula revealed that many proposed transportation projects provided extremely high returns. But some, such as increasing long-distance high-speed rail service, did poorly. In general, a variety of smaller transportation initiatives provided better returns than larger projects.

extremely high returns

The evaluation system is not a one-time phenomenon on new projects. Rather, it involves continual collection of data on performance of the transportation network, needs of users, and the effectiveness of the policies being applied.

The British formula is not critique-proof, of course; the NGO community, for example, has suggested that it undercounts the impact of carbon, noise, and landscape factors. In the U.S. context, the tradeoffs between safer and more convenient urban roadways on one hand and roads facilitating added suburban sprawl on the other might be particularly difficult to quantify.

undercounts the impact of carbon

Still, the idea of a system that does not pick modal winners and losers in advance, that is based on objective data, and that seeks to judge where the greatest transportation need lies proved immensely appealing to Summit transportation experts.

A related set of fresh approaches, such as factoring in impacts on housing and economic development issues, and giving metropolitan regions special consideration, was introduced to the panel by officials of the German government.

Summit participants adopted the European approaches, in fact, as a cornerstone of their proposed new federal transportation policy, declaring "no more transportation for its own sake. Transportation dollars must lead to improved outcomes for the entire nation, including resilient metro regions."

FRAMEWORK FOR REFORM

How, then, can transportation dollars and planning be positioned to serve key national goals—a more competitive U.S.

Germany's Federalist Solution

COULD IT BE? A federalist system of government that minimizes frictions, takes planning seriously, integrates transportation with critical housing and economic development agendas, and gives metropolitan areas special attention in the process?

Global Urban Summit participants were treated to a description of just such a system by Lutke Daldrup, the German federal government's state secretary of Transport, Building, and Urban Affairs. Daldrup, the former mayor of Leipzig, described Germany as a nation "highly urbanized but decentralized politically," a country that has begun in recent years to take metropolitan regions far more seriously. Why? His answer: "Metropolitan regions are laboratories for the global economy. They are powerhouses of economic change, centers of innovation, and centers of poverty, social exclusion, unemployment, even criminality. Metros combine great opportunities and problems of our society."

The German Federal Republic, said Daldrup, originally delegated most future planning roles to its *Länder*, or state governments, with little federal assistance except for major roads and waterways. For 40 years after World War II, federal attention actually focused on economically lagging areas, and after reunification on the revitalization of the former East German *Länder*. But in recent years the focus has shifted to economic growth and innovation, and the role of metropolitan regions in achieving both.

There is now agreed definition of 11 metropolitan regions within the country, including the "decision and control powerhouses" of Frankfurt, Dusseldorf, and Munich, the political power poles of Berlin-Brandenburg and Bonn, and major regional centers such as Stuttgart. The mayors and other political leaders of the Nuremberg area actually came together and asked for recognition as a metropolitan region. Asked why, Daldrup replied: The Nuremberg leaders realized that their entire region is competing with the rest of Europe, as well as the rest of the world; that both the historic city center and suburban areas recognized they had a contribution to make; and that they needed to stick together to advance the area's promising economic innovation clusters.

Germany's actual division of funding responsibilities between the federal, state, and local levels shifts from time to time. Historically, major decision-making power over large projects was vested in the Länder. But increasingly the federal government formulates national plans for major roadways, waterways, and rail systems, placing a major emphasis on maintenance and use of existing infrastructure. Compact cities, less spatial separation, lower energy use, and cost and green agendas to reduce carbon footprints are factored in, along with ties to housing and overall economic-development planning. There appears to be direct, intensive work with officials and planners in key metro areas—as in the planning and construction of major new railway stations tied to ambitious urban renewal projects in Berlin and Stuttgart.

For regular transportation, housing and related economic development initiatives, Daldrup's ministry formulates five-year plans based on extensive research and analysis, working with members of the *Bundestag* (parliament) to ensure that decisions are responsive, to a practical degree, to local concerns. Partisanship was once more apparent, with Social Democrats regarded as the leading party of the cities and Christian Democrats the reverse. But the Social Democrats have recently lost power in several key areas to the Christian Democrats, who are seeking to improve their image as more liberal and urban.

A major problem now confronting the Germans, without clear resolution, is how to deal with the new roadway congestion triggered by the fast-increasing flow of freight-bearing truck traffic, projected to grow 40 percent in the next years.

On all transportation-related fronts, however, the government sees a need to keep improving Germany's already high-quality data collection system over the next five years. The principle of tying major transportation, land use, and environmental issues together for action in a coordinated place-sensitive manner, in vivid contrast to prevailing U.S. custom, seems solidly entrenched.

Election Season Messages

COULD THE IDEA OF TRANSPORTATION REFORM reach the masses—especially in the context of a U.S. presidential campaign? Two political leaders, one a Republican, the other a Democrat, gave imagined campaign speeches with overlapping themes.

Pat McCrory, Republican Mayor, Charlotte, North Carolina

Five new urgent challenges demand a new transportation strategy for our nation. First, there's globalization. We Americans are used to getting ahead by working hard. But countries in Asia, Europe, and South America are doing everything they can to catch up with us. Second, energy independence: Our economy depends on oil supplies from unstable nations such as Iran and Venezuela. Third, we must keep our air clean, and the fact is auto emissions are dirtying our air. Fourth, transportation must strengthen our communities and help our families. Congestion robs us of time with our families. And fifth, we are a growing nation. By 2050 demographers say there will be an additional 120 million of us. We must think ahead.

The way Washington thinks about transportation is broken. From the Big Dig to the Bridge to Nowhere, Congress spends your tax dollars in haphazard ways. Our transportation trust funds are turning into slush funds.

We must maintain the phenomenal interstate system President Eisenhower left us. We need to invest in new infrastructure more intelligently. When I'm president, we're going to measure how well our transportation system is performing and target our resources to where the data shows we need to invest.

We're going to bust up bureaucracy in Washington. The Department of Transportation is organized around building projects, not moving people. The bureaucrats care about modes, not mobility. We will move much of the decision-making down to the local level, with the caveat that local decision-making must fit our national goals.

And we must have smarter growth. Our local governments are letting sprawl eat up our countryside, causing traffic jams that are difficult to build our way out of. We must break the cycle and grow in more intelligent ways.

Tom Ceis, Democratic Deputy Mayor, Seattle, Washington

America's families are worried that the gap between the wages they earn and the prices they pay for transportation is growing. It's not just rising gasoline prices. Families are forced to move further and further away from the job centers in search of housing they can afford. They're frustrated that they need to drive everywhere for everything, whether for jobs, school, shopping, or health care. They're spending more time on the road, and less time together with families and loved ones.

Business is just as concerned. The cost of transport has gone up considerably, squeezing the ability to invest in new products, new services, innovation, technology, and workers. Business leaders who return from traveling abroad ask me, "Why are our airports and seaports and transit systems and commuter rails and highways not up to the standards of a fiercely competitive world?"

It's time again, as Eisenhower did with the interstates, for a president to lead. We need to maintain and preserve what we have. But we also need new state-of-the-art infrastructure. And to get rid of bottlenecks, we should fix the interchange that backs up every day at 4 p.m.

I propose an "Invest in America" program, a partnership with states and metropolitan regions, giving them much more power over transportation decisions with the tradeoff that they'll be accountable for every dollar they spend, for the results they get. Results will be measured against national priorities: economic competitiveness, job growth, climate change, energy security, congestion relief, health, and safety.

And Invest in America will put transportation in service of livable communities where people can fulfill their dream—to walk and bike where the air is clean, where there is a neighborhood park, a library nearby, and a grocery down the street.

economy, improved access, health and safety, strengthened communities, more conserving land use, minimized energy use, reduced CO_2 emissions, and less dependence on foreign oil suppliers? A range of ideas, ways, and means resonated with participants:

- Make transportation policy bolster the economy and match key national goals on the basis of strict cost–benefit ratio analysis. Let the policy be officially neutral or "agnostic" as to modes.
- Focus the United States' transportation policy on the viability of metropolitan areas and prime transportation corridors between them, recognizing metros' key role in national economy security and progress.
- Promote new "user pays" forms of traffic regulation, including 1) tolled lanes on very busy freeways, 2) congestion pricing (tolls for private vehicular use of heavily traveled urban centers) based on the model of efforts in London, Stockholm, and Singapore, and 3) emissions-based tolls on heavy trucks on freeways (based on a German program).
- Make "fix it first" a national standard, and assume costs of repair and maintenance of the existing interstate system as a federal responsibility.
- Establish safety as a national priority to sharply curtail traffic injuries and deaths and reduce vehicle-triggered diseases such as asthma; add explicit wellness goals through walking and cycling to cut government costs and enhance national competitiveness.

- Create a federal sub-cabinet to deal with transportation that includes the secretaries of Transportation, Energy, Housing and Urban Development, and the administrator of the Environmental Protection Agency. Require that they provide Congress with an annual report on how they are integrating their efforts in a cross-cutting way.

- Fill a major information gap by creating a comprehensive new federal database covering all aspects of transportation and transportation-related business and personal usage, including travel patterns, infrastructure maintenance and backlogs, energy use, CO_2 emissions, freight, links to housing, city, and town planning, and other relevant issues.

- To promote a true program of national transportation priorities (as opposed to Congressional earmarking), consider an entity modeled after the federal government's BRAC procedures for closing of military bases. This way, the commission would consider the broad range of proposed major transportation infrastructure projects and then prepare a list of fundable projects that Congress must approve or reject on a single up or down vote.

- Rather than turn to the automatic choice of major new superhighways to relieve congestion, assess all available choices, starting with targeted construction at serious bottleneck locations, almost all of which are located within metropolitan regions. Aim transportation planning and budgeting at significant reduction in goods movement time by highway and/or rail, both for economic efficiency and to reduce polluting emissions. A program of combined bottle-neck relief (improved freeway-to-freeway interchanges and significant port and intermodal terminal access roads) might require a $60 billion to $80 billion program, some partici-pants suggested.

- Commit to a national passenger rail plan to connect the nation's largest metros on trips of less than 500 miles. Encourage partnerships with states to leverage rail expan-sion efforts and coordinate on commuter rail. A credible U.S. intercity rail system would cost $50 billion to $60 billion, according to a 2002 report from the American Society of State Highway and Transportation Officials. Many of the corridors identified in the city coincide with megaregion corridors, including those where intercity travel is congested.

- Give state governments and the MPOs chief responsibility for allocating funding among highway, transit, and other transportation proposals. As federal transportation funds are released to states, stipulate that the state governments con-trol the priorities and fund flows to smaller metro and rural areas. But the federal funding would go directly to, or be specifically designated for, all metros of 1 million residents or more. The metros of significant size would then have full power to determine (using new and improved outcomes-based criteria) the exact road, bridge, transit, or related projects that would work best for their areas. Companion proposals include the following: 1) Congress should set a limit of one MPO per metropolitan area, solving the problem of two or more (generally politically motivated) MPOs in some regions, an arrangement that makes rational region-wide decision-making almost impossible; 2) MPO membership should be required to reflect the population weights of the localities represented; and 3) MPOs should be assisted in gaining the analytic capacity, based on cost–benefit analysis, to judge and compare varied road or transit proposals.

- Create incentives for metropolitan regions to overcome the parochialism of dozens or hundreds of local governments in a single region by offering greater or quicker federal or state support to metros that are able to reach internal agreement on voluntary comprehensive and integrated transportation, land-use and economic-development plans.

- Encourage metros to consider transit options as a way to 1) provide a mode choice for commuters and travelers, 2) relieve some roadway congestion, and 3) encourage and accommodate higher densities in fast-developing areas (such as the Southwest United States), where transit-oriented locations have the potential to absorb a significant share of the country's growing population. Common-sense rules of flexibility would also dictate that MPOs be allowed to set their own match ratios for the investments they make, both in highways and transit. (Significantly, when a broad-based bipartisan federal transportation commission mandated by Congress unveiled the nation's first-ever long-range transportation plan in January 2008, calling for dramatic funding increases for multiple modes of transportation including rails as well as roads, one glaring omission was any focus on metropolitan regions or improvements of the MPO system.)

- Publicize value-recapture strategies, special taxing districts, or similar devices to recoup a fraction of the public's major investment in new light-rail lines (the announced plans for new rail line rights-of-way in the Denver, Dallas, and Charlotte regions have stimulated literally billions of dollars in private investment, for example).

- Reduce the growing transportation burden on Americans' family budgets by synchronizing transportation and housing policy, with a premium on locating affordable housing close to employment areas, schools, community colleges, shops and services, and in walking range of public transportation.

- Establish an explicit transportation goal of serving communities' land use objectives and honoring citizens' sense of place in their cities and towns.

- Support modern, inclusive planning tools such as alternative growth scenarios to give officials and citizens a clear vision of choices.

- Encourage local transportation planning to value and provide safe routes that accommodate foot travel and bicycling to and from transit, work, schools, and town centers, both to reduce traffic burdens and improve Americans' health.

CHAPTER 8

U.S. Metros: Building Blocks of American Prosperity?

city-suburb ties

place-based assets

a more competitive national economy

The city skyline with the Spring Mountains as backdrop, Las Vegas, Nevada, U.S.A.

environmental stress

U.S. is a metro nation

reformed, remade federal government

quality of place

equity

metros matter

CAN METROPOLITAN REGIONS—AMERICA'S "REAL CITIES" of the 21st century—be the centerpiece of the United States' positioning for prosperity in a challenging global era?

Yes, they can, and indeed they must. The great cities and their suburban rings—reservoirs of the nation's greatest wealth, higher learning, cultural institutions, corporate skill, and talented professionals—encompass the central core of the assets that the United States needs to mobilize effectively if it hopes to face rising worldwide economic competition, deal with environmental perils, and build a more inclusive, more resilient American society.

metros matter

The "metros matter" message, conceived by leaders of the Brookings Institution's Metropolitan Policy Program, was examined, debated, and enthusiastically endorsed by a group of public officials, business executives, foundation officers, and policy experts at the Summit. Their deliberations contributed to a Brookings policy initiative launched publicly in November 2007 with a tantalizing objective: "Blueprint for American Prosperity—Unleashing the Potential of a Metropolitan Nation."

The goal, said Bruce Katz, director of the Metropolitan Policy Project, which planned this Summit session, is: to inject a new metropolitan-based view to influence the focus of debate—but not the outcome—of the 2008 presidential election. It will be, Katz noted, the first election since 1952 without an incumbent on either major party's presidential ticket, opening up the possibility for a serious discussion of new and potentially exciting policy directions.

MAJOR U.S. METROS AS NATIONAL PROSPERITY DRIVERS

Percentage of national activity in 100 largest metro areas, various indicators, 2005

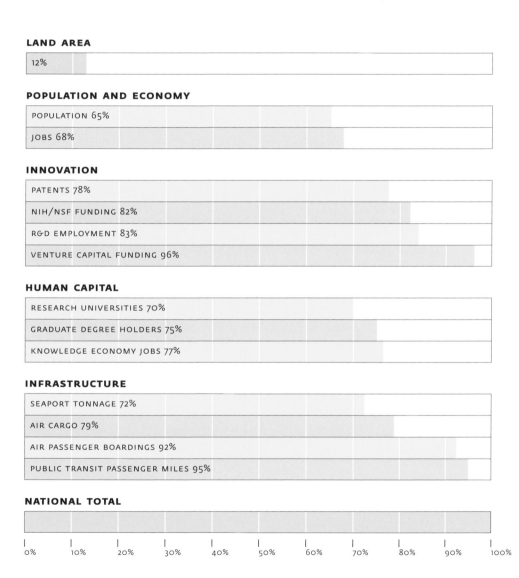

LAND AREA

12%

POPULATION AND ECONOMY

POPULATION 65%

JOBS 68%

INNOVATION

PATENTS 78%

NIH/NSF FUNDING 82%

R&D EMPLOYMENT 83%

VENTURE CAPITAL FUNDING 96%

HUMAN CAPITAL

RESEARCH UNIVERSITIES 70%

GRADUATE DEGREE HOLDERS 75%

KNOWLEDGE ECONOMY JOBS 77%

INFRASTRUCTURE

SEAPORT TONNAGE 72%

AIR CARGO 79%

AIR PASSENGER BOARDINGS 92%

PUBLIC TRANSIT PASSENGER MILES 95%

NATIONAL TOTAL

0% 10% 20% 30% 40% 50% 60% 70% 80% 90% 100%

Credit: The Brookings Institution, Metropolitan Policy Program

But the objective, participants repeatedly underscored, was not to magnify the role of metropolitan regions for their own sake. Rather, "it's to win, compete, and move the country forward," generating broadened personal opportunity and sustainable development, noted Rey Ramsey, technology expert and founder/chief executive officer of One Economy Corporation. Or, in the words of Jeremy Nowak of the Philadelphia-based Reinvestment Fund, to demonstrate to ourselves "that America is a country organized for success."

National policy innovation, Robert Yaro of the New York City–based Regional Plan Association commented, has been paralyzed by a generation-long "disbelief in and disdain for federal leadership." The moment is ripe, he argued, "for an activist government that rises above the dogma of Left and Right and spells out a role for the federal government in which it doesn't dominate metro areas and states, but charts a course for the whole country—a program of activist, progressive leadership."

U.S. CHALLENGES AND SHORTCOMINGS

By some measures the United States seems so economically strong it should have few concerns. Its economy has long been the world's most productive; in terms of total output the U.S. Gross Domestic Product (GDP) of $12.4 trillion in 2005 was nearly triple that of Japan's, the closest competitor. Twenty-two of the world's most productive city regions (measured by GDP per capita) are in the United States, including such globally connected metros as New York, San Francisco, Washington, Los Angeles, Seattle and Houston.

Metros Triumphant—and Challenged

A DISPERSED AMERICA—people continuing to spread out, leaving metropolitan areas—was widely prophesied in the 1970s. But the projections were dead wrong, Brookings' Bruce Katz noted at the Summit. Despite popular writing about a "flat" world, he said, population *and* economic activity actually moved increasingly into metropolitan centers, both in the United States and internationally. The more relevant metaphor is author Richard Florida's word—*spikiness*—as a glimpse at a world map of economic activity clusters suggests. On the population side, latest figures indicate North America is now 81 percent urban, Western Europe 77 percent, and Australia/New Zealand 88 percent.

But why—again in Katz's words—are metro regions, especially the top 100 in population, "punching way above their weight in innovative value-laden growth"?

It's their high productivity per worker, and their capacity to take advantage of worker specialization in an ever-more variegated global economy, Alan Berube of Brookings explained. With substantial population and thus many workers, larger metro regions provide an easier "match" when companies look for employees with particular skills. Major financial and service institutions are more likely to be present. Knowledge "spillover" occurs more spontaneously among the many people and firms of a denser area. Big, high-quality facilities—major highways, leading universities, top-tier libraries, auditoriums and museums, quality public transit systems as an alternative to auto use—are feasible because many people share their costs.

As Berube noted in a research paper for the sessions, "Today *information*—for instance the price of light sweet crude oil on the New York Mercantile Exchange—can be transmitted quickly and cheaply over long distances, reducing the need for proximity to facilitate those exchanges. But knowledge, especially *tacit knowledge*—that which cannot be codified, but only understood through training and personal experience—is notoriously averse to transmission over long distances. Thus, IT consulting firms might outsource the development of discrete modules to programmers in India or Estonia, but still continue to rely on in-house, face-to-face interaction between highly trained workers and clients in order to develop sophisticated systems design."

Larger metros draw more venture capital investment, direct foreign investment and R&D funding. High land costs, which one might assume would be a major competitive downer for these larger metros, are not the problem one might assume, Berube noted. The host of industries in which the United States increasingly specializes—high technology, life sciences, finance, consulting, and the like—are not land intensive. That sets them apart from manufacturing, which has increasingly decamped for small metropolitan and rural areas in the South, Midwest, and abroad.

Quality of place spells another major plus for many metros. Highly educated workers, able to find work in any region (or for that matter any nation) they prefer, often opt for places with diversity, broad ranges of housing styles, varieties of neighborhoods, and strong cultural and entertainment offerings. Two-earner, college-educated couples, rising in numbers in recent years, are drawn to larger metro areas and their potential for superior job matches. Skilled young workers are able to switch jobs and increase their incomes more easily. And there is strong evidence, Berube reported, that large cities and metros innovate more—produce more patents, for example—because their dense clusters of employment promote productive knowledge "spillovers" between firms and professions.

It is true that a number of smaller metropolitan and micropolitan areas—St. George, Utah; Bend, Oregon; Hanover, New Hampshire; for example—have grown rapidly in recent years, either because of major universities or exceptional natural amenities. But in a nation with rapidly growing minorities (by 2050 only 48 percent of working-age Americans will be non-Hispanic white) and dramatically declining household sizes (3.4 in 1950, 2.6 today), it is very likely that demand will remain strong for the diverse array of quality places that large metropolitan areas provide.

Yet for all their advantages, the nation's metros face a range of major challenges holding back their collective prosperity—and thereby the United States as a whole.

Collectively, metros have experienced a slowdown in productivity growth since mid-decade. Most have pockets of mediocre if not extremely poor schools, with alarmingly low graduation rates. Significant numbers of their residents exhibit poor credit histories (a situation exacerbated by the 2007 to 2008 subprime mortgage lending emergency). Many road-ways are in poor condition and often congested, and most metros' public transit systems lag far below the quality level of other industrialized nations. The sprawling development patterns and high per-capita vehicle miles traveled leave the areas extremely exposed in the event of a global energy crisis, even while generating heavy amounts of greenhouse gases.

Thus there is a need, the Summit panelists agreed, to develop an aggressive, metro-focused U.S. development policy on every front, from research-and-development breakthroughs to human capital develop-ment to more conserving transportation land use policies.

stiff new global competition

Still, the American economic powerhouse faces stiff new global competition. Market reforms in China and India have unleashed awesome new investment and economic power; overall the size of the global labor force has doubled in a decade and a half, with more and more educated workers—for example, there are currently some 2 million Chinese university graduates a year. Indian universities produce 260,000 engineering graduates yearly, compared to a disappointing total of 200,000 in the United States. And in terms of basic infrastructure investment—new roads, railways systems, ports, and airports—Asia and other world regions are leaping ahead of the United States, which often seems unable to maintain the facilities it built decades ago.

Growing inequities in the labor market

Growing inequities in the labor market throw a long shadow over the image of the United States as a land of opportunity for the broad masses. The nation's highly educated workers have seen their wages rise sharply over the last three decades, while those of less-educated workers have stagnated or, in real dollars, deteriorated, with housing, transportation, and medical care consuming more and more of their disposable income. Wealth building is proving especially difficult for immigrants and African-Americans, a problem of growing scale as African-Americans and Latinos expand to make up an estimated 40 percent of the national workforce by 2050.

U.S. skills for global competitiveness may well suffer in the coming decades as baby boomers, the 78 million Americans born between 1946 and 1964, retire in high numbers. Overall workforce growth will slow dramatically, raising the specter of severe shortages in some high-skill areas. By 2050, non-Hispanic whites will be a minority of the labor force. New workforce entrants will be heavily Hispanic and African-American—a severe handicap unless radical improvements can be made in these groups' seriously lagging educational attainment. High proportions of Latinos and African-Americans drop out of school before high school graduation, and fewer still (ten or fewer out of 100 who entered ninth grade in 2001, for example) are expected to both complete high school and earn a post-secondary degree, according to the National Center for Public Policy and High Education.

Finally, the United States may be headed into severe and threatening environmental stress. Even as rising carbon-dioxide emissions exacerbate perils of coastline flooding, droughts, and wildfires, the country remains, on a per capita basis, by far and away the world's largest single emitter of greenhouse gases. It continues to be reliant on highly costly and unreliable oil supplies for more than 60 percent of its petroleum use. Rising world energy prices may pose serious threats to the national economy; a major global oil crisis could deal a crippling blow. With dangers to U.S. ecosystems already on the rise, environmental pressures are sure to intensify as the country adds its projected 120 million additional people by 2050, a population rise only India and China are projected to exceed.

workforce
growth
will slow
dramatically

environmental
stress

A NEW GROWTH SCENARIO

What policies would unleash American skills, intelligence, and knowledge to provide a more secure and prosperous future for the nation's citizens and communities?

Three types of growth are critical to achieving true prosperity for the United States, the Brookings researchers concluded. And they are all closely interconnected, and interdependent:

- Productive growth: not just in raw numbers, but growth that is centered in innovation and entrepreneurship that generates high-quality jobs and helps the United States maintain its global economic leadership.

- Inclusive growth: conscious outreach to racial minorities, struggling recent immigrants, and others lagging in education and income to help them gain qualifications for higher-income work and become part of a strong and diverse American middle class.

- Environmentally sustainable growth: conserving the nation's natural resources, growing green, advancing efforts to address climate change and greater U.S. energy independence. Quality infrastructure, including world-class roads, transit and ports, and telecommunications and broadband networks, is a critically important element because it determines how efficiently goods, people, and information can travel within and across markets.

But sustainable growth underscores the need for infrastructure and growth patterns that improve air quality, conserve land and natural resources, and reduce Americans'

Euro Models: Discreetly Pro-Metro

METRO REGIONS as key to national and continent-wide prosperity have risen rapidly in recent years on the agendas of several European nations and the European Union—though in a fairly quiet way, partly to avert resistance by more rural areas.

Germany, for example, developed a finely attuned post–World War II federal system: strong states (*Länder*) and local governments with clear planning powers, increasingly recognized metropolitan regions, and a federal government seeking to aid and abet without stirring up political disputes. Without a great deal of publicity the federal government has a key focus "on creating clusters of knowledge, to foster cooperation, so that our 11 metro regions are able to compete with international mega‑regions," Oliver Weigel, head of the German Federal Ministry of Transport, Building, and Urban Affairs, told the Global Summit panelists. (See Sidebar, "Germany's Federalist Solution," p. 305 in Chapter 7.)

Great Britain, by contrast, shifted dramatically with Labour's rise to power in 1997. Up to then, the prevailing notion had been of England as a rural nation with cities relegated to the margins; in 1986 Prime Minister Margaret Thatcher actually abolished the Greater London Council, the capital region's governing body. Tony Blair's government shifted radically, first with an array of disparate urban initiatives, then in a more deliberate process of negotiated Local Area Agreements. But Labour's goal apparently remained constant: to encourage not only London, but other city regions to reposition themselves as engines of the country's prosperity.

The emerging British vision, as Bob Kerslake, chief executive of the Sheffield City Council, explained to the panelists, was a national mission to encourage cities, facilitate local public–private partnerships, and create a vision of "prosperity, inclusion and sustainability" (all three values, he said, are "integrally linked—you can't have one without the other").

Kerslake used the revival story of Sheffield—520,000 people in a region of 1.7 million, Britain's fourth largest city—to illustrate the British urban revival. At one point Sheffield dominated world steel production, only, in the 1970s, to lose a full quarter of its jobs, "knocking the stuffing out of our formerly very proud city." A first revival step was to tamp down business–government hostility. And second, to rebuild confidence, "from revival to regeneration with a new economy resilient to market changes."

A Magnificent Seven Projects program—a new Town Hall, Peace

Gardens, and others—was initiated in 2000 as a "visible symbol" of progress, the city declaring itself ideal territory for the private sector to fill in. Major public investment, including British government support and £900 million from European Structural Funds, helped stimulate nearly £2 billion in private funding. Diverse economic projects appeared, including an infusion of financial and legal services. Wages rose, and unemployment fell sharply.

Kerslake did comment that "London is both a massive advantage and a challenge for us. No country can succeed without a global city, with the huge gateway advantages, resources, investment it brings." But, he added, there is also a disadvantage because London "is such a magnet for people, innovation and investment—it makes it hard for us to get the critical mass now." His example: "If I'm in London and I get a job in Sheffield, where's my next job? We need to retain a critical mass of our own knowledge workers." Sheffield is, though, in the early stages of building its links to Leeds and Manchester, both within a 30-mile radius, adding a region of up to 5 million people that could represent a more powerful collective economic draw.

The European Union, in the meantime, has moved beyond its early (and successful) program of targeted aid to lagging countries—the focus under which Ireland and Spain benefited most dramatically. The participants heard from Joist van Iersel, member of the European Economic and Social Committee, that E.U. leaders grasp that even strong areas have their weaknesses, so therefore it is imperative for strong regions to remain strong. The E.U.'s 2000 Lisbon Strategy actually articulated a top "strategic goal…to become the most competitive and dynamic knowledge-based economy in the world."

As yet, said van Iersel, there is no formal E.U. competence, or formal declaration, to focus heavily on assistance to cities and their regions. Yet there's growing recognition, he added, "that metros are the driving forces in the economic development of Europe."

In the meantime, he named Germany the star on working directly with its metros, followed by France, Poland, Italy, and the Netherlands. Examples of urban regions significantly aided by their national governments include Bilbao, Stuttgart, Helsinki, and Copenhagen.

The implicit challenge: If Europeans can move in a relatively brief time frame to a competitiveness agenda that increasingly promotes the critical role of metropolitan regions, why not the United States?

world-leading consumption rates of gas and electricity.

quality of places

And it ties directly to focus on the *quality* of places: creating and sustaining vibrant downtowns, attractive town centers, and neighborhoods with parks, stores, schools, and places of worship within easy reach. Workers in today's knowledge economy, it's suggested, are increasingly seeking communities of density, diversity, and distinctiveness, even as sprawling, less energy-efficient suburban development, often encroaching on rural lands and valuable ecosystems, declines in relative popularity.

But here is the crux, according to the Brookings analysis: Productivity, inclusivity, sustainable growth are all chiefly attainable in the context of *metropolitan areas*—the collections of our more densely developed cities, suburbs and counties, tied together by commuting, common-labor markets, shared environments, and civic cultures. And it is within those metro areas that the nation will be able to leverage its key potentials and challenges: economic innovation, human capital, infrastructure that is up to new-century demands, and quality places.

Metros' critical importance, by virtue of their scale, is hard to question. They may also be described—as the writers of this report have in writings over the past two decades—as the "citistates" of the modern global economy. The U.S. Census Bureau defines 363 metros, primarily regions with urban centers of at least 50,000 people and strong area-wide commuting ties. Whole counties are either included or excluded. Alternatively, metros or citistates can be viewed more organically, with more fluid borders; essentially "the citistate is what the economy does."

Metros are present across all 50 states—from one in Hawaii to 24 in Texas. And their dominance is indisputable. Cumulatively the top 100 represent just 12 percent of the nation's land cover, but they also represent

- 65 percent of total U.S. population
- 74 percent of the nation's GDP
- 74 percent of the nation's college graduates
- 77 percent of all good-paying "knowledge jobs"
- 78 percent of all patent activity
- 79 percent of the nation's air cargo
- 79 percent of performing arts establishments
- 82 percent of National Institutes of Health and National Science research funding
- 89 percent of passenger air boardings
- 94 percent of U.S. venture capital funding

Bottom line of the case that the Brookings group presented: "Metros are not part of the national economy. They *are* the national economy. ... America is a metropolitan nation."

FEDERAL BARRIER—AND CHALLENGE

But there is a massive problem: America's federal government is too often a *non*-partner with regions that are working hard to pull together their resources and address critical problems.

National officials, the Summit participants agreed, are strangely oblivious to the reality that the United States is not so much a single national economy as a collection of unique and varied metropolitan economies, each dependent on its particular mix of firms, trained workers, quality infrastructure, R&D centers, and sources of capital investment working together.

economic clusters of metros

The dominant economic clusters of metros illustrates their individuality and special challenges: the New York region in financial services; Twin Cities in biomedical devices; Chicago and San Francisco in pharmaceuticals; Seattle, Dallas, Los Angeles, and Hartford in aerospace; Detroit in motor vehicle parts; Akron in polymers. Specialization also makes the United States competitive globally: the country's ten top metros alone generate 45 percent of the nation's employment in legal and accounting/consulting services.

In regions nationwide, alliances of business, civic, environmental, and neighborhood groups have come together to focus on solving pressing problems and improving competitiveness. The numbers and effectiveness of the alliances have grown exponentially in recent years.

Just a few examples: Greater Dallas, Denver, Charlotte, and Seattle have relied on civic alliances to remake traditional downtowns and catalyze support for new transit systems. Greater Cleveland, Milwaukee and Raleigh-Durham have partnerships focused on research universities, community colleges, and job training to strengthen their economic specialties. Greater Chicago's Metropolis 2020 organization, formed out of

broad civic and labor support

the business community but with broad civic and labor support, has worked on such issues as workforce housing, public

The Federal Conundrum

IF METROS ARE TO BE EFFECTIVE PLAYERS in a 21st century world, how do they cope with the state governments that hold the vast reservoir of constitutionally grounded power in the United States?

Ideally, state governments would recognize metros for what they are: immensely productive wealth producers, partly because of what they still produce through manufacturing, but more so because of all the specialized skills and services, as well as academic and specialized research capacities, that are centered in their cities and suburbs. Metros are the bedrock of states' economic strength.

A smart state would not only seek ways to free its metros to be more productive but would create incentives to make them even more so. One way to do that would be by creating incentives to encourage central cities and inner- and outer-ring suburbs to form alliances for progress—and possibly adding disincentives if they do not.

Sadly, that is seldom the formula. State legislators from urban areas rarely form cohesive teams, and rural state legislators too often view the metros as adversaries, not allies. It is difficult for some metro areas to get permissions to tax themselves—with no burden to taxpayers elsewhere in the state—for roads or public-transit expansion and upkeep.

Ironically, the federal government often treats the states much as the states typically treat their metro regions: with indifference and lack of concern to help them prosper.

Could a new national consensus—to value, challenge, and assist both states *and* metros—be formed? That is an open question the Brookings' *Blueprint for American Prosperity* raises. The core idea: leadership from the "top," to help the "bottom" function well, to achieve a more prosperous American future. But would such initiatives have any chance in the complex world of U.S. politics, encumbered as it is with well-developed special interest politics and the constitutional system's built-in checks and balances?

The easy answer is no; such efforts would be unprecedented, doomed from the start. On the other hand, as Summit sessions underscored, the United States (and its global neighbors) face 21st century challenges of unprecedented breadth.

transit, curbing sprawl development, and prisoner reentry. The University of California, San Diego, collaborates with local businesses to breed and grow start-up technology firms by connecting them with faculty research skills and outside corporate investors.

The imperative of this moment, venture capitalist Karen Mills told her fellow panelists at the Summit, "is to integrate around place. Metropolitan transportation, housing, clusters of economic development work most effectively together. Place is central—and the place-based assets have to be aggregated to work well in today's economy."

place-based assets

But does official Washington encourage, aid and abet, even recognize place-based efforts? Rarely. Almost without exception, federal policy fails to see how metro clusters function to sustain and grow the nation's economy. Programs and policies that the metros need to mix and match for their particular needs are compartmentalized and fragmented at the federal level. Research, job training, economic development, housing, transportation, and other infrastructure programs are all separated into their own organizational and programmatic boxes. Brookings notes that federal policy related in some way to economic development is spread across nine departments, five independent agencies, and 180 distinct programs. Plus, the federal focus often seems clearly out of date—housing programs pushing to add affordable units just in cities, for example, when more poor people today are living in suburbs as jobs have decentralized.

Nor has official Washington acted early or forthrightly on pressing national issues that impact all regions: boosting the wages of lower-income workers, building state-of-the-art transportation systems linking metros, border-to-border broadband access, or responding to the overriding challenge of climate change.

The Brookings team summarized their case against today's federal government in this way: It is very often absent when it should be present in helping address new issues. It is frequently present when it should be absent (imposing environmental or workforce requirements, for example, that regulate in a way that stunts or distorts local problem-solving). And it is stovepiped, fragmented, unaware of the place-based implications of its policies, and oblivious to the role of constructive local partnerships.

place-based implications

The federal establishment is even deficient on the most basic services, shortchanging budgets of such core statistical agencies as the Census Bureau and Bureau of Economic Analysis, which metro regions rely on for transparent and accessible data to guide their policies and decisions. One participant derisively called today's United States "a fact-free zone."

The conclusion: The federal government needs a major overhaul to make it far less formulaic and "one size fits all" as it works with distinctive regions and their distinctive needs. A reformed, remade federal government would lead where it must, engage in crucial areas that demand vision, scope and capacity, and empower metros so that cities and suburbs have

reformed, remade federal government

the ability to respond to local priorities with federal tools. The United States needs a national government that is organized for success, determines ways to maximize its own effectiveness, and acts to enhance the creative energies of America's states, metros, and the private sector.

One example: Washington should provide metros and local governments with incentives to form and pursue broad partnerships that address core challenges ranging from green building and energy conservation to targeted educational opportunities for new immigrants.

"Critics may say such a policy is about dumping money on 100 or 362 metro regions," Alan Berube, research director of Brookings' Metropolitan Policy Program said. "Our answer must be: these are investments critical to use the advantage of place." Or as another panelist noted: "Each federal investment must be evaluated with transparency for an outcome-based approach. The approach is not a blank check for regions, but a process that evaluates the dollar return, progress in labor market returns, using new green infrastructure, saving energy. And applying the federal data that's lacking today to make sound decisions, to judge efforts realistically."

MAKING THE METRO CASE

popularize the metro message

To popularize the metro message across the United States, interjecting it into 2008 election debate and beyond, the Brookings team described an elaborate campaign to "grow a network" and build partnerships in several dozen regions,

Henry Cisneros on a Metropolitan Nation

Excerpts from remarks by former U.S. Housing and Urban Development Secretary Henry Cisneros at the November 2007 Brookings Institution launch of its Blueprint for American Prosperity:

OVER THE LAST DECADES, metropolitan areas that were little more than towns 50 years ago have become pillars of the national economy: Atlanta in communications, Charlotte in finance, Miami in trade and banking, San Diego in the biosciences, and San Jose in technology. The evidence is abundant: In American history the metropolitan economies drive the way the nation works.

In American history urban places have been home to our churches, temples, museums, symphony halls, opera houses, ballparks, stadiums, convention venues, and conference centers. Imagine how much poorer our nation would be without the National Cathedral in Washington, the Getty Center in Los Angeles, the Statue of Liberty and Central Park in New York, the Museum of Natural History in Chicago, the Opera House in San Francisco, Camden Yards in Baltimore...

Our urban places give us identity and celebrate our common purpose. We capture that magic even in the names of the athletic teams that describe our urban history: the Pittsburgh Steelers, the Seattle Mariners, the Dallas Cowboys, the San Francisco Forty-Niners, and, yes, the New York Mets—the Metropolitans. The metropolitan places are where America comes together.

Metropolitan areas provided the stepping stones to a better life, the route to American middle class for so many—the route of the Irish of Boston, the Poles of Detroit, the Slavs of Cleveland, the Jews of New York, the Germans of Milwaukee, the Swedes of Minneapolis, the Chinese of San Francisco, the Latinos of San Antonio, and the Vietnamese of Anaheim.

Just as metropolitan areas have been engines for some of the greatest advances in American history so too can they serve the 21st century imperatives of national progress.

Metropolitan areas can sustain work and the hope of advancement when 76 percent of the nation's knowledge jobs are in the 100 largest metropolitan areas.

Metropolitan areas can support learning that will unleash human ingenuity when 74 percent of the tier-one research institutions are in those 100 largest.

Metropolitan areas can uplift our spirits when critical masses of the nation's creative talent flourish there.

Metropolitan areas are home to the neighborhoods where we can preserve safety and dignity and family peace of mind.

Metropolitan areas are places where we must govern ourselves with optimism and inclusiveness when 76 percent of our GDP is generated in only 100 urban places.

Metropolitan areas are the places where our nation can address the challenges of our times. In the new century, we can be a nation with an economy that has the competitive attributes to succeed in global competition, even as we prepare the way for a new middle class.

There is no question that we Americans are facing massive competition in the years to come. Yet even as we compete with forces that drive wages down in a global context, we must build the new American middle class. To do so we have to energize metropolitan schools and build the urban technological infrastructure.

We can be a nation that integrates its people and that helps lower-income families and immigrants raise their incomes and accumulate assets. We must create excellence in urban schools from kindergarten through college, extend home ownership, create pathways to higher education, open access to the financial system, and strengthen the portal role of urban areas for immigrants.

We can be a nation that wisely uses its physical gifts, uses less land, uses fewer natural resources, and creates sustainable places. To do so we must modernize our infrastructure and build smartly.

The Brookings Institution is right to drive a national conversation about a new partnership, about how we use our national resources rather than leave urban governments on their own, about how we create incentives to cooperate across the boundaries of city and suburb, artificial boundaries that disappear when an urban area is viewed from a plane at night.

Some of our nation's great historic epics, the truly important dynamics that have built the foundation of our way of life—our economic maturation over time, our acceptance of immigrants, the processes of democratic participation, the ascent of the middle class, the emergence of public education as the force it has been—have been so transformative because of our urban and metropolitan places.

The continuing challenges before us in the new century—creating inclusiveness of opportunity, harnessing human potential, integrating new Americans to play their part in civic action and leadership, growing in wise and responsible ways—must be addressed in the metropolitan places, the places that we built, the places that we need, and the places we love. In this way we will keep our country strong.

building (or connecting to) broad coalitions of business, university, and public officials in each. The media—including major newspapers, whose own market areas are naturally metrowide—would also be engaged, starting with meetings with editorial boards.

Moving beyond the message, the campaign would work to empower metro coalitions by providing them with quality research and important connections to help them 1) develop initiatives tailored to their own regions, and 2) combine their efforts so they can more effectively express their priorities on the national stage.

Then, from the Washington side, Brookings' campaign would seek to convince federal policy makers of the critical role that metros play in achieving key national goals.

The Summit participants, however, had no illusions about the potential difficulty of promoting the idea of metro

promoting the idea of metro regions

regions—all evidence notwithstanding—as centerpieces of the future national economy. In fact, it was noted, metros are *not* often recognized for their value, not in local politics, not in state politics, and rarely in national policy.

The Advisory Commission on Intergovernmental Relations, which had begun examination of metros' roles, was allowed to expire under the Reagan administration. Very few of the Metropolitan Planning Organizations (MPOs) designed in federal transportation legislation since the first ISTEA (Intermodal Surface Transportation Act) legislation in 1992 have gone far beyond a log-rolling exercise in choice of local transportation projects. And in general American life, the word *metro* hasn't and doesn't generate warm feelings.

Another danger several participants saw: The "nightmare," in the words of former Washington, DC, Mayor Anthony Williams, "that this initiative gets labeled tax and spend—more money for big cities and housing."

Others cautioned: make sure the agenda is not seen as a "command economy" effort, but rather an effort to give choices and opportunities to metro areas, allowing them to fulfill their potential as the nation's cutting economic edge.

Strategies must also be found, participants said, to make clear to the "white areas" on the map—those outside the United States' 362 metropolitan regions—that they, too, will benefit from a more competitive national economy in which the metros will inevitably take a lead role. The Brookings team has sought to lessen any anti-metro backlash with three points:

a more competitive national economy

1. Much of rural America lies within metropolitan America. Fifty-one percent of all U.S. rural residents actually live in suburban or exurban counties located within metros.

2. Many professionals who prefer small-town or rural environments work there, contribute to local economies and civic life, sometimes starting local firms, even though they may continue to commute electronically, or occasionally in person, to headquarters in larger metro areas. Globally competitive firms, typically headquartered in large metros, often have manufacturing or other spin-off activities (call centers, for example) in less-urban places to take advantage of their

lower-cost labor and less-expensive office space. Often their operations become mainstays of rural-area employment bases.

3. Agriculture ties rural places (producing most of the nation's food supply) to urban places (the chief consumers). Increasingly, urban farmers' markets and niche grocers have become major new customers for rural growers' sale of fresh and/or organic foods. Rural and small-town places with natural resource attractions also depend on metro areas for the bulk of their customers.

Still, the Summit panelists saw compelling need for a proactive education and advocacy campaign to sell all Americans—residents of metro areas included—on metros' importance to American life and economy. Critical to the metro "sell": The idea that these regions are not only critical to the national economy, but able to play that role because of their multiple assets and connections.

The overarching themes, developed by participants: "Unleashing America's Prosperity," "Metros Are Connected Places," and "Together We Win." Or stated a bit differently: "The world is changing. What we value is at stake. We're connected by where we live. Overwhelmingly, we live in, or we relate to, metro areas. Metro areas drive the economy. America must invest. Unleash the potential."

The group also sought to redefine "metro" with connective, appealing language, deliberately downplaying the city-versus-suburb themes that have been popular in media and in

Lurie Garden in Millennium Park, Chicago, Illinois, U.S.A.

The Olympic Sculpture Park, with a permanent collection including Alexander Calder's "Eagle," has revived the historic waterfront, Seattle, Washington, U.S.A.

local political standoffs through many of the post–World War II decades. The new and alternative "shorthand" embraced by the panelists centered on the concept that "Metros Are Connected Places." They envisioned a public relations campaign "jolting" Americans in a friendly way to recognize that they do not live in a single city or suburb, but rather in geographically expansive metro regions that enable them to share all manner of valuable resources:

- One or more lively downtowns
- Mixes of historic center-city and ring-city neighborhoods
- Universities and community colleges
- Theaters, museums, and libraries
- Job-providing employment clusters and corporate offices
- A regionwide array of parks and waterfronts
- Interconnected transportation systems
- Sports teams, often the focus of the liveliest regionwide conversations

If "metro" embraces all those, the group was suggesting, what's *not* to like? Or if the metro has problem neighborhoods, pollution perils, or common economic challenges, why not work on those challenges together, with shared resources?

work on those
challenges
together

A NATIONAL–METRO POLICY MIX

At and following the Summit sessions, the Brookings policy analysts began to enumerate (and prepare papers on) a broad range of initiatives that a metro-sensitive federal government *could* and *should* consider adopting. A sampling:

Boosting innovation, productivity, and growth through a national innovation foundation. It is an axiom of modern economics: Innovation sparks productivity. But the United States is slipping behind major nation competitors in R&D expenditures as a percentage of the GNP—an untenable position for a high-wage, developed 21st century society. One solution: a National Innovation Foundation—a federally funded, "nimble, lean, and collaborative" entity to catalyze cutting-edge productivity growth among firms, industry groups, research universities, and new public–private partnerships.

Energy discovery institutes: repurposing federal energy research for today's economic and climate challenges. The scale, pace, and design of U.S. energy research is insufficient to ensure the nation's competitiveness, national security, and ability to respond to global climate change. To reverse that situation, the nation needs both enhanced funding for advanced energy research and a bold new development of highly networked "discovery–innovation institutes" that link research universities to energy labs, venture capital, and the private sector. Two major U.S. regions that might be prime candidates for special analysis and activities: the Great Lakes and the Intermountain West.

Clustering for competitiveness. Regional networks of businesses, industry associations, colleges, universities, and other R&D organizations, even with very informal networking, have been shown to have strong potential in growing industries and service areas appropriate to their specialties, infrastructure,

Revitalizing Urban Centers: Investing in Education, Housing, and the Environment

Richard M. Daley

Mayor of Chicago, Illinois, U.S.A.; plenary speaker

EDUCATION HAS BEEN MY NUMBER ONE PRIORITY as mayor of Chicago. Why? Because it is the only long-term solution to ending poverty and, in a world based on information, it's the key to the city's economic success. Without a good education, a person cannot enter the work force. But while the United States boasts the best higher education in the world, basic education is often a third or fourth priority, with high-rated schools often reserved for the privileged.

I was told that it would be a political risk to take control of Chicago's schools away from the independent school board. But the public school system was in total disarray. The deteriorating physical condition of the buildings told children that education didn't matter and the poor academic state seemed to confirm this. I had to do something drastic to transform this huge obstacle to the city's long-term vitality.

With business leaders joining in, we persuaded city taxpayers to spend more than $5 billion on new construction and major renovations of 45 schools, adding laboratories and gym facilities, converting more than 100 asphalt playgrounds to green campus parks. In turn these improvements to school buildings helped spur revitalization of the surrounding neighborhoods.

On the academic side, our appointed management team emphasized basics such as reading and math, ending the practice of social promotion. Principals and teachers were held accountable for student performance. Other innovations, including charter schools, military academies with tight discipline, and single-sex schools, were encouraged. Despite high poverty rates, the results were better test scores and climbing graduation rates.

My administration also focused on neighborhood facilities beyond schools, since education should not end when school is out. I'd rather see a child with a book than in front of a TV, so we built 52 new libraries, offering free wireless Internet access and rooms for neighborhood groups to gather. Our efforts to leverage city-supported facilities as community anchors continued as we remodeled police and fire stations, making them more people-friendly.

To aid older residents the city built eight senior centers and added more than 5,000 units of senior housing. In 2000 a major transformation plan for public housing began, another move that political consultants warned me against. But I was deeply disturbed by the state of the high-rise public housing units that Chicago had built from the 1950s to the 1970s, which had become crime-ridden danger zones.

The city began to demolish these high-rises, replacing them with low-rise apartments and townhouses, mixing subsidized units with market-rate rental housing. Our goal was never to blame the people who had been caught in degraded public housing but rather to create attractive new environments to help rebuild souls. Some 15,000 of a planned 25,000 housing units have been rehabilitated or constructed with an effort to integrate developments with new and renovated schools, libraries and fire stations to create a self-sustaining cycle of renewal.

To show how a large city can live in harmony with nature, we also embarked on a major beautification and greening effort. We began one of the nation's most aggressive programs to transform industrial brownfields. We created dedicated nature areas along the banks of the Chicago River. We closed Meigs airfield and plan to turn it into a nature and wetlands area. We reconfigured commercial thoroughfares with planters, street lights, and bike racks. And Chicago is now among the world leaders in green-roofed buildings, with some 400 either built or being developed, including the pioneer rooftop garden at City Hall and the widely acclaimed new Millennium Park, where the nation's largest green roof replaced a gravel parking lot. Next, as part of the ongoing modernization plan for O'Hare Airport, we intend to replace 154 acres of low-quality, inaccessible wetlands currently on airport property with nearly 450 acres of higher-quality wetlands throughout the Chicago area.

It is the cities that pay attention to quality of life—good schools, safe streets, strong neighborhoods, and pathways for walking and biking—that will thrive in the 21st century.

and skilled worker pools. The federal government currently spends more than $80 million annually on local economic development efforts. But the programs are fragmented, under-leveraged, and unaligned.

Federal funding might prove far more productive if it were shaped and coordinated to stimulate and support cluster activities in promising competitive industries. There is a current model in the Department of Labor's competitive WIRED grants to regions, nominated by their governors, with partnership plans to transform their communities. A broader program might provide one-time $10 million awards to regional industry clusters on the condition they be industry-led, involve collaborations with multiple research, workforce, and regional development entities, and have the potential create well-paid jobs in the sector.

Community School Compacts. Kalamazoo Progress, launched in 2006, guarantees up-to-100 percent financial support at any Michigan college or university for students who graduate from Kalamazoo's public schools and retain a minimum grade point average. The program has already shown it can motivate students to stay in school, even attracting middle-class families back to the city with its program. Pittsburgh Promise, an effort to adapt the Kalamazoo approach for that city, is being launched with a $100 million commitment from the University of Pittsburgh Medical Center, contingent on other fund-raising success. An early idea is that the federal government, in partnership with 100 to 300 underperforming inner-city and older suburb areas, could emulate these types of initiatives. Assuming, for example, the effort were financed as a 50–25–25 federal–state–local matching program, the total cost to all, with 1.5 million students participating, might be about $15 billion annually. Arguably, the long-term payoffs, in future worker productivity alone, would justify the national and state investment, even while the metropolitan areas stabilize their neighborhoods and build their prospective economies.

"Metro raise." One of the most successful federal programs in helping low-income families make ends meet in a world of low wages and fierce globalization pressures has been the federal Earned Income Tax Credit (EITC). Especially effective in high-cost-of-living regions, the credit could be expanded to boost incomes, reduce poverty, and make housing more available for metro workers on the low end of the wage scales.

Immigration. The heavy debate about federal immigration policy obscures a critical issue: How will the millions of immigrants of recent years, mostly legal, adjust to life in the United States? They and their children will constitute a growing share of local populations, but federal assistance is scarce to nonexistent. A nationally supported "New Americans Initiative" could help seed state–level public–private partnerships, increasing immigrants' English language skills, assisting on employment, citizenship, skills training, and related issues, with major benefits to economies from the metro to the national level.

Green building. Detached single-family homes—"the American Dream"—account for nearly half of the 43 percent of carbon emissions arising from the nation's built environment. A typical home emits 20,000 pounds of carbon annually; just 1 percent of homes are built to green standards. In an era of pressing climate change, the "dream" may require reinvention, starting with a broad variety of already-available but thinly spread energy-saving practices.

Brookings will propose using federal regulatory and fiscal policy to encourage capital markets to invest in green market products, to modernize underwriting and energy-efficiency mortgage lending, give Federal Housing Authority a new energy-efficiency mission, and establish strong incentives for stem-to-stern green features in the millions of homes projected to be built in the next years. In addition to reduced carbon footprint, significant savings for fiscally-pressed homeowners could be achieved.

consumer demand

sustainability

stark class differences

improved satellite data

CHAPTER 9

Building Evidence to Sustain an Urban Future

crosscutting elements

a scholarly network

consumer demand

true mobility

urban research mission

An aerial view of Paraisopolis, a slum with some 60,000 residents, São Paola, Brazil

A GLOBAL URBAN RESEARCH COMMONS for the 21st century is

a Web-based resource

critically needed. The commons would be a Web-based resource that would gather papers, databases, and other information that have never before collected in one place. It would also encompass publications that synthesize new research findings. It would convene researchers and practitioners in virtual and face-to-face meetings on a regular basis.

The reasons are compelling. The urban research/prac-

disseminating its findings

titioner community needs to be as efficient in disseminating its findings as are major corporations that employ worldwide supply chains for their products. On-time knowledge is critical to shaping rapidly urbanizing places. The sustainability of cities has become, with the vast rural-to-urban migration of the times, close to synonymous with the sustainability of the human enterprise. Cities' spatial form, technologies, and resilience in the face of climate change are ripe for intense global debate and exchange. And because poverty in the 21st century will overwhelmingly be *urban* poverty, a global wave of examination of its roots, development, evolution, and long-term solutions is essential.

informal contacts

Much can be learned through informal contacts—mayor-to-mayor, expert-to-expert networks. But a global urban research commons requires rigorous academic attention to decipher emerging key questions, test hypotheses, monitor experiments, and raise the level of analysis of the critically pressing urban issues.

To test this idea, the University of Pennsylvania's Institute for Urban Research, led by professors Eugenie Birch and Susan

Wachter, organized the weeklong Summit session exploring urban research themes. Urban researchers from five continents, from both Global South and Global North, from varieties of disciplines such as demography, economics, health, education, environment, geography, city planning, health, and housing took part.

a scholarly network

They identified a need for a scholarly network that crosses geographies, disciplines, and private and public sectors. Participants discovered that researchers in Latin America, Africa, China, and India felt a need to understand developments elsewhere, and that numbers of Global North scholars share many of the same concerns.

Four core questions for a global urban research commons were identified before the session, and addressed by the network of scholars in their preparatory papers and during the session:

- Where will the new urban dwellers find a place to live and will these places be sustainable?
- In what conditions will they live in their fast-growing cities?
- What basic urban services will they need to allow the improvement of their standard of living and life prospects?
- How will those services be financed and supplied?

focused research

The participants observed that urban growth and challenges have *not*, until now, been a target of focused research or action plans among scholars. Much research, noted Schuaib Lwasa of Uganda's Makerere University, is skewed with a rural bias, while censuses often have difficulty reaching informal settlements, meaning that slums are often undercounted and therefore underrepresented politically and in provision of services. There has been some effort to address data shortfalls as urban researchers drawn from academia, the United Nations, the World Bank, and other interested institutions have undertaken important studies tracking urban growth. In fact, one participant, city and regional planning expert John Landis, observed, the world is awash in data, including the UN-HABITAT's Global Urban Laboratory's demographic surveys and demographic analyses that assemble existing research country by country. But U.N. data, researcher Mark Montgomery noted, often just covers center cities, not the total metropolitan areas—a practice symptomatic of a general lack of uniformity and breakdown by spatial factors in currently available data.

One goal, for example, would be to come to a common global definition of what constitutes urban as opposed to rural population. Current definitions not only vary wildly, but often fail to get at the expansive, de facto way that urban regions are forming globally.

crosscutting elements

The missing crosscutting elements of research are also broad and problematic. As Birch observed, numbers are often available on how many households in a particular city have people with specific diseases. But the numbers are rarely applied to specific neighborhoods or city sections. It is rarely known, for example, where concentrations of tuberculosis are in an urban area. High-quality epidemiology would look for clusters of sickness. Instinctively, it is known that the highest concentration is in slums. But even within slums, where are

Some 25,000 people take to the streets and parks to draw attention to global warming on Earth Day, April 20, 2008, Budapest, Hungary

Solar panels installed on the roof of the Daegu Exposition and Convention Center, Daegu, South Korea

the incidences highest? What are the appropriate crosscutting factors to tie in—thematically and at various points in time, and related to interventions that authorities may have attempted, or reforms slum dwellers themselves have inaugurated? What lessons do such data offer for comparable areas of the same cities, or indeed others with similar demographic profiles worldwide?

So a central need emerges: to start defining (and then communicating to national and city governments) just which types and varieties of data are needed to assist in more effective governance and planning. The research that does exist, participants observed, tends to focus on overall trends of population growth, development, and poverty demographics, but is not up to now on the critical spatial—place-specific—analyses and comparisons that may be vital for the welfare of future city dwellers and the earth.

A starting point was suggested: determining a limited number of critical statistical measures of demography and spatial distribution of population, data that should meet many local government needs but also facilitate statistical comparisons worldwide, nationally, regionally, and locally.

VISUALIZATION TOOLS AND CHALLENGE

For sustainability it is imperative to know not just the overall magnitude of urban population growth but where it is most likely to occur and its impact on the environment. What will be the human imprint on the land as a result of the additional

types and varieties of data

sustainability

1 to 2 billion people coming to the cities? How can the exciting visualization tools, such as GIS or Google Earth, now made available by technology, be applied to the actual form of development, especially in a world of exploding Global South populations? What are and will be the demands for land, especially in vulnerable places? Can an urban spatial build-out data tool for these times be created, and then be applied for improved decision-making? The questions were a major theme of the Summit research discussions.

Satellite photography, for example, can show actual land area that is covered by buildings, as opposed to rural or undeveloped territory. One instance is the LandSat-based analyses of selected world cities developed by Summit participant Stephen Sheppard of Williams College and his associates. Such data are extremely useful in showing spatial expansion over time, and would seem ripe for worldwide application covering *all* cities— a development that could be aided, participants said, if NASA, with its constant global satellite monitoring, took a greater interest in urban observations.

Already researchers at Nairobi's Regional Center for Mapping of Resources and Development (RCMRD) are using high-resolution satellite remote sensing data from LandSat and the QuickBird (launched in 2001 by DigitalGlobe) for their city. Wilber Ottichilo of RCMRD told participants how the data, interpreted through GIS, has been applied in such areas as natural-resources management, utility mapping, and hydrological studies.

Improved
satellite data

Improved satellite data is made all the more imperative by the recent-day decentralization of power from central to local governments across the Global South, emphasized in the sessions. Yet the data from the sky cries out for integration with basic demographic information to help cities improve their service delivery, health, and economic prospects—for example, numbers of households, age distribution, fertility and mortality rates, and other drivers of urban growth.

Providing quality GIS data systems and tools to Global South cities could increase their municipal governance capacities dramatically, it was suggested. But latest technology might deliver even more. One example: two- and three-dimensional visualization of city form and its incremental change over fairly brief periods of time. Architects, urban designers, and public and private decision makers could all benefit, seeing ways to think beyond their individual projects to an entire district, city, or region. The process could also be democratized, exposed to a cross section of city residents for their reactions.

ISSUES OF SUSTAINABILITY

What are the issues that call for immediate investigation? For example, what are the environmental and social impacts of rapidly growing slum settlements on the Global South cities'

long-term
sustainability

immediate and long-term sustainability? Conversely, for people moving to cities from rural areas, what are actual quality-of-life prospects? Cities can be the world's most formidable wealth creators, but they are also subject to deep divisions and areas of grinding, fearsome poverty. For instance, research tells us that people experience better health in cities than in rural areas but worse health in urban slums than anywhere.

One critical question: Is there a typical life cycle of a slum? Historically, most urban settlements shift from primitive to mature over time. But what happens to people within the life cycle? The improvement in favela conditions and living standards over time, cited by Susanna Pasternak of the University of São Paulo, was an example. She reported that most adults in Brazilian *favelas* are gainfully employed, some have cars, and their makeshift homes have added rooms, with stoves, radios, refrigerators, color TVs, even computers. Such advances are clearly tougher to register in such deeply poor countries as those of sub-Saharan Africa and Southeast Asia. The challenge is all the tougher for slum residents living without any kind of land title or way to provide collateral for a loan for basic home improvements. Microfinance and housing microfinance still make a difference. A study of the variables and trends could yield extraordinarily valuable insights into the potential of innovations in this area.

Closely related is the now-intense issue in many Global South cities: Should slum areas be demolished in the name of urban renewal and economic development—or is slum upgrading, tapping residents' entrepreneurial skills, a better course? There is widespread belief, based on sterile high-rise settlements for poor families that spread across the Global North after World War II, that the high-rise buildings

Construction workers at Sai Gon South, a mixed residential and commercial urban development covering 8,154 acres, South Saigon, Vietnam

themselves spawn negative social conditions. But are other factors—accessible jobs, schools, parks, for example—more critical? If low-income people in Hong Kong can live successfully in very high buildings, why not in other parts of the developing world? A careful analysis of varying countries' and cities' experiences, both with removal and upgrading, could provide a powerful tool for current-day debates.

Related questions are clear: In cities with slums and restrained government resources, what is known of most productive first steps? Are they provision of effective water supply, sanitation, education, or providing public transportation links to jobs? Or is providing self-help resources to organized tenants more critical? Or concerted efforts to provide land-tenure rights to residents? How can these programs be paid for? How can credit markets be galvanized, so that when microfinance is used, it can be extended from microenterprises' microfinance to housing and communities? And when public–private partnerships are employed, can these strategies compliment one another?

ENTER THE MARKET—AND INEQUALITY

The fortunes of today's cities, the participants agreed, are heavily determined by globalized market forces that create new economies and opportunities and are especially powerful when wedded to the surge of consumer demand of rising middle classes in many Global South cities. Clearly they are a part of cities' seeming magnetic power in these times.

consumer demand

A GLOBAL URBAN SUMMIT SAMPLER

Observations of Research Session Participants

Quandaries of Urbanization

UN-HABITAT's Urban Indicators Data Base suggests the global rural-to-urban transition is almost complete in Latin America but continuing full steam in Africa and Asia. The most stunning figures come from the cities of sub-Saharan Africa, with an overall annual growth rate of 4.6 percent. The explosive growth of such cities as Dhaka, Bangladesh, and Lagos, Nigeria, is leading to extreme problems of adjustment, including plummeting conditions in housing, health, and education. Yet there are alternatives. Bogota, for example, is a world leader in slum prevention. An agency controls the perimeter of the city, locating small pockets of growing slum populations, then providing those areas with an office providing technical services such as design, critical services, and land-development advice. The resulting communities are low-income, but not slums.

Why do some countries have slums and others not? China has few. Governance and financing are important.

—NEFISE BAZOGLU, UN-HABITAT

Chinese Growth Dilemmas

There are 600 million people in China's cities today; by 2050 there could be 1 billion. And there is strong growth of per capita GDP. The overt national government policy has been to restrain the growth of large cities and instead encourage the development of small- and medium-sized cities incentivized, by land leasing first introduced in 1988, to make deals for new commercial enterprises. The result: urban sprawl as local governments try to capture new industries and revenues, allowing most new development to go to their outskirts.

—ANTHONY YEH, UNIVERSITY OF HONG KONG

The average size of an apartment in China today is four times per person larger than 20 years ago. Office space per worker is also much larger.

—DOUGLAS WEBSTER, ARIZONA STATE UNIVERSITY

One-eighth of the urban population of the Urban South live in megacities; they're actually a relatively small part of the population.

—STEPHEN SHEPPARD, WILLIAMS COLLEGE

The Ugandan Example

Lots of research is skewed with a rural bias. Censuses have great difficulty reaching informal settlements, meaning slums are underrepresented in many statistics. We do know in Uganda that although the country is just 13 percent urbanized now, the population of Kampala, our prime city with 1.2 million people in 2002, is exploding: now it accounts for 39 percent of the nation's total urban population. The city is growing rapidly, with promotion of industry and the private sector driving some of the real estate growth. Uganda is also seeing growth of trading centers with populations comparable to urban areas. We experience such problems as major outbreaks of cholera, malaria, and dysentery in urban areas. High percentages of the population are without fresh water supply or sewer service. Yet we have a transportation problem, with more and more private cars.

—SHUAIB LWASA, LECTURER AT MAKERERE UNIVERSITY, KAMPALA

India's Planning Challenges

About 12 percent of the world's urban population growth is occurring in India; three of its 393 cities with more than 100,000 people are among the eight largest on the planet and contribute significantly to the global economy. But the state of urban public services is far from satisfactory. There is a major nationwide reform, the Jawaharlal Nehru National Urban Renewal Mission, providing reforms-linked financial assistance to state governments and some localities. But multiple public institutions are professionally weak, lack financial resources, and have limited autonomy and financial powers. The states are slow in devolving functions and funds to municipalities. Most local bodies are weak, with multiple managers, overlapping functions, and lots of time off for lunch. Urban infrastructure is lagging badly. Almost all city areas have treated water supply, but the quality and distribution are inadequate. Thirty to 50 percent of solid waste remains untreated.

—VINOD TEWARI, THE ENERGY AND RESOURCES INSTITUTE (TERI), INDIA

Small-City Quandary

The Global South's smaller cities, where most early 21st-century population growth is projected, are seldom equipped with highly qualified municipal staff. They often lack basic capacity. With decentralization by central governments, smaller cities are being asked to pay more of their own costs without an adequate revenue base.

—MARK MONTGOMERY, POPULATION COUNCIL AND SUNY AT STONY BROOK

Fate of Cities

Most national governments have lost the power to decide on the size or territory of cities. Cities are becoming multi-nodal, dynamic, with the historic center meaning less.

—STEPHEN MALPEZZI, UNIVERSITY OF WISCONSIN-MADISON

Coastal Boom

Roughly 2.7 percent of the world's land area is urbanized. But 64 percent of coastal systems are urban. And the world is likely to continue to draw people to coastal areas, with relatively high densities, already the pattern in every continent of the world. Imagine a 10-meter sea level rise: 60 percent of the people of Bangladesh live within the 10-meter zone. China is experiencing 1 percent a year overall population growth, but 2.4 percent in its low-elevation coastal zone.

—DEBORAH BALK, BARUCH SCHOOL OF PUBLIC AFFAIRS, CITY UNIVERSITY OF NEW YORK

Climate Change

The Chinese and Southeast Asians are not talking much about climate change. Remember that the average building in China lasts for economic purposes just 15 years. So to move millions of people is perhaps no big deal. Imagine a 6-to-10 meter sea rise, endangering 85 percent of China's output? It would not happen; the Chinese would see it coming, build dikes, move their factories.

—DOUGLAS WEBSTER, ARIZONA STATE UNIVERSITY

Urban Growth Models

Models are good at characterizing and comparing urban change processes over place and time. But they need serious improvement to anticipate the future and simulate the effects of varied inputs. Planners can produce an end-state vision—of how a city might look and function in 2030 or 2050. The question then is how to get to that point? The problem is that today's models are good at showing factors that have impacted growth patterns in the past. But they are not so good on forecasting or comparing alternative futures.

—JOHN LANDIS, UNIVERSITY OF CALIFORNIA, BERKELEY

Age

An aging population is often missing from projections of demographic change in the next half century. It is increasingly agreed that we will have 2.5 billion or so more people, the world population growth rate will slow, population increase will end in the developed world while slowing in the developing world. But we will have a three-time increase in the numbers of the old. Slums are now overwhelmingly composed of young people, but that may change. Aging and urbanization will integrate in ways we haven't begun yet to imagine.

—JOEL COHEN, ROCKEFELLER UNIVERSITY

Health

Is urbanization good or bad for health? The evidence is not clear. Cities in some areas are better; diarrhea is a grave problem in rural areas, and far lower in urban. Motor vehicle and pedestrian accidents are high in urban areas, a bit lower in rural. (Hanoi, for example, has moved from rickshaws to racing motor bikes in just ten years.) The risk for diabetes rises sharply with urbanization—overweight conditions are much greater in cities. But in many rural areas, especially less-developed ones, undernutrition is an issue. Mental health problems rise in urban areas: old people are often found dead, with lack of any social connection. Urbanites also contract HIV/AIDS much more than rural people. The same is true of substance abuse.

—TIMOTHY EVANS, WORLD HEALTH ORGANIZATION

In health field, prevention of HIV/AIDS, the use of preventive models is difficult. What helps? Partnership in development of knowledge, data work with affected communities. Not recommend: just an academic point of view. Engage the local constituency at the start rather than as an expert at end, so you come to conclusions at the same time. Second, engage the media right from the beginning so they can help in the translation because academics cannot do that.

—AFAF MELEIS, UNIVERSITY OF PENNSYLVANIA, SCHOOL OF NURSING

Education Opportunities

Government and society have no choice—we *must* address the need for education of the urban poor. No country can develop without engaging the majority of its population. But there is a huge equity problem: the affluent go to the best schools and universities, and there are far too few places for the poor. Government has to do more even though education consumes the largest part of budgets. The rich should be taxed more for schools and scholarship programs. And the poor themselves have to learn to pay where and as they can to qualify for specialized advanced education.

—KILEMI MWIRIA, MINISTRY OF EDUCATION AND PARLIAMENT, KENYA

Education of Girls and Women

Kenya made a big step forward in 2003, introducing free universal primary education and abolishing school charges. But in urban slums schools have low enrollment, high rates of waste due to high numbers of dropouts, absenteeism, and low completion rates and achievement. A vital next step: strong focus in developing nations, and especially the slums, on education of girls and women as a key to the future. Girls' education raises economic productivity, reduces fertility rates, lowers infant and maternal mortality, and improves health and nutrition. And it sets the stage for women's absorption into the economy, self-employed or as employees. This is critical because women are the foundation of life in urban slums due to their multiple roles as family homemakers, caretakers, workers, and producers and managers of food. It is especially distressing that more than 30 million girls in sub-Saharan Africa are missing from school. When uniforms are required but hard to afford, the boy is usually sent to school while the girl stays home. Often girls don't dare to go to school because of lack of toilet facilities.

—FAITH MACHARIA, FORUM FOR AFRICAN WOMEN EDUCATIONALISTS, KENYA CHAPTER

Housing

Housing finance has expanded throughout the world in recent decades, but a large share of the low-to-moderate income urban population in developing counties still has very limited access to long-term housing finance. Subsidized loans have proven ineffective in improving overall housing finance because they operate on a limited scale only and are not sustainable. The U.S. subprime lending sector provides affordable financing options for moderate-income households and immigrants without adequate proofs of income, but the associated risks have proven to be substantial. On the other hand microlending has emerged from an innovative idea to become a viable financing option for the poor over the past decade.
—KYUNG-HWAN KIM, SOGANG UNIVERSITY, SEOUL, KOREA

Houses in Brazil's squatter settlements in the year 2000 were usually made of brickwork, often with two stories, and were served with electricity, drinking water, and garbage collection. The critical problem: Only a little more than half were connected to public sewage systems.
—SUSANA PASTERNAK, UNIVERSITY OF SÃO PAULO

The dilemma is that left unguided, market forces may produce highly inequitable impacts. The market, for example is increasingly providing serviced townships for rising middle-class population groups in such nations as India. Yet there is a profound irony: Because of the paucity of basic urban services such as clean water and sanitation offered to the entire population, and especially those living in slums, those who cannot afford to buy into the new serviced townships will end up being forced to pay more for public services than the wealthier households negotiate, in effect, for themselves. The most pressing need is to provide services for the poor who cannot depend on the market. In the absence of such provision, the resulting divisions, some noted, could well be kindling a political crisis for India—and the world.

highly inequitable impacts

Already, in many developing nation cities, the poor—especially those without land tenure—are reported to pay as much as 20 to 30 times what middle-to-upper class people do for basic services. So what reforms, accomplished either by local government or self-organizing of the poor, can be developed to provide critically needed services to all, not just the privileged groups and classes?

critically needed services to all

The issue is sharpened by the competition of cities as they work actively to attract knowledge workers to bolster and expand their local economies. The more highly skilled workers, whether native or immigrant, almost instinctively look for safe compounds—for example, India's "serviced townships," or gated communities, around Johannesburg—where they will be isolated from crime and enjoy better schools and higher-quality services. Yet the vivid differences in lifestyles and circumstances can lead directly to serious crime threats from some of the underprivileged and hopeless peoples of these cities. Even militarylike armaments appear around homes of the privileged. The idea of a shared civil society suffers.

Research on alternative development plans—or ways of organizing with these communities to provide for themselves and link to public services—is critical to deal with the stark class differences apparent today. Because if properly channeled, market forces, in today's world, are what provide the critical capital for cities to shake poverty and develop more coherent and strong societies.

The dilemma seems to be that at the individual and family level for rural residents, moving to cities can result in less hunger, better health, and more educational and economic opportunities. The entrepreneurial vigor and determination of the Global South's country-to-city movers is a strong force. But for sustained growth in levels of achievement, the building of networks, sharing of skills, and support of local government are vital if the society is to offer true mobility and be sustainable.

Also to be considered: Ordinary crime, terrorism, government instability, and ethnic/tribal rivalries are deeply disturbing factors in many of the world's growing cities today. Extreme density among recently arrived slum dwellers can exacerbate such problems. One can imagine targeted research on the best global models to build both self-help mechanisms

stark class differences

true mobility

deeply disturbing factors

A cyclist uses his passcard to rent a SmartBike parked outside the Reeves Center, Washington, D.C., U.S.A.

Two workers locate a bike in a bicycle parking area during "No car day," Bogota, Colombia

A China Railway high-speed bullet train at the rail station in central Beijing, China

A new means of urban transportation, the Trixi, takes passengers through the city Barcelona, Spain

and more cohesive societies in fast-growing areas, thus avoiding as many of the threats as possible.

NEW CHALLENGES

A variety of other challenging new research questions emerged from the Summit, including these:

- What drives urban form in the Global South cities? Is it development of land at the urban periphery? Jobs? Friends and relatives urging new residents to join them? It is not clear how close Global South growth incentives are to those in the Global North. In the United States, for example, investment in a new road provokes investment. Is the same true in developing countries, or are other forces, magnets, stronger? And are the patterns different between larger and smaller, growing cities?

- Should megaregions be considered in the Global South as they are in the Global North (See Chapter 5)? The Chinese have already begun to do so, as Douglas Webster, a professor at the Arizona State University related at the sessions, noting rapid growth of the Beijing–Tianjin–Hebei megalopolis in particular. (That megaregion's rapid rail system links cities of 10 million each by a mere 29-minute ride.) Along with urban analyst Robert Lang of Virginia Tech, Webster has identified 12 megaregions in China; three of them will account for 65 percent of the GDP but only 18 percent of the country's population by 2020. Megaregion analysis could be helpful to focus transportation priorities, decide on areas for development, identify environmental priorities, analyze watersheds, and the like.

The clear determination at the end of the Summit research week was to push forward with a global urban research commons to consider, test, and evaluate all these topics, and more. The model would include a major focus on strong academic standards on the one hand, but also be characterized by total willingness to collaborate and work with practitioners of urban arts in cities across the globe. The objective would be to make the research accessible, practical, and informed by practice—thus useful to public and private decision makers upon demand.

There was simply zero likelihood, University of Pennsylvania's Birch and Wachter noted after the week's meetings, that the scholarly network to study and develop the array of issues highlighted in the Summit sessions could develop without the real-time interchange of views on global urbanization and its challenges that was the focus of the Summit sessions.

Whether the future funding is foundation, international organization, NGO, or private, there was broad and strong agreement among participants that the urban research mission they identified is critical for 21st–century cities, and by extension to the world they lead.

So what would a global urban research commons be? It would be a network of analysts and scholars at work in varied cities united through virtual and physical meeting. The Commons would serve as an umbrella or clearinghouse for

global urban research commons

real-time interchange of views

urban research mission

a network of analysts and scholars

existing efforts. It would seek to bring together research on issues that link urban-planning needs and applied research from across the global research community. And it would promote data sharing and purchase of needed data sources. It would translate and disseminate data widely, and seek to do so in a very timely manner, helping scholars and practitioners enrich one another's ideas. It could, for example, take the research, Podcasts and other products from the collaboration laboratories ("co-labs") around the world that were described in Chapter 5, and make them quickly but also permanently available for researchers, governments, NGOs, and other interested audiences.

What binds all of this together? Susan Wachter offered a concise summary of the desired outcomes of urbanization: economic growth, sustainability, and equity.

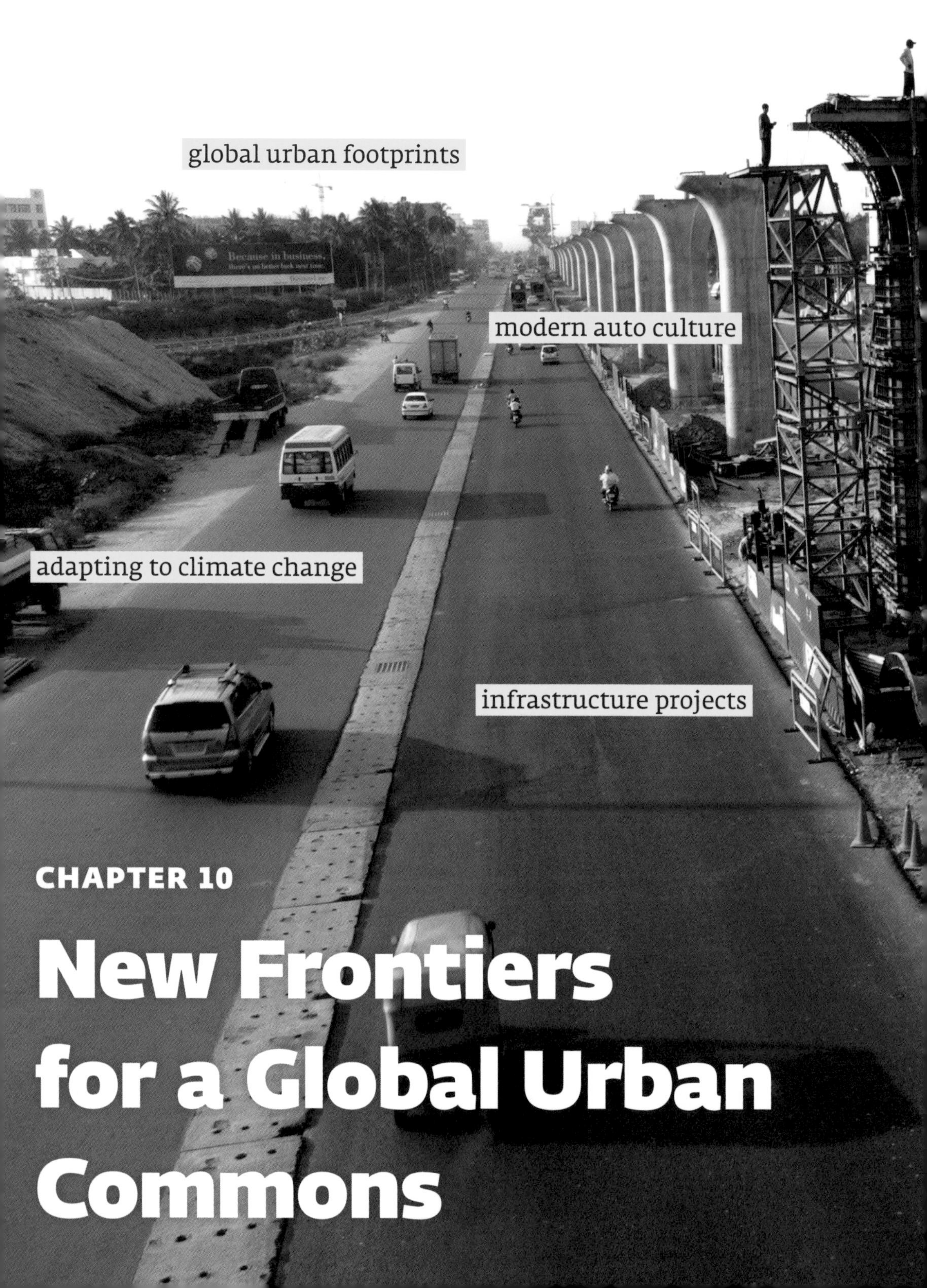

global urban footprints

modern auto culture

adapting to climate change

infrastructure projects

CHAPTER 10

New Frontiers for a Global Urban Commons

privatization

a full range of voices

quality pedestrian spaces

city-to-city learning

expanding living standards

An elevated road is being built to ease traffic congestion, Bangalore, India

WHAT POLICIES AND APPROACHES MIGHT WORLD CITIES— Global South and Global North alike—share and learn from this century of the city?

This book has cited many, from building climate change resilience to rethinking transportation, from improving urban health to enhancing professional planning. But each of those topics and more raise new possibilities of coordination and mutual learning—and intriguing questions:

coordination and mutual learning

Who are some of the critical players for cities now? Might not many be women—caregivers and social capital creators and potentially great income producers, *if* cities clear the way for their education and advancement? Or a combination of mayors, *and* leaders in civil society, *and* grassroots organizations communicating more closely and constantly, city to city, continent to continent, in the new global urban commons?

global urban commons

This chapter explores some of these possibilities.

SMART LOCAL ECONOMICS IN A CENTURY OF MARKETS
There is no doubt that the forces of globalization have plunged the world into a century of rapid worldwide exchange. Capital by the trillions circulates in global markets, looking for targets of opportunity, and—as we noted in Chapter 2, "Water, Sanitation, and Shelter: A Fresh Look at Finance"—could be tapped in part for development in some of the world's most deprived urban neighborhoods. Manufactured goods carried through international trade keep multiplying in volume. Even sophisticated

services such as information technology are now up for grabs globally with 24-hour Internet connections.

Many less-developed countries have benefited, in terms of new jobs produced and foreign exchange earned, from the economic revolution sparked by globalization. The dramatic economic surges in such countries as China and India testify to the broad benefits. The smaller Asian dragons of Singapore and South Korea, plus to some extent Malaysia, Thailand, and, in South America, Brazil and Chile, also showed that advancing modern economies are hardly a Global North monopoly.

For cities, there is risk in the game. The globally mobile investments that hit them tend to be tremendously agnostic— what makes money gets money, whether it is green or polluting, supportive or destructive of local businesses, exacerbating or smoothing out social inequities. Sheer economic *growth* is substantially different from *development* that builds local skills, creates new capacities, does not pollute, and benefits more than a narrow cut of the city's population. But the raw forces of globalization make no differentiation.

The special challenge for developing world cities in the intense competition of the times is to develop niches that accentuate positive impacts, do not create the severe industrial pollution reported in fast-growing metropolises (most vividly reported from China), and help their burgeoning low-income, less-educated populations move toward secure, healthy, and dignified lives.

creates new
capacities

accentuate
positive
impacts

Cities, communicating across the globe, should be able to inform each other on multiple levels. Which are the exploiting or polluting industries that need to be accepted with great caution, if at all? Even on the high-technology side, what are the environmental dangers? What smart principles of regulation are emerging from cities' experience worldwide?

smart principles of regulation

One important reminder: Cities are critical economic actors themselves. The infrastructure they choose to build (or not build) has a major economic—and often social—impact. The thoroughness of the environmental regulations they establish can make significant differences in public health. The services they do or do not provide (for example, effective water, sanitation, and inspections to avert disease-producing waste accumulations) can play a major role in the sheer survival prospects in some slum populations. Their willingness to hear a full range of voices in their own citizenry, not just favored classes, can be critical to their morale *and* prospects for prosperity.

critical economic actors

a full range of voices

As Mark Roseland and Lena Soots note in the Worldwatch Institute's 2007 *State of the World,* the tax decisions urban governments make can have profound outcomes. Are the heaviest levies laid on the "bads"—pollution, waste, urban sprawl, resource depletion? Conversely, is there an effort to keep the burden lighter on the "goods"—jobs, income, investment, good urban development, and resource conservation? And do local tax structures impede or facilitate entry of the poor—slum dwellers included—into the labor market?

The globalized economy delivers numerous opportunities to today's major cities—oftentimes investors dangling jobs and investments before officials' eyes. A worldwide exchange of experience among cities might well deliver a message of caution: *Look and analyze before you leap.* The best course is proactive, to take seriously the modern method of "cluster analysis" of a region's best industrial/business prospects that Harvard University economist Michael Porter developed, asking basic questions: which industries "fit" the particular attributes, specialized knowledge, and workforce capacities of a city region? Where are the long-term wealth-building potentials? What changes in the city's education and worker training programs are necessary to realize the knowledge and wealth-building potentials?

A companion principle: Municipalities, watching developers with a careful eye, can work to grow and sustain development from within. That means starting with a preference for locally owned businesses, which in most instances are more likely to be stable, lasting generators of wealth, more likely to train and develop local talent, and less likely than outside-owned firms to close up shop abruptly.

Active exchanges of experience and findings of what works, what doesn't, and how to finance and regulate smartly— both among city governments *and* such interested observers as universities, public staff, even organizations of slum dwellers— are likely to pay the greater long-term dividends.

globalized economy

cluster analysis

long-term wealth-building

sustain development from within

CLIMATE CHANGE AND ITS MANY CITY FRONTIERS

The world's cities—their buildings, factories, cars, and trucks—consume roughly 75 percent of the world's energy and account for 80 percent of the carbon emissions and consequent dangers of serious global warming. The big hemispheric issue is that the Global North, with its centuries of industrialization, bears most responsibility for causing the problem, while the Global South is likely to bear the early, severest brunt of climate change damage.

causing the problem

But despite differing North–South emphases, climate change presents such massive challenges to cities that a big part of all 21st–century urban agendas will revolve around the issue. Direct city-to-city learning will be critical on many fronts: for example, the role of coastline levees, "moving" of whole neighborhoods (or indeed downtown sections) out of harm's way, protection of roadways and railroads, and radical energy-saving designs for buildings (whose power requirements generate the most greenhouse gas emissions of any major source, well beyond transportation, the most obvious culprit). New York City, for example, has an ambitious green agenda that includes making virtually all new *and* existing buildings far more energy efficient; the added insulation and equipment costs will be financed with inventive financial instruments by which the owner is held harmless while the debt is paid off out of the building's all-but-assured energy cost savings.

city-to-city learning

an ambitious green agenda

Even in China, facing some of the world's grimmest environmental challenges due to rapid industrialization, there are islands of hope. Near Shanghai, a world model of a sustainable, non-carbon emitting city is about to rise on an island three-quarters of the size of Manhattan. With a team of specialists from Europe, North America, and Asia, the London-based design firm Arup is working with the Shanghai Investment Corp. on the project. The goal is to create the world's first fully green city, every block engineered in response to China's environmental crisis. It is expected that Dongtan (as it is to be named) will have a half million residents by 2050 and will be powered totally by local and renewable energy, with clustered, dense neighborhoods, a program that recycles 90 percent of all waste, a network of high-tech organic farms, and a ban on any vehicle that emits CO_2.

the world's first fully green city

U.N. Secretary General Ban Ki-moon argues that such constructive responses to climate change—"green economics"—can actually pay dramatic dividends. Citing the International Panel on Climate Change, co-recipient of the 2007 Nobel Peace Prize, Ban argues that growth in global energy demand could be cut in half over the next 15 years by deploying existing technologies in buildings, transport, and appliances, all the investments returning a 10 percent yearly return or better.

deploying existing technologies

MYSTERIES OF THE GLOBAL URBAN FOOTPRINT

From a city planning perspective, the issue of the century may be that of the global urban footprint: how large an area of the world's land surface is required for cities' dramatic population growth. Cities still occupy a small portion of land

global urban footprint

on the planet (even though, if their needs for food, fuels, water, and waste areas are included, they require vast areas of the world's surface). But cities' immediate footprint is also critical. The more they spread out physically, the more impervious land cover is created, the greater is the urban island heat effect, the greater the chances of harmful runoffs and compromising of stream and river quality, and greater the likely impairment of the "green lungs" of surrounding natural area.

urban island heat effect

Complicating the footprint issue is that of expanding living standards. As incomes rise, people automatically demand increasing amounts of living space. The average size of a single-family American home rose from 983 square feet in the 1950s to 2,329 square feet in recent years (add to that the space to park and run the average family's autos in overwhelmingly suburban, spread out places). Shanghai's average dwelling size increased from roughly 4 square meters to 16 square meters from the mid-1990s to the mid-2000s—growth ameliorated only in part by the city's heavy emphasis on high-rise structures.

expanding living standards

The urban footprint and its implied (though not yet calculated) impact on global warming emerged as a particularly compelling finding of an early week at the Global Urban Summit focused on worldwide research needs. Stephen Sheppard reported on how he and his Williams College colleagues, employing Landsat satellite images of a sampling of 120 world cities (one set taken around 1990, another around 2001) were able to show global cities' dynamic form of growth—

how much they move to the urban periphery ("outspill"), or, alternatively, find space inside ("infill").

Additionally the Landsat readings permitted intensity light readings indicating types of land use, pixel by pixel, down to very small areas. Then the Williams team matched its images with local census information from each city to estimate actual population and per capita income.

A major finding: New residents don't cause a city to expand physically at quite the rate of population growth. But they still cause, on a worldwide average, seven times more outspill than infill (and in the East Asian cities measured, 15 times more outspill). The study also permitted a rough approximation of how rapidly population increase may force cities to infill or expand onto new territory. Sheppard described a "half and half urban preparation rule:" Take the average of a city region's population growth and income growth, and one can conclude approximately how fast population growth will probably force a city to expand onto new territory. That means that São Paulo, at current trends of building mostly "out" rather than "up," may well need 7.5 square miles, and Shanghai an even more startling 14 square miles of new development, *every year*.

The impacts of cities' physical expansion—locally and in relation to global warming—do invite city-to-city learning on the role that good planning can play. A hands-off, let-development-go-anywhere approach leads to accelerated land consumption and increase carbon footprint through

infill or expand

383

new roads, loss of natural landscape, and longer travel times.

sound plans and policies

Sound plans and policies, conversely, can recycle underused urban land or schedule better use of expansion areas to achieve much greater people-carrying capacity. Good planning can avoid some of the worst modern traffic jams by putting public transit first, making walking and biking convenient, channeling solar lighting into enclosed and underground living spaces, and preserving pockets of green critical to humans' physical and emotional health.

An immediate conclusion: The 21st century needs to be a century of renewed, effective city planning, the challenge

renewed, effective city planning

described in Chapter 5, "Designing the Inclusive City."

It is clear, however, that methods of government finance also play a major role in the speed and nature of urban expansion. In countries in which central governments set land use rules and provide a major share of municipalities' funding, growth tends to focus heavily within existing city lines. This tends, in general, to be the European pattern; serious government-set growth limits have, in fact, led to concentrated, dense cities.

But in a system like that of the United States', in which most land controls are local, and municipalities are largely self-financed, the welcome mat is out for proposals by private industries or developers that will increase the local tax base. Since green fields on the edge of an area are cheaper to develop, that is where the lion's share of the new growth goes, resulting in sprawl.

Now versions of the U.S. practice appear to be spreading. China has been allowing industrial parks, joint ventures, even the creation of new cities, not by central government decision but whenever a local Communist party chooses to make a deal with private investors. India, on a parallel track, is moving toward independently financed, suburban-style

service townships "service townships"—indeed the private sector is being allowed to create whole new gated towns for the country's more affluent classes.

Post-apartheid Johannesburg, South Africa, not only suffers from huge housing and infrastructure deficits centered in its formerly all-black townships. Its high crime rates were a major factor in moving South Africa's stock exchange out of the city and into a suburban enclave, Sandton—in the process changing the name from Johannesburg Securities exchange to the more anonymous corporate title "JSE Limited." *Urban Age* reports the city "contends with glaring disparities in close physical proximity—gated and electrified suburban residential affluence stands within ten-minute driving distance of dense inner-city neighborhoods teeming with street life and informal commerce," even while "suburban building projects, replete with pseudo-Tuscan moats and escapist Balinese themes, increase in velocity and geographic spread."

Serious social issues arise: How, for example, will urban services be provided for the 80 percent of the population that lacks even a fraction of the wealth to buy into the new privately provided townships? Cities worldwide might ask, Do we wish

divisive "gated community"

to emulate the socially divisive "gated community" phenomenon that has become so prominent in newly built U.S. areas in the last decades? What is our formula to avoid 21st-century socioeconomic apartheid?

socioeconomic apartheid

The difficult bottom line is that the Global North and Global South have a common challenge: to convert more outspill to infill. Growth areas across the globe need to guide the "once in a world" urban expansion now under way so that it consumes the least feasible amount of land and encroaches on fewer of the wetlands and estuaries and deltas that provide the cleansing kidneys, as it were, for human existence. This must be done in a way that triggers the least amount of new asphalt and concrete cover, stimulates shorter auto and truck travel, and relies more on public transportation, thus generating fewer greenhouse gas emissions.

INFRASTRUCTURE: CRITICAL, BUT ALL PUBLIC?

Adequate roadways, railroads, public transit, seaports, airports, water and sewage treatment plants, electric grids, schools, and hospitals—21st-century cities face staggering challenges to create and maintain the basic physical infrastructure they need for safety, mobility, health, and advancement.

Consider first the Global South. Total *yearly* needs to build and maintain basic infrastructure in the developing world's cities has been estimated at some $200 billion. And small wonder: fresh water (as of 2000) was reportedly lacking for up to 150 million African slum dwellers, for 700 million in Asia's cities, and for as many as 120 million in Latin America. The comparable deficit figures for sanitation facilities suggest they are missing for up to 180 million slum dwellers in Africa, 800 million in Asia, 150 million in Latin America, according to "indicative" (unofficial) estimates compiled by David Satterthwaite and Gordon McGranahan for the Worldwatch Institute.

Only China, pushed by national pride and an ebullient, perhaps once-in-history economic growth rate, appears to be building infrastructure adequate for future generations, the Urban Land Institute (ULI) notes in its *Infrastructure 2007* report. Even then, accompanying environmental safeguards have been widely criticized. India, also growing rapidly, is struggling to add infrastructure quickly enough, yet despite some advances, it appears hampered by corruption and bureaucratic delays.

infrastructure adequate for future generations

The nations of the Global North, by contrast, have witnessed a marked slowdown in infrastructure building and upkeep in recent decades. The biggest laggard of all appears to be the United States, presumably riding on the wave of overconfidence and "assumed superiority" described in Chapter 7, "U.S. Transportation Challenge: Better Outcomes for Billions Spent."

communicating oft-neglected priorities

So how can cities help each other? Communicating oft-neglected priorities is a good start. One example: the major advantage of creating inventory lists of deficient and needed infrastructure, each project matched to an updated cost estimate. Keeping the big picture in focus discourages fast political runs for marginally useful projects. A second example, underscored in the ULI report: to suggest how vital it is to think and plan metro-region-wide, analyzing the functional interrelationships of infrastructure elements (roads, public transit, land-use planning, and location of housing, schools, and offices all seen as an interconnected, regional whole). A third idea for cross-city counseling: Protect local government budgets by insisting on truly efficient land use. American laissez-faire suburban growth patterns have, for example, run up infrastructure costs exponentially. Why? No premium is ever charged for the dramatically higher per-mile or per-unit cost of providing water, sewer, electric, police, and other systems to strung-out settlements. Compact development in towns or cities involves substantially lower costs. If sprawling development had to pay its own way, there would unquestionably be less of it. Forewarned of sprawl's big cost premiums, growing cities around the world might be prompted to hold it in check.

Privatization is the "hot" new infrastructure idea of recent years, initiated in Great Britain under Prime Minister Margaret Thatcher and spread to the United States, Canada, Australia, and India since. Either the private sector finances construction of infrastructure projects or purchases or leases existing government-financed infrastructure, charging tolls to recoup its investment. Private management is often sold as a way to get tighter management and higher performance of roadways (and more recently ports). Political leaders are drawn to privatization as a way to keep roads and other infrastructure operating or to build anew, without incurring taxpayer wrath for raising new taxes.

cross-city counseling

compact development

privatization

Tolls have one great virtue: the user pays directly for the public good he or she is using. But there is no "free lunch"—one way or another, the public ends up paying for the cost of infrastructure. There is also some danger that privatization offerings may lead to agreements that foreclose better alternatives (exclusive bus lanes rather than new tolled lanes along a highway, for example). Also it is rare that privately financed infrastructure will find the profit it seeks in serving low-income areas.

And, there are only so many infrastructure projects investors would find attractive in the first place. "Even investment bankers, who gorge on healthy fees from these transactions, warn that privatization 'will not be a panacea'," author Jonathan D. Miller notes in the ULI report. It is estimated that only 10 percent of U.S. roads could attract public–private partnership type deals; basic street grids, for example, will likely never qualify.

Such reservations do not mean, however, that public–private partnerships will not expand; the U.K. model suggests that in one form or another, they are likely to be proposed for water supply and sewers, for schools and hospitals.

Privatization presents one rich opportunity for exchange of counsel by cities and their allies around the world. Individuals with extensive experience in financial houses of such cities as New York, London, and Hong Kong could offer pro bono counsel to cities, especially those of the Global South, that are considering privatization deals, often for the first time. Knowing the field, the investment veterans would be able to help the

The Velib program allows residents and visitors to pick up and drop off bicycles at over 700 locations throughout the city, Paris, France

Repair technicians deliver a monitor to a client after servicing it, Bangalore, India

cities avoid serious beginners' errors, briefing them on criteria to consider before deciding to make a deal and, if the deal is decided on, how to structure it so that the city gets the best possible terms.

Concurrently, whether the issue is privatization or just helping other cities persuade their national government to assist in financing their immense infrastructure needs, the
need and opportunity is clear. It is to exchange ideas with cities that have more extensive experience dealing with investors, banks and institutions; it is the chance to get counsel from civil service veterans and other volunteer advisers who really grasp the infrastructure issues that cities in developing nations face, and how to overcome them.

SPACES FOR PEOPLE IN A MOTORIZED WORLD

More than 1 billion motorized devices travel the roads of the world. There were more than 600 million automobiles—24 percent in the United States alone—at last count in 2002, though the global count now is surely far higher with rapidly rising car sales from Eastern Europe to India to China. (Some 1,000 additional cars take to the streets of Beijing daily. A $2,500 personal auto is being marketed in India to meet fast-rising middle-class demand.) The worldwide totals for mopeds and motorcycles, as well as for trucks, buses, and vans, each topped 200 million in 2002, and are all on the rise today. The speed of change is illustrated in cities such as Hanoi, transformed from rickshaw culture to racing motor bikes in just the last decade.

No doubt exists: We live in an age of motors. The personal convenience, added economic activity, and quality of life they deliver are vital and prized across the continents. Few humans would now choose to "de-invent" motorized vehicles.

But modern auto culture has not been kind to cities. Autos' impact in the Global North, especially after World War II, went far to shatter the historic strength of urban centers—their close geographic concentrations of people, attractions and economic activity, and a shared public realm. Suburban outspill (and in the United States sterile single-purpose zoning) created vast new areas of auto-accessible-only residences, shopping malls and business parks. Public transportation often atrophied as the lion's share of public investment went into motorways serving the rising tide of cars and trucks. The motors-first trend was most pronounced in the United States, more restrained in Europe, and moderate in geographically closely packed Japan.

Recent years have seen some counter movements. Strong efforts at urban revitalization—restoring traditional city centers, strengthening cultural facilities, and building neighborhoods at a more compact, human scale—have strengthened many of the world's historic cities in recent years. Fast-rising gas prices have discouraged automobile use. Car-free zones have been established and "congestion pricing" introduced (first in Singapore, later in London and Stockholm) to keep center cities more mobile. The New Urbanist town design model and shifting consumer preferences have led to more land-conserving developments in many parts of the United States. Brookings

modern auto culture

public transportation

car-free zones

Institution fellow Christopher Leinberger argues in a recent book (*The Option of Urbanism*) that the "one size fits all" formula of "drivable suburbanism," dominant for the past 60 years, is fading in popularity and sustainability. In its place, he suggests, a new "walkable urbanism," focused in reviving cities and new transit-connected suburban towns, is emerging.

But the global auto push has remained powerful: Witness the Chinese government's declaration of car production as a pillar industry. Explosively growing Shanghai doubled its car use between 1995 and 2004 even as it publicly sought to repress bicycle use. The vast expansion of international trade has led to motorways clogged with truck traffic to and from ports.

One oft-cited consequence: Sheer urban congestion has become so serious that traffic in many world cities often moves at the speed of horse-drawn carriages. Or, in many cases, at even slower speeds—with alarming environmental consequences. Jakarta is faced with geometrically expanding vehicular use—so drastic and with such severe daily traffic jams that a former governor has warned that the city's roadways may come to a complete standstill in 2014. Jakarta's mass transportation grand design includes widespread busways, a subway, and a monorail. But still the city administration has announced plans for six inner-city turnpikes to create more spaces for cars and trucks, a step critics contend will worsen both the congestion and already severe air pollution. In the United States the legendary gridlock around the hypergrowth region of Atlanta, Georgia, has become so extreme that

expanding
vehicular use

businesses have begun to shun the area. Some 1.7 million drivers clog that area's roadways at rush hour; the answer has been to add freeway capacity, by one proposal favored by the Georgia Transportation Department, up to 23 lanes at one stretch in suburban Cobb County.

tame auto use

Can cities move more aggressively to tame auto use and reclaim more of the public realm for pedestrians and bicycle users? Given the automobile's high popularity among economically rising classes, it is a difficult challenge, made all the tougher by the tens of billions of dollars that globally active automobile companies pour into advertising glamorizing the comfort and speed of their products.

bike-for-hire stations

But counter efforts are beginning. Handy bike-for-hire stations are proving instant hits in crowded inner cities. The Paris "velib" bike rental program—the name combines "velo" (bicycle) and "liberte" (freedom)—registered an astounding 2 million trips in the first 40 days after its 2007 opening. With almost identical systems sprouting up from Barcelona to Vienna, Oslo to Washington, D.C., with interest expressed in London, Rome, Moscow, and Beijing, the bike rental push seems likely to spread across all continents.

And some urban leaders have begun major efforts to tame the autos' total dominance. Most prominent among them in recent years was Enrique Peñalosa, mayor of Bogotá, Columbia, from 1998 to 2000. When he took office, Peñalosa quickly vetoed a pending proposal to construct seven elevated highways over the city. Instead he made an absolute priority of creating walkable spaces: pedestrian streets, sidewalks, greenways, bicycle paths, metropolitan-scale and neighborhood parks, and citywide car-free days. He forced removal of autos on sidewalks which, as he explains, "car-owning upper classes had illegally appropriated for parking."

Building on the highly successful citywide bus system of Curitiba, Brazil, Peñalosa pressed to create a "TransMilenio" system of buses on exclusive right-of-way in the center of major streets, with special entry platforms and wide-opening doors that permit 100 passengers out of a bus and 100 to enter within a few seconds. The highly efficient system (financed in part by a city-earmarked national gas-tax increase that Bogota encouraged) carries 1.4 million passengers a day. (The exclusive busway model is proving increasingly popular in Global South cities that can't afford rail systems; a peripatetic Peñalosa is credited with helping to popularize the busway system in such cities as Jafkarta, Beijing, Delhi, Cape Town, Lima, and Dar es Salaam in Tanzania.)

"A city can be friendly to people or it can be friendly to cars, but it can't be both," Peñalosa insists. He notes that for some 5,500 years, cities were built chiefly for pedestrians—and with shared streets. The upper classes could retreat to country houses or other exclusive locations; the poor, without alternatives, had only humble homes to retreat to. But all classes had to use the street; it was the place that all met as equals. Because, in Peñalosa's view, quality pedestrian spaces not only show respect for the poor but "create quality of life, create social integration, create happiness because we all need to walk, to be with people, to see people."

But, he argues, the automobile went far to destroy the equalizing effect of public space as it filled boulevards and streets with dangerously fast-moving traffic, crowding out sidewalks, filling vast spaces with parking, subjugating the cities' own people to its voracious space demands. And those demands, he asserts, "are making today's developing cities sadly into a second-rate copy of developed cities" in which "governments are often spending huge amounts of money on road infrastructure to benefit cars, money that could be going to schools, parks, hospitals." The pattern is even evident, he suggests, in very poor African cities that lack even basic running water, sewers, or sidewalks.

second-rate copy of developed cities

Yet there *are* better models available. As Ricky Burdett and Philipp Rode note in the Urban Age's 2008 book, *The Endless City*, the record of reviving aging public transit systems in New York City and London, Shanghai's rapid development of a vast underground network, and Bogota's bus and cycle network "all show how city governments have prioritized public transport not simply as an end in itself but as a form of social justice, providing millions of people with access to jobs and amenities."

The alarming fact, they note, is that the idea of the "compact, mixed-use, well-connected, complex and democratic city ... runs counter to what is happening on the ground in the vast majority of urban areas." Rather, they observe, Western-developed models of single-function zones, elevated

Peace Corps and Beyond

Reel back to the 1960s and the United States' contact with the developing world—outside of congressional foreign aid grants—was in its infancy. The Peace Corps, born in the Kennedy presidency, had begun to send out idealistic youth to developing nations across the world. Some American youth were learning foreign cultures through such programs as the Experiment in International Living. A handful of NGOs were providing a degree of assistance, especially in low-income rural areas around the world. Levels of idealism, especially in the Peace Corps, were extraordinarily high.

Today the picture is vastly more complex. The Peace Corps lives on, though its ranks are roughly 8,000, a far cry from the 100,000 President Kennedy had hoped to see in a decade. Yet the opportunities remain rich. The World Bank in 2007 reported that of the world's 1.5 billion youth ages 12 to 24, an unprecedented 1.3 billion live in developing countries. This "youth bulge" may not expand much further in absolute numbers because it is will reach a plateau as global fertility rates decline. But today's opportunities for young Americans to travel and work through the Global South, engaging directly with other young people in their home cities, are immense. One immediate connecting point: technology. It has been said that among youth in particular, "text messaging now rules the world." The step to Internet and cell phone use and their dramatic learning and development opportunities is not difficult.

Some of the most difficult challenges are in the Global South nations with the world's most rapidly rising populations. Total population is projected to triple or more between 2005 and 2050 in such nations as Afghanistan, Burkina Faso, Burundi, Chad, Democratic Republic of the Congo, Liberia, Niger, and Uganda. Bangladesh, Pakistan, and Ethiopia will also see large absolute increases.

Yet the range of Americans' present-day global involvement is not trivial. One example: World Learning, currently headed by Carol Bellamy, former investment banker, New York City Council president, director of the Peace Corps and executive director of UNICEF. World Learning focuses on "the human face" of such challenges as poverty, HIV/AIDS, environmental degradation, and ethnic conflict through a range of training and exchange programs touching more than 75 nations each year.

Exciting new forms of outreach are developing. One example: the Acumen Fund, a project incubated at the Rockefeller Foundation by program officer Jacqueline Novogratz, a Stanford Business School graduate who noted in her early career (working with an international unit of Chase Bank) that millions in loans were going to the wealthy with scarcely any benefit to the desperately poor. But in Rwanda, where she met a group of poor women struggling with a church-subsidized, money-losing bakery, she experimented with a new business approach that turned the bakery profitable, boosting the women's incomes, within six months. "I saw the power that markets can have to bring people out of poverty, the discipline that running a business provides, and the pride that results from ownership." Now, through the Acumen Fund that she created—she terms it a "philanthropic venture capital fund"—Novogratz works to help start (and counsel) health care, housing, and water enterprises by and for the poor in India, Tanzania, Pakistan, and other nations. Major philanthropies, from Rockefeller and Cisco to Google and Gates, have all lent a hand.

More new, high-profile U.S. involvement with critical global issues has emerged in recent years with the Clinton Global Initiative. Its annual meetings in New York draw some 1,000 world leaders: current and former heads of state (led of course by former President Bill Clinton himself), prominent business executives, scholars, and NGO representatives. Major commitments for worldwide outreach in such areas as education, energy and climate change, global health, and alleviating poverty have emerged.

The Ashoka program, begun in 1980 by American Bill Drayton, has recognized and provided start-up funding for more than 1,700 social entrepreneurs—individuals in 60 countries devising system-changing solutions to some of the most urgent social challenges of the times. The social entrepreneurs become lifelong members of Ashoka's global fellowship.

A single example of an Ashoka fellow may be worth noting. Sanjay Bapat of India created a virtual meeting ground for citizen groups, poor communities, corporations, funding agencies, and interested global citizens, communicating through his Web site, IndianNGOs.com. The goal: an Internet-age tool to help India's citizen-sector groups learn from one another and form partnerships. While most information-exchange Web sites are supported by funding agencies or run by volunteers, IndianNGOs.com charges fees, modest ones for small start-up groups, larger ones from corporate members to keep the enterprise strong.

Now there are also a number of internationally focused U.S.-based charities inspired by the success of the French-born, 1999 Nobel Peace Prize–winning Doctors Without Borders (Médecins Sans Frontières). Engineers Without Borders USA, formed in 2000, has grown to 8,000 volunteer members in more than 200 chapters in which professional engineers and their students work together. In 2007 they were engaged in 250 projects—water, sanitation, energy, and housing—in 43 countries.

The engineers' first step is always meetings with local residents. It is critical, says Bernard Amadei, the group's founder, to devise systems the residents understand and can fix, and which will help them create local businesses and job creation. The big challenge, Amadei told a Lehrer News Hour correspondent, is to ensure "that whatever technology or solution we bring over is appropriate to the community, is respectful of the community, respectful of the culture, respectful of the people, does not divide people, creates more unity, more peace in a community."

motorways, and gated communities are commonly being "dumped…on the fragile conditions of the exploding cities of the Global South."

ROADWAY SAFETY: NEW-CENTURY CAUSE

Beyond questions of money and land use, a motorized world raises a massive safety problem: how often cars kill. The problem is severe in the developed world (more than 42,000 fatalities in the United States annually, for example). But cars and trucks are especially lethal in developing countries as they accelerate on roadways filled with pedestrians, cyclists, jitneys, and sometimes farm animals and hand-drawn wagons (and on some continents even camels and elephants). The worldwide fatality rate inflicted by vehicles is 1.2 million, plus 50 million serious injuries (by World Health Organization estimates). Highway deaths, WHO projects, may well pass death tolls from HIV/AIDS in the next two decades.

often cars kill

Dr. Mark Rosenberg, founder and former director of the National Center for Injury Prevention and Control at the United States' Centers for Disease Control and Prevention and a panelist at the Summit sessions, has made a life cause of fighting the vehicular death toll.

The world needs, he argues, to emulate Sweden's spectacular progress in recent years, "Vision Zero," a goal of no more deaths from highway accidents. Sweden has driven its roadway death loss down to 440 in a year, the lowest figure since World War II. How? Tough seat-belt and helmet laws as obvious first

Vision Zero

Young women share a motor scooter as they travel through a monsoon rain, Amritsar, India

steps. But the Swedes also started remaking their roads. They replaced red lights at intersections (which encourage drivers to accelerate dangerously to "beat the light") with traffic circles. They installed four-foot-high barriers of lightweight but tough mylar down the center of roadways to prevent head-on collisions, and as side barriers at critical locations. On local streets, narrowed roadways and speed bumps, plus raised pedestrian crosswalks, limit speeds to a generally nonlethal 20 miles an hour. Britain, New Zealand, and the Netherlands are also registering major success with safety redesign and tough roadway rules.

success with safety redesign

If the world could eradicate smallpox, Rosenberg argues, it is reasonable to make zero traffic deaths a next global public health target. He reports substantial international action since the U.N. General Assembly first debated the issue in 2004. A U.N. Road Safety Collaboration was brought together by WHO. The World Bank is mobilizing resources to help developing countries in particular. George Robertson of Britain, a former Secretary-General of NATO, chairs a new Commission on Global Road Safety. There will be a 2009 U.N. Ministerial Conference on road safety, a first-ever meeting of cabinet-level officials from both developing and developed countries to set a global strategy.

zero traffic deaths

But, Rosenberg notes, if the world's cities established direct links, comparing notes on how to implement safety measures, overcome opposition, and make their streets dramatically safer, they "could make a tremendous difference in taming

comparing notes

this entirely predictable worldwide epidemic of needless road-way deaths, saving thousands or tens of thousands of lives."

more humane roads and public spaces

In one respect the movement to create safer, more humane roads and public spaces for the world's people has never been riper. The urbanized areas of places such as India, China, Vietnam, and African countries must expand dramat-ically and rapidly to accommodate their added hundreds of millions of people. With an intense worldwide dialogue among cities on best development practices, the century's new city-scapes might be made dramatically safer. And cities could plan early and well for clear physical separation between lanes of vehicular traffic, bicycles, and pedestrians.

In fact, there is a U.S. organization with that very mission: the "Complete Streets" movement, an alliance of organizations of bicyclists, senior citizens, landscape architects, and smart-growth advocates. Complete Streets "are about a right-of-way for everyone out there traveling, walking, or bik-ing," says Barbara McCann, the movement coordinator. All users of all ages and abilities, she asserts, need to be able to move safely along and across a complete street. Indeed, she adds, "safety is a huge reason."

"Complete Streets" movement

In response six states and some 50 localities have adopted Complete Streets policies requiring that transportation plan-ners include bicycling and walking facilities in all their urban-area projects. Chicago, for example, is moving to narrower traffic lanes, median "refuges," and curb extensions for pedes-trians, as well as converting four-lane roadways into three lanes with marked bike lanes. Advocates say the improvements are great, but that potential cyclists are so fearful of traveling within a hair's breadth of fast cars and big trucks that bike lanes offering physical separation—a higher curbed strip or even the small vertical separation posts as Paris is trying—are mandatory. Few women, seniors, children, or more cautious men, they argue, will use bike paths without those protections.

street crimes

What about protecting walkers and cyclists from muggings or other street crimes? It can be a problem. But experience shows: the more walkers and cyclists "out there," the less the crime incidence. And basic law enforcement is always a necessity. Plus, the public payoffs from increased walking and cycling can be significant: more efficiently used roads and public space, a decrease in personal obesity owing to lack of physical exercise (a massive public health problem in itself), and reduction of the greenhouse gas emissions and global climate impact of per-

fighting obesity and carbon emissions

sonal cars. Fighting obesity and carbon emissions in a single approach, argues Jonathan Patz, president of the International Association for Ecology and Health, "may present the greatest public health opportunity that we've had in a century."

share the public realm

But the opportunity is arguably wider: building civil society in which peoples from all walks of life can share the public realm with safety, dignity, and respect. Peñalosa argues that as new communities are built (or older ones retrofitted), the moment is ripe to lay out long (20-mile or longer), 50-foot-wide exclusive pedestrian and bike roadways through new

new green strips

neighborhoods and city sections. Ideally these new green strips would link residential areas, parks, waterfronts, shopping areas, schools, and libraries. Older citizens could walk safely to a cafe and parents could take babies out for fresh air in their carriages. Such roadways, argues Peñalosa, "could completely transform a neighborhood's life and even significantly increase property values. Yet the cost of creating them in newly urbanizing areas would be minimal."

GOING GREEN: WATER AND ENERGY

The green aspiration list for the century seems daunting, at first glance unachievable. Saner transport systems, parks, high energy–efficiency building standards, wind- and solar-power generation, cleanup of power plants and factories whose emissions spell illness and death for hundreds of thousands of humans each year—all, and many more, are the list.

Yet constant reminders are necessary: Climate change is a full-blown global emergency. Among its many imperatives, says Terry Tamminen, former chief policy adviser to California Governor Arnold Schwarzenegger: Stemming "our wasteful use of electricity and our stubborn refusal to generate power with something cleaner and more sustainable than flaming chunks of coal."

Cities, which by virtue of their intense economic activity are the chief generators of pollution on the planet, need to be the lead agents of reform. And not just in a vacuum, addressing issues within their borders, but by working with the rural regions around them.

the lead agents of reform

The welcome news is that a host of creative, green, adaptive strategies have been invented around the world and could be boosted significantly by increased, direct city-to-city communications.

Consider water and sanitation issues. A good part of the learning needs to occur in Global South cities in which huge populations still lack either adequate fresh water supply or systems to dispose safely of human waste. Big, highly engineered water and sewer systems are often unaffordable or impractical in rapid, unplanned development around the peripheries of Global South cities. Local activists could benefit from advice from peers in other cities on how to organize to demand attention and get responsive service from city water and sewer agencies that are often more likely to serve the more affluent and disregard "informal settlements."

And across the Global South models of self-organization by slum dwellers need to be expanded radically. One example: "condominial" water supply systems, initially developed in Brazil, in which the public water agency is persuaded to provide water pipes to an organized group of households, which then take the responsibility for installing the pipes to individual homes or yards. The result is a huge advance for peoples' standard of living over communal or public standpipes. And it reflects the ideal of mixed "macro" and "micro" public utility systems—citywide on one side, localized on the other. On the waste water side, observers for years have been intrigued by the cooperative model for installing sewer pipes for a neighborhood,

highly engineered water and sewer systems

waste water

A toddler rides in a wooden cart that his father uses to peddle bottled water and other drinks along the city's seaside, Manila, Philippines

Workers try to repair one pipe in the city's large, aging network of pipes, Moscow, Russia

developed by the Orangi Pilot Project, in Karachi, Pakistan (see Chapter 2, "Water, Sanitation, and Shelter: A Fresh Look at Finance").

learning new models

But in an age of climate change, learning new models may be important for privileged communities as well. The Global North has become accustomed to massive, highly centralized systems of water and waste water service. Many residents have minimal, if any, knowledge of how those systems function. Yet such single systems could prove enormously vulnerable in an era of radical weather change—either drought-imperiling single-source water systems or massive floods drowning out waste water treatment facilities. In adapting to climate change, redundant, smaller and flexible technologies may prove a critical backup. Indeed, in Bangladesh (annually clobbered by typhoons) and Calcutta (now Kolkata), India, local, cooperative minisystems have shown they can recover from heavy storms more than easily inundated macro water utility systems.

adapting to climate change

"Leapfrogging" of Global North infrastructure systems may be practical in some fast-growing Global South cities that face big infrastructure deficits—cities such as Lagos, for example, in which the majority of the city has no sewer service. The Western development model, established in a few years at the end of the 19th century when there was little concern about the limitation of natural resources or the ultimate size of cities, was (and remains) essentially linear: water, energy, foodstuffs, and other solids enter the city, get consumed once, and then

infrastructure deficits

are discharged as waste. The alternative is a more circular system in which the output of water or waste or energy is recycled, so that sewer water, for example, can be used to cultivate fish and plants, or solid wastes recycled to create methane gas, without the massive costs of centralized systems.

It is not difficult to imagine how models like these, described, depicted graphically, and analyzed for costs and benefits on Internet sites across the world, could make major contributions to 21st-century sustainability across all continents.

Energy issues—steps that cities can take to protect against shortages, high prices, pollution, and greenhouse gas emissions—are especially compelling. On the one hand, there are still hundreds of millions of city dwellers who lack electricity or other conventional heat sources. Often they are obliged to burn kerosene, charcoal, wood scraps, or dung for cooking or warmth (processes that cause indoor air pollution that triggers a massive annual death toll). On the other hand, 150 years of rising electricity demand has left cities across the continents dependent on major fossil-fuel burning, pollution generating power plants and transmission systems, most built with now outmoded technology and subject to blackouts or other sudden failures.

Yet a plethora of more efficient, less polluting, and less dangerous power sources are being developed around the world. Solar orientation and power, new power from wind or geothermal sources, green roofs and walls, reflective paints, natural daylighting, efficient lighting—the list of potential technologies and approaches continues to lengthen. And

protect against shortages

solar orientation and power

409

reliable indoor light for families that have never known it is in sight: in India, for example, distribution has begun of a new type of solar-powered lamp that uses LEDs (light-emitting diodes). The lamps are reportedly four times more efficient than an incandescent bulb.

"model" energy cities

Many "model" energy cities, exhibiting new technologies or other radical saving plans, have emerged around the world, among them Barcelona, Melbourne, Chicago, Cape Town, Copenhagen, and Daegu, South Korea. Some 65 cities took part in a two-day Local Government Climate Session in connection with the worldwide climate change conference in Bali in 2007. U.N. Environment Program director Achim declared, "As champions of the climate cause and centers for innovation, efficiency, investment, and productivity, cities are posed to play an increasingly prominent role in the international climate change debate. It is in cities that climate and sustainability solutions for more than half of the humanity will be found."

And surely there is global potential in rethinking basic energy distribution systems. In the United States, asserts Richard Munson of the Northeast–Midwest Congressional Coalition, "the average generating plant was built in 1964 with 1950s technology. Two-thirds of the fuel we burn is wasted."

distributed energy

A major solution the critics recommend: distributed energy. The idea is to supplement overloaded and polluting major power stations by local generation of power in small power plants. The installations are typically constructed to serve individual hospitals, campuses, apartment houses, factories, or entire neighborhoods. They have an efficiency level double or better than that of regional power plants, because they practice cogeneration, producing electricity and steam simultaneously. Many have run, up to now, on increasingly scarce and expensive natural gas. But they're ideally suited for several emerging energy technologies: fuel cells, wind turbines, rooftop solar electric devices, and microgenerators.

Distributed generation, analysts Janet Sawin and Kristen Hughes report for the Worldwatch Institute, not only improves reliability, it also reduces vulnerability to accident or sabotage. Because the installations are modular and fairly easily installed, they are well-suited to fast-developing cities as migration pushes power demand up rapidly. "And distrib-

local control and ownership uted systems," it is noted, "provide local control and ownership of energy resources, encouraging community level economic development." Distributed generation is not, however, a *total* alternative. As David Morris, director of the Institute for Local Self-Reliance, notes, local power plants can be set up so they can both draw power from and contribute power to larger electric grids: "a two-way electricity system" that is "distributed, decentralized, and democratic."

collaborative models Indeed, it is precisely the new "leapfrogging" and collaborative models of serving cities, rarely mentioned by the big power companies and international engineering and construction firms, that is a natural for a debate engaging citizen activists and entrepreneurial city officials through informal global city exchanges.

A woman in a field near the site of Dongtan, the planned "eco city" being designed by Arup, a British engineering firm, Chongming, China

Bangokok, Thailand

GREENER STILL: METRO FOOD

The globalization and industrialization of food, with vast nation-to-nation shipments of such basic commodities as rice and wheat, raise major concerns about the security and cost of critical food supplies for city populations. The alarming escalation of global food prices in the spring of 2008 highlighted the problem, one potentially even more serious as the spatial footprint of the world's city regions expands, consuming lands once devoted to agriculture. Major environmental issues are raised as well, with the diversion of many farmlands to bio-fuel production and the environmental dangers of rapid conversion of carbon-conserving tropical forests to crop production.

The issue is hardly one that cities can ignore. With rapid urbanization, where will they turn for adequate food supplies? How secure will their supply chains be? Should a premium be placed on food grown within cities or their immediate hinterlands?

escalating food needs

The escalating food needs of such expanding megacities as Jakarta, Bangkok, Karachi, Mumbai, and Shanghai already pose serious challenges, dependent as those metropolises are on 1) increasingly distant rural areas, many of which face their own water- and climate-sustainability issues, and 2) massive fleets of literally tens of thousands of trucks—diesel powered with serious emissions, sensitive to rapid increases in global energy pricing—to bring in sufficient food supplies for millions of people.

metropolitan agriculture policy

A prime U.S. advocate of an explicit metropolitan agriculture policy is Representative Earl Blumenauer of Oregon, a plenary speaker at the Global Urban Summit. Blumenauer argues that federal agriculture subsidies flowing to large commodity crop operators should be shifted "to build sustainable agriculture, create a farmers' market in every community, help farmers protect our land and water, preserve our viewsheds, foster land banks, and control erosion."

A metro focus fits history: In a pattern familiar across the world, most U.S. cities were founded not simply as centers of commerce but because areas of fertile fields, often in lush river valleys, had flat lands relatively easy to build on (and in easy range of food supplies). Especially following World War II, however, large portions of North American urban fringe land once devoted to farming were converted to suburban development. Modern transport made it relatively easy to ship in— by truck, rail, or ships—foods from distant locations.

producer-to-customer ties

The direct producer-to-customer ties in farmers' markets strengthen cohesion and civic capital for people who share a geographically expansive metro region but may otherwise never meet. Local food is a metaphor for the entire region's economic interdependence. Studies indicate conversations occur as many as ten times more often at farmers' markets than at regular grocery chains, a not insignificant psychological boost in an increasingly impersonalized world. Civil society and food? The 21st–century connection, Global North and Global South, may turn out to be not just a challenge, but an answer.

URBAN HEALTH: LOOKING "UPSTREAM" AND FACING UP TO THE DRUG ISSUE

A 21st-century global health agenda will be tough to devise because, as we note in Chapter 4, "Urban Health: Learning from Systems that Work," any purely "medical model" is grossly inadequate to deal with the dire conditions of sanitation, poor water, pollutants, floods, and droughts that threaten many parts of the Global South. If these basic conditions generating human suffering and disease can't be brought under control, medications, clinics, and doctors' diagnoses will be of limited help.

public health issues

But the need to focus on basic public health issues and all the "upstream" factors that contribute to health are hardly constrained to the Global South. In the United States, with health care soaring to 16 percent of GNP and projected to keep on rising, there is serious question about the sanity of the entire system. It is widely estimated that an extraordinary amount of health care dollars—by some estimates 90 percent—go to expensive hospital diagnosis, treatment, and surgical procedures. Yet clear evidence exists that the chronic diseases of the times—heart disease, stroke, diabetes, and many types of cancer—are largely preventable by smart diet, regular exercise, moderation in alcohol consumption, and not smoking.

triple threats

Some of those same issues, with globalization, are now starting to affect the Global South. Dr. Julio Frenk, former Secretary for Health of Mexico and plenary speaker for the Summit week focused on health, noted the presence of triple

415

threats: such historic diseases as malaria, modern communicable diseases including HIV/AIDS, and in today's cities a startling array of conditions ranging from malnutrition to obesity, air pollutants to mental illness.

Yet even if public health answers to most of those challenges could be developed, and widely applied, Frenk agreed that another deep and global challenge would remain: addiction to legally prohibited drugs. The issue is not only the serious physical harm to individuals of addiction to mind-altering drugs, but as some Global Urban Summit participants noted, the broad impact the drug trade has had on the cities of the world.

the drug trade

Imagine, for example, living in everyday fear of dying in crossfire between drug dealers and police or between rival gangs. That is the situation Summit participant Janice Perlman described in the three favelas of Rio de Janeiro she analyzed from 1968 to 1969 and then revisited, with many of the same families, in 2001 to 2003. The fear of military government demolishing homes had been replaced by fear of the lethal violence perpetrated either by the drug gangs or bribed police. Residents told Perlman that seeking retribution from the courts is futile, indeed that identifying the dealers is a death sentence. Result: shrinking personal freedom, fear of using public space, social capital decimated.

drug gangs or bribed police

But that situation, while extreme, is echoed in depressed inner-city neighborhoods across U.S. cities where the trade in illicit drugs (often sold to suburbanites driving by for their "hit") has flourished. Narcotics dealers and their runners struggle violently to gain and keep control of their lucrative markets. Death by gunfire is common. Bystanders are frequently killed. Threats of retaliation create a code of silence so that police cannot solve murders. Civic life is strangled. The parallel to the favela situation is almost painfully perfect.

The U.S. Government has pursued a policy of total prohibition and criminalization of both dealers and users, domestically as well as in its foreign relations, over the past four decades. Yet the United Nations estimates the value of the global market in illicit drugs at $400 billion, or 6 percent of global trade. The extraordinary profits, Ethan Nadelmann writes in *Foreign Policy*, "enrich criminals, terrorists, violent political insurgents, and corrupt politicians and governments."

illicit drugs

Bearing the brunt of today's drug wars, the cities may have to take up the cause and become major pressure points on their national governments for change. They have the biggest stake: They are the primary killing fields of the drug wars; it is their police and legal systems that prohibition corrupts. Strong voices of civil society, especially the medical community and social service groups, organized city by city, will likely be needed to give elected leaders political cover and mobilize national and global coalitions for sweeping reform.

become major pressure points

WOMEN OF AN URBAN WORLD: ASSET, CHALLENGE FOR CITIES

The welfare of women—their health, rights, education, opportunity—is critical to world cities. And the connection is straightforward: stable neighborhoods and a talented work force are prerequisites to cities' economic competitiveness. And neither can be fully realized unless women are valued.

unless women are valued

There remain major threats to women's welfare, however, greater or lesser in varying societies but reflected worldwide and recounted in some detail during the Global Urban Summit sessions. There are low-wealth cities, in struggling parts of Africa, for example, in which girls are lucky to even enter school. (Of the 115 million 6- to 12-year-old children not in school in the developing world, UNESCO and UNICEF estimate three-fifths are girls.) Girls often lack basic supplies and books, or are denied required school uniforms in favor of boys. Some schools do not even have separate latrines for girls, a subject of daily humiliation and even worse during the days of the month when girls have their menstrual periods. And if there are family needs—ailing parents, for example—girls are often pulled out of school, even at quite young ages, to perform household chores.

girls often lack basic supplies

Yet there is solid evidence that the more years girls can be kept in schools, the greater the chance they will refrain from early sex and will use contraception. The later they wait to have their first child, the smaller and more economically secure their families are likely to be. And greater self-confidence and lower birthrates for young women translate into less overall population growth, and a relief of severe pressures on local governments. Plus, studies have shown that smaller families are substantially likelier to move out of poverty than large ones.

greater self-confidence

A woman sells drinking water, Port-au-Prince, Haiti

multiple disadvantages

But girls across many continents face multiple disadvantages. There is often lack of preventive care for girls or instruction in building self-esteem, learning to respect and be defensive about their bodies, and how best to avoid rape or other male-inflicted violence. These girls suffer from the lack of counsel on avoiding sexually transmitted disease; the absence of help on such lifestyle issues as the importance of exercise and avoiding becoming overweight (with obesity a growing problem even in cities of less developed countries); and limited access to basic health services, including childhood vaccinations, prenatal and postnatal care, and coaching for motherhood.

Virtually all these negative conditions are within the power of cities to address. Across the world, women are demonstrating their capacities and talents in businesses, academic settings, and in political life. In the Global South they not only provide the relationship-building and community-building skills critical in all communities, but in settings of extraordinarily rapid change in which chaotic social conditions easily develop. In slum settings they are typically the leading edge in forming residents' groups willing to pool modest resources to obtain varieties of financing for housing, water, or sanitation service (as noted in Chapter 2, "Water, Sanitation, and Shelter: A Fresh Look at Finance").

relationship-building and community-building skills

Recent decades have seen a meteoric rise of women in the Global North, and some Global South nations, in higher education, corporate life, and government. Astoundingly (at least from the viewpoint of earlier generations) women now constitute the majority of students in U.S. colleges and universities, and are approaching half of new entrants in most professions. There is now scarcely any dispute that women are adding significantly to the quality, innovations, and positive

positive growth rates

growth rates of their economies and society.

Places around the globe that still accede to attitudes rooted in male superiority—that a woman's primary role is for sex, bearing children, and fetching water, for example, or that girl children are less desirable than boys—are choking the collective future potentials of their cities and regions. The cures that cities can apply, while sometimes expensive, are not complex: adequate neighborhood services, including

adequate neighborhood services

water, sanitation, parks, police presence to prevent attacks on women, decent schools, basic legal equality, and provision of basic health care and childcare services that serve women and families effectively. Active city-to-city how-to exchanges on

city-to-city how-to exchanges

these topics, globally but especially in the Global South, could help to hasten the paradigm change.

MAYORS AND BEYOND: THE CRITICAL NEW-CENTURY NETWORK

The case for learning and exchanges—city to city across nations, continents, and the globe—is hard to dispute. Many world cities today have populations far exceeding those of nation states just a few decades ago. The variety of hard-to-resolve issues they face is extraordinarily broad. Knowledge of solutions, approaches, and experiences from other cities and

Students at Ibhongo High School, in the heart of the country's largest township, Soweto, Johannesburg, South Africa

A slum dweller uses her mobile phone after a fire gutted her house, along with almost 500 other homes, Kolkata, India

continents could well make a critical difference in facing the toughest issues of the century.

Two recent mayors of Athens, a quintessential city-state and seedbed of modern democracy, have made the case eloquently in recent years.

One was Dora Bakoyannis, the first woman mayor of Athens in its 3,500-year history. Elected in 2002, she faced the megamanagement challenge of bringing off the 2004 Olympic Games on schedule. Confounding outsiders' prediction of failed deadlines and security breaches, she succeeded, leaving a legacy of a new metro subway system, a completely nonpolluting bus fleet, 80 acres of new parks—and a newly confident Athens.

"The leaders in the future of environmental protection will be the world's great cities," Bakoyannis told us in 2005. Why? Because, she replied, citizens find it much easier to influence local government than national on the new century's green issues. Dimitris Avramopoulos, Bakoyannis' predecessor, asserted it was necessary for 21st century cities to reflect "new global reality" by talking directly with one another other, past nation-states and their entrenched bureaucracies, seeking shared solutions to shared problems: unemployment, crime, drugs, illegal migration, and degradation of the environment.

In the Athenians' spirit, 2,000 mayors, city councilors, and regional leaders from around the globe who attended the second World Congress of United Cities and Local Governments (UCLG) in October 2007, in Jeju, Korea, showed no shyness in their official declaration. Prepare for climate change, the

influence local government

World Congress of United Cities

423

group said, by increasing urban density. Use clean and renewable energy. Expand public transport systems. Reform the practice of overwhelming national government fiscal control that disadvantages cities, even while they bear the brunt of fast-rising slum populations. Safeguard cultural diversity and affirm the full rights of women; build "inclusive cities for an inclusive world." "We call on nation-states and armed groups," the UCLG declaration read, "to cease considering cities as military objectives—*'cities are not targets'*."

Sister Cities International was an early leader in developing international exchanges. In the wake of the September 11, 2001, attacks on the United States, it began an Islamic Peace and Friendship initiative, fighting upstream but resolutely against prevailing waves of hostility and misunderstanding. On another track, it started a "Network for Sustainable Development" to help citizens exchange ideas on such topics as global warming, air quality, clean water, renewable energy, affordable housing, and town redevelopment. Organizations such as ICLEI (Local Governments for Local Environmental Initiatives), City Mayors, and the Global Forum are all among the global networks of officials now active.

The emerging paradigm appears to be celebrating mayors' contacts on one side, but also bringing direct civil society—business, professionals, youth, environmental, and slum dwellers' groups—into the active exchanges, supplementing official mayor-to-mayor exchanges with expert-to-expert, activist-to-activist exchanges on topics ranging from housing

citizens exchange ideas

mayors' contacts

active exchanges

The Top Urban Global Networks

Organizing cities from around the world is no easy task. But energetic officials have been at the task ever since the formation of the International Union of Local Authorities, in 1913.

By the 1990s a range of other organizations had emerged and officials sensed the need to form an umbrella organization that could, as a top function, represent the world's cities to the United Nations. The result, after some years of difficult negotiations, was founding the United Cities and Local Governments (UCLG), in 2004. It includes the International Union of Local Authorities, the World Federation of United Cities, United Towns Organization, and Metropolis (the World Organization of Major Metropolises). With eight vice presidents representing all world regions, UCLG identifies itself as "the main local-government partner of the United Nations" and proponent of decentralization, a "quiet democratic revolution," as UCLG describes it, enhancing local versus nationally centralized governments' authority. The group's membership encompasses half the world's population through its 1,000 city members and 60 organizations of cities from 127 U.N. member states.

City Mayors (London-based) is an international network of professionals helping city mayors develop innovative approaches to such areas as housing, transport, and education. Its Web site gets some 2.5 million "hits" a year.

The Global Forum (Rome-based), with 140 cities and some 100 other public- and private-sector partners, points to mayors as "the new diplomats of our world" but also seeks to act as a network of city leaders and young citizens trying to strike a balance between local autonomy and sharing benefits of globalization.

Based in Washington, D.C., the Cities Alliance, a global coalition of cities and their development partners, is committed to scaling up successful approaches to poverty reduction, enabling cities of all sizes to obtain more international support, and helping local authorities plan and prepare for future urban growth.

For international advocacy on a wide range of sustainability issues, the lead organization is the International Council for Local Environmental Initiatives (ICLEI), an affiliate of UCLG. Its interests include climate, water, biodiversity, renewable energy, and disaster-risk and participatory governance; it reports some 700 member governments worldwide. Among other activities, it has worked with more than 170 U.S. governments on steps to cut back their greenhouse-gas emissions and improve environmental stability.

Sister Cities International is the United States' premier citizen-to-citizen exchange organization, formed at the inspiration of President Dwight Eisenhower in 1956. Currently 800 American communities are engaged in 2,200 sister-city relationships, focused on cultural contacts and exchange visits. Participants range from high school students to members of chambers of commerce, with partners in 134 nations around the globe.

A new international network, BeGlobal.net, scheduled to go public in 2008, is a social network modeled on the popular Internet site Facebook, but "with a purpose," in the words of founder Tim Honey, former leader of Sister Cities International. Its purpose? To identify and link "global cities," not by the familiar definition of their "command and control" weight as business centers but rather, regardless of size, their assets in every field from arts and culture and business to scientific research, tourism, peace organizations, and community-service groups. BeGlobal will give special attention to international links or activities.

The nonprofit information site GuideStar.org reports that there are 13,000 internationally focused nonprofits in the United States; the BeGlobal idea is that many are exemplars of global commitment and engagement on pressing issues ranging from global warming to building a sense of global citizenship. Many Peace Corps retirees, for example, have remained internationally engaged, including doctors who volunteer time for overseas missions. "The old Internet," Honey asserts, "was a series of portals; social networking goes further by letting people connect and stay connected, city to city and across continents."

Noteworthy in all the existing and emerging global networks are possibilities of interchange that go beyond familiar "North–North" or "North-to-South" patterns to allow burgeoning "South–South" ties and learning as the developing world's cities and their civil societies employ modern, highly affordable communications—especially the Internet—to link their own cultures and fast-evolving urban institutions and health to water and energy. That point was made explicitly in the Summit's Global South sessions, and it was reflected in the mix of people present: participants ranging from high-level U.N. officials and government policy leaders to scholars, as well as business leaders and even slum dwellers, all bringing their diverse viewpoints to the table and searching out directions all find constructive.

ELECTRIFYING THE GLOBAL NETWORK

Can the cities of the world rise to the grand hopes of the Rockefeller Foundation Global Urban Summit—to be the 21st century's dynamic centers of human equity and opportunity, eradicators of human poverty, proving grounds of environmental sustainability?

Immense population increase, global climate change, perils from pandemics to the turbulence of international economics all cloud the prospects.

mutually derived agendas

But *connectedness*—mutually derived agendas for reform, efficiency, developing collaborative human capacities—should offer rich opportunities. Just as cities themselves first brought mankind together, incubated the world's most exciting skills, cultural breakthroughs, and dynamic economies, today's networking of world cities and their peoples—the idea of the global urban commons developed at the Summit—provides extraordinary opportunity for these times.

electronic communications

Face-to-face meetings remain powerful learning tools. Yet practically, electronic communications will be the dominant medium of the times. Nothing like it has ever been seen in world history: the Internet's direct messaging and capacity to post compelling visual and text bulletins, leaping barriers of space in mere seconds. And it is not just people of similar position or specialty who can communicate across seas and continents with a flick of a computer key. The "mix and match" potentials of officials, academics, business, citizen groups, and activists have hardly any limit.

Not all of this is automatic; some coaching on how to make contacts or find relevant new Web sites may be necessary (and that assumes all groups have broadband access, not yet a foregone conclusion). But information is power; resourceful players will learn the electronic ropes. The medium is too powerful (and refreshingly uncontrolled) to be contained. Dramatic new Internet-based information systems on cities' operations are beginning to appear. Citizen appetite for direct inputs are sure to rise, matched in many cities to numbers of adventuresome bureaucrats communicating with each other and with the citizenry outside of official channels. Inevitably, citizen complaints, sometimes uncomfortably vivid, will make some of the exchanges a challenge for officials. The combination of growing contacts—including world mayors, Internet-empowered citizen groups, and government workers and their allies exchanging information and insights—represents one of the most promising of all 21st-century urban frontiers.

The positive news is that the groundwork for the global urban commons has been laid, ranging from intense and increasing academic analysis to mutual learning among mayors, from idea exchange by activist NGOs to idea exchange among the poorest of the world's peoples. Literally thousands of world networks, by profession, interest, official role, or shared cause now exist. What an exciting century!

Yet as participants in international exchanges all know, challenges of language, culture, perception, even national pride, can often blur the learning that occurs. Champions—idea translators—are required for even the most brilliant academic research. The same need exists on the database front. Even cleverly kept and cross-referenced on computers, data accomplish little just as stored words; they require product advocates, trusted intermediaries to monitor the idea flow and provide a "high-tech, high-touch" interface to keep promoting the information and then guide interested parties in the best ways to use it. This is a function that large, bureaucratic institutions perform poorly.

The irony is that even as we become one world electronically and by profession and interest, it is not standardized tactics but rather a "letting many flowers bloom" approach—sponsoring new and inventive partnerships, jumping silo barriers of professions prizing both intellect *and* passion among the networked communicators of the times—that may yield the broadest and most lasting impact. The openness of cultures, peoples, ideas of the Rockefeller Foundation Global Urban Summit symbolized this type of exchange—not as an end in itself, but as a beginning.

thousands of world networks

idea translators

we become one world

lasting impact

Acknowledgments

We are confident that the urban leaders and activists from across the hemispheres who participated in the Rockefeller Foundation Global Urban Summit of 2007—in four weeks of sessions that sparked the ideas this book reflects—join us in thanking the Rockefeller Foundation for its extraordinary initiative.

Not only was the array of participants remarkable: officials, scholars, *and* grassroots leaders from cities as diverse as Seattle and Kampala, Mumbai and São Paulo. So was the Foundation's vision in seeing that today's new urban-majority world needs an actual agenda. The Rockefeller Foundation leaders insisted that the panelists not simply identify the most pressing problems facing global cities, but also explore varieties of specific ways to address them.

Our job was to capture those ideas and illuminate the threads that connected them, identifying elements of a specific action agenda. The Summit participants, both in the sessions and in follow-up conversations (face-to-face and later electronic), helped us immensely in that task.

We are grateful to our colleagues (and their colleagues) from the partner organizations of the Global Urban Summit for their day-to-day efforts during the Summit, their assistance in elucidating ideas, and their comments on our manuscript drafts—particularly Elliott Sclar, Nicole Volavka, and Gabriella Carolini of the Columbia University Center for Sustainable Urban Development; Eugenie Birch, Susan Wachter, and Kendra Goldbas of the University of Pennsylvania Institute for Urban Research; Robert Yaro and Petra Todorovich of the Regional Plan Association; and Bruce Katz, Mark Muro, Robert Puentes, Alan Berube, Amy Liu, and Julie Wagner of the Brookings Institution Metropolitan Policy Program. Bill Cote and John Cheshire of BC Video, who filmed the Global South sessions, also kindly shared their footage with us, allowing us to get more direct quotations from participants.

Our major collaborator in monitoring the Summit sessions and book preparation was our Citistates Group colleague, Farley Peters, who sorted through an alpine mountain of our session computer notes, interviews, and background materials, organizing everything so that themes emerged for us to write around. She also checked all our manuscripts for thoroughness and balance, and was our principal liaison with the Rockefeller Foundation in the conference planning stages.

We also greatly appreciated the assistance of Lenneal Henderson, a Citistates group associate and professor of Government and Public Administration at the University of Baltimore. He monitored all the Global South sessions, applying his own international consulting experience to several vital interviews with panelists and later lending his insights to building this book's narrative.

The magic of the Rockefeller Foundation Bellagio Center setting, and the thoughtfulness of the staff there led by Pilar Palacia, will remain with all of us for years to come.

We wish to recognize stalwart allies on the Rockefeller Foundation staff who assisted in our endeavors, including research associate Anna Brown, Rachel Christmas Derrick, editor of this volume, and Katherine Snider, who coordinated the book's design and production. The engagement of Maria Blair and Ariel Pablos-Mendez also proved invaluable.

Finally, all who read this book should know that without the vision of Judith Rodin, recognizing the emergence of an intensely urban world, and of Darren Walker, who conceptualized and led the entire effort, the new light of *Century of the City* would never have been lit.

Neal R. Peirce
Curtis W. Johnson

Authors

NEAL R. PEIRCE

A journalist and speaker, Neal R. Peirce focuses on the national and global roles of cities and metropolitan regions. With Curtis W. Johnson, he has co-authored 26 newspaper series—"Citistates Reports"—on strategic issues facing individual metropolitan regions, including articles for the Seattle *Times*, Philadelphia *Inquirer*, Miami *Herald*, Charlotte *Observer*, and Phoenix *Republic*. Together, Peirce and Johnson wrote *Citistates: How Urban America Can Prosper in a Competitive World* (Seven Lochs Press, 1993). With Farley Peters, they organized and lead the Citistates Group, a network of journalists, speakers, and civic leaders committed to building competitive and sustainable 21st century regions (www.citistates.com).

Peirce's ten-volume series on the states and regions of the United States culminated in *The Book of America* (W.W. Norton, 1983). He also wrote *The People's President*, on the electoral college in U.S. history and the direct vote alternative (Simon & Schuster, 1968), *Corrective Capitalism*, on the rise of community development corporations (Ford Foundation, 1987), *Breakthroughs: Re-Creating the American City* (Rutgers University Center for Urban Policy Research, 1993), and (with Johnson) *Boundary Crossers: Community Leadership for a Global Age*, a project in partnership with John W. Gardner (The Academy of Leadership Press, University of Maryland, 1997).

Since 1975, Peirce has written the United States' first national newspaper column on city and state local themes (Washington Post Writers Group syndication and Citiwire.net). Peirce was a founder of *National Journal* and served in the 1960s as political editor of *Congressional Quarterly*. He has been a trustee of the German Marshall Fund of the United States, member of the executive committee of the National Civic League, and three-time faculty member of the Salzburg Seminar.

CURTIS W. JOHNSON

Curtis W. Johnson's career plays on a split screen—half devoted to being a leader in the public sector and the other half as analyst and commentator. His public service culminated with four years in the mid-1990s as chairman of the Metropolitan Council, which coordinates land use and operates wastewater and transit systems in the Twin Cities (Minneapolis-St. Paul) region of Minnesota.

Following ten years as a college president in the 1970s, Johnson for 11 years led the Citizens League, a well-known public affairs research organization in the Twin Cities; and then spent three years as policy adviser to Minnesota Governor Arne Carlson, including a period as chief of staff.

He co-authored *Disrupting Class* (McGraw Hill, 2008), with Clayton Christensen of Harvard Business School and Michael Horn. The book lays out why and how the process of learning will see fundamental changes in the 21st century.

With columnist Neal R. Peirce, Johnson has written "Citistates Reports," published in leading newspapers in 26 American regions since 1987. Covering locally significant challenges ranging from regional collaboration to land use and growth practices, these reports have consistently demonstrated an agenda-setting impact. He co-authored with Peirce *Citistates: How Urban America Can Prosper in a Competitive World* (Seven Lochs Press, 1993) and *Boundary Crossers: Community Leadership for a Global Age* (The Academy of Leadership Press, University of Maryland, 1997), showcasing ten lessons learned from citizens making an impact on public policy. Johnson is president of the Citistates Group, a former Salzburg Seminar faculty member, and a frequent public speaker.

The Rockefeller Foundation Global Urban Summit
Bellagio Center, Italy, July 2007

Participants

GLOBAL SOUTH TRACK

**Financing Water,
Sanitation,
and Shelter**

Graham J. Alder
Consultant
MATRIX Development
Nairobi, KENYA

Joel Leslie Bolnick
Co-ordinator
Community
Organisation Resource
Centre
Shack Dwellers
International
Cape Town, SOUTH
AFRICA

Anna Brown
Research Associate
The Rockefeller
Foundation
New York, NY

**Antony Jonathan
Bugg-Levine**
Managing Director
The Rockefeller
Foundation
New York, NY

Bruce Daniel Cameron
Deputy Director of
Housing Programs
Overseas Private
Investment Corporation
(OPIC)
Small & Medium
Enterprise
Washington, DC

Gabriella Y. Carolini
Columbia University
The Earth Institute
Center for Sustainable
Urban Development
New York, NY

John Cheshire
Producer
BC Video
New York, NY

Bill Cote
President
BC Video
New York, NY

Franck Daphnis
President & CEO
Development
Innovations Group
Bethesda, MD

Barbara E. Evans
Dean of Graduate
Studies
University of British
Columbia
Faculty of Graduate
Studies
Vancouver, CANADA

Mila Emilia Freire
Senior Adviser
The World Bank
Sustainable
Development Network
Washington, DC

**Ravinath Jayasri
Goonesekera**
Member
Municipal Council
Moratuwa, SRI LANKA

Sumila Gulyani
Urban Planner
Columbia University &
The World Bank
Washington, DC

Lenneal Henderson
Citistates Group
Baltimore, MD

Barbara C. Hewson
Managing Director
and Principal
NewLine Capital
Partner, LLC
Emerging Markets
Housing Finance
New York, NY

Curtis W. Johnson
Citistates Group
Minneapolis, MN

Rajivan Krishnaswamy
Senior Urban
Finance Advisor
The World Bank
Cities Alliance
Washington, DC

**Mary Wairimu
Mathenge**
Chief Executive Officer
National Cooperative
Housing Union LTD
Nairobi, KENYA

Diana Mitlin
Professor
Manchester University
International Institute
for Environment and
Development (IIED)
London, ENGLAND

Rakesh Mohan
Deputy Governor
Reserve Bank of India
Former Secretary-Dept.
of Economic Affairs
in the Union Finance
Ministry
Mumbai, INDIA

**Rose Sessie
Molokoane**
Co-ordinator
Shack Dwellers
International
Cape Town,
SOUTH AFRICA

Mark R. Montgomery
Professor of Economy
Stony Brook University
Dept. of Economics
New York, NY

Michael Mutter
Senior Advisor
UN-HABITAT
Human Settlements
Financing Division
Nairobi, KENYA

James Mwangi
Managing Director
& CEO
Equity Bank Limited
Nairobi, KENYA

Ravi Narayanan
Former Chief Executive
now Vice Chair
WaterAid, Asia Pacific
Water Forum
Bangalore, INDIA

Cyrus Njiru
Principal Water
Management Specialist
African Development
Bank
Operations Policy &
Compliance Dept.
Tunis, TUNISIA

Nikki Ortolani
Administrative
Coordinator
Columbia University
The Earth Institute
Center for Sustainable
Urban Development
New York, NY

Ana Puszkin-Chevlin
Senior Research Fellow
Florida Atlantic
University
Center for Urban
& Environmental
Solutions
Boca Raton, FL

Lisa M. Schineller
Director
Standard & Poor's
New York, NY

Elliott Sclar
Professor
Columbia University
New York, NY

David A. Smith
Founder
Affordable Housing
Institute
Recapitalization
Advisors, Inc.
Boston, MA

Alfredo Stein
Project Leader
University of Lund
Housing Development &
Management Dept.
Lund, SWEDEN

**Anna Kajumulo
Tibaijuka**
UN-HABITAT
Nairobi, KENYA

Nicole Volavka-Close
Columbia University
The Earth Institute
Center for Sustainable
Urban Development
New York, NY

Darren Walker
Vice President
Foundation Initiatives
The Rockefeller
Foundation
New York, NY

Melanie Walker
Senior Program Officer
The Bill & Melinda Gates
Foundation
Global Development
Seattle, WA

Jane Weru
Executive Director
Pamoja Trust
Nairobi, KENYA

Christopher Williams
Ag. Director SP4
UN-Habitat
Washington, DC

GLOBAL SOUTH TRACK
Building
Climate Change
Resilience

Mozaharul Alam
Research Fellow
Bangladesh Center
for Advanced Studies
(BCAS)
Dept. of Climate Change
Dhaka, BANGLADESH

**Narayana Susith
Arambepola**
Director
Asian Disaster
Preparedness Center
(ADPC)
Urban Disaster Risk
Management (UDRM)
Pathumtani, THAILAND

Maria Blair
Associate Vice President
and Managing Director
The Rockefeller
Foundation
New York, NY

Anna Brown
Research Associate
The Rockefeller
Foundation
New York, NY

Paul R. Brown
President
CDM's Public
Services Group
Carlsbad, CA

Gabriella Y. Carolini
Columbia University
The Earth Institute
Center for Sustainable
Urban Development
New York, NY

John Cheshire
Producer
BC Video
New York, NY

Bill Cote
President
BC Video
New York, NY

Jo Da Silva
Associate Director
ARUP Group
Arup International
Development
London, UNITED
KINGDOM

Rohinton Emmanuel
Professor of Architecture
University of Moratuwa
Dept. of Architecture
Moratuwa, SRI LANKA

Roland J. Fuchs
Director
International START
Secretariat
Washington, DC

Michel Gelobter
President
Redefining Progress
Oakland, CA

Margaret A. Hamburg
Senior Scientist
Global Health & Security
Initiative/NTI
Washington, DC

Jorgelina Hardoy
Researcher
IIED-América Latina
Buenos Aires,
ARGENTINA

Madeleen Helmer
Head Red Cross/Red
Crescent Climate Centre
The Hague,
NETHERLANDS

Lenneal Henderson
Citistates Group
Baltimore, MD

Margit Hentschel
Western States
Regional Director
ICLEI - Local
Governments for
Sustainability
Dept. of Western States
Regional Capacity
Center
Fort Collins, CO

Carol A. Howe
Switch-Project Manager
UNESCO-IHE-Institute
for Water Education
Switch Integrated
Project
Sustainable Urban
Water Management
Delft, NETHERLANDS

Saleemul Huq
Head, Climate
Change Group
International Institute
for Environment and
Development
Climate Change Group
London, ENGLAND

Curtis W. Johnson
Citistates Group
Minneapolis, MN

Stephen Kabuye
Mayor
Entebbe Municipal
Council
Entebbe, UGANDA

Nancy Kete
Senior Fellow and
Co-Director
EMBARQ (also WIRI)
World Resource
Institute
Washington, DC

Mark R. Montgomery
Professor of Economy
Stony Brook University
Dept. of Economics
New York, NY

Maria Neira
Director
World Health
Organization
Public Health and
Environment
Geneva, SWITZERLAND

**Erin Nicholas
Novakowski**
Senior Consultant
Chreod Ltd.
Ottawa, CANADA

Nikki Ortolani
Administrative
Coordinator
Columbia University
The Earth Institute
Center for Sustainable
Urban Development
New York, NY

Rajendra K. Pachauri
Director
Tata Energy Research
Institute
New Delhi, INDIA

Ana Puszkin-Chevlin
Senior Research Fellow
Florida Atlantic
University

Center for Urban
& Environmental
Solutions
Boca Raton, FL

Aromar Revi
Director
TARU
New Delhi, INDIA

Debra C. Roberts
Head
Ethekwini Municipality
Environmental
Management
Department
Durban, SOUTH AFRICA

**Patricia Romero
Lankao (de Duffing)**
Deputy Director
UCAR/ISSE
Boulder, CO

**Cristina Maria
Rumbaitis del Rio**
Senior Research
Associate
The Rockefeller
Foundation
New York, NY

David E. Satterthwaite
Senior Fellow
International Institute
for Environment and
Development (IIED)
London, ENGLAND

Elliott Sclar
Professor
Columbia University
New York, NY

James S. Traub
Contributing Writer
The New York Times
Magazine
New York, NY

Lawrence J. Vale
Professor
Massachusetts Institute
of Technology
Head of Department
of Urban Planning
Cambridge, MA

Nicole Volavka-Close
Columbia University
The Earth Institute
Center for Sustainable
Urban Development
New York, NY

Darren Walker
Vice President
Foundation Initiatives
The Rockefeller
Foundation
New York, NY

Rusong Wang
Professor
Chinese Academy of
Sciences
Research Center for Eco-
Environmental Sciences
Dept. State Key Lab on
Urban and Regional
Ecology
Beijing, CHINA

Urban Population Health

Siddharth Raj Agarwal
Executive Director
Urban Health
Resource Center
New Delhi, INDIA

Katherine C. Bond
Associate Director,
Health Equity and
Southeast Asia
Regional Program
The Rockefeller
Foundation
Nairobi, KENYA

Anna Brown
Research Associate
The Rockefeller
Foundation
New York, NY

**Waleska Teixeira
Caiaffa**
Assistant Professor
of Epidemiology

Federal University
of Minas Gerais
Belo Horizonte, BRAZIL

Gabriella Y. Carolini
Columbia University
The Earth Institute
Center for Sustainable
Urban Development
New York, NY

**Subramaniam
Chandrasekhar**
Assistant Professor
Indira Gandhi Institute
of Development
Research
Mumbai, INDIA

John Cheshire
Producer
BC Video
New York, NY

Bill Cote
President
BC Video
New York, NY

Tamara C. Fox
Program Officer
Hewlett Foundation
Menlo Park, CA

Julio Frenk
Minister of Health
Fundacion Mexicana
para la Salude
Mexico, D.F. MEXICO

Amlan Kusum Ganguly
Director
Prayasam
Dept. of Civil Society
Organization
Kolkata, INDIA

Michel Garenne
Director of Research
Pasteur Institute
FRANCE

Gordon McGranahan
Head
International Institute
for Environment and
Developement
Human Settlements

Group
London, ENGLAND

Trudy Harpham
Professor of Urban
Development and Policy
South Bank University
Dept. of Urban Studies
London, ENGLAND

Leo Heller
Professor, Department
of Sanitary and
Environmental
Engineering
Universidade Federal
de Minas Gerais
Belo Horizonte, BRAZIL

Lenneal Henderson
Citistates Group
Baltimore, MD

Curtis W. Johnson
Citistates Group
Minneapolis, MN

Felicia Knaul
Chief Economist
Mexico National
Foundation for Health
and Welfare
Mexico, D.F. MEXICO

Anthony A. Kolb
Urban Health Advisor
U.S. Agency for
International
Development
Dept. of Urban
Programs Team
Washington, DC

Yao Lan
Project Manager
National Center for
Women and Children's
Health
China/UK Urban Health
& Poverty Project
Beijing, CHINA

Gora Mboup
Senior Demographic &
Health Expert
UN-HABITAT
Human Settlements

Officer, Monitoring &
Research
Nairobi, KENYA

Qingyue Meng
Professor and Director
Shandong University
Center for Health
Management & Policy
Shandong, CHINA

Susan P. Mercado
Team Leader
WHO Center for Health
Development
Urbanization and
Health Equity
Kobe, JAPAN

John Monahan
Executive Director
O'Neill Institute
for National and
Global Health Law,
Georgetown University
International Health
Program
Washington, DC

Mark R. Montgomery
Professor of Economy
Stony Brook University
Dept. of Economics
New York, NY

Brigit Obrist
Assistant Professor
University of Basel
Institute of Social
Anthropology
Basel, SWITZERLAND

**Francis Gervase
Omaswa**
Director General
Ministry of Health
Wandegaya-Kampala,
UGANDA

Nikki Ortolani
Administrative
Coordinator
Columbia University,
Earth Institute
New York, NY

Ariel Pablos-Mendez
Managing Director
The Rockefeller
Foundation
New York, NY

Marilyn Rice
Regional Adviser
PAHO (Pan American
Health Organization)
Healthy Municipalities
Washington, DC

Mark Lewis Rosenberg
Executive Director
Task Force for
Child Survival and
Development
Decatur, GA

Elliott Sclar
Professor
Columbia University
New York, NY

Justin P. Steil
Ph.D. Student
Columbia University
Urban Planning
Brooklyn, NY

Paul Taylor
Cap-Net Director
United Nations
Development Program
Pretoria, SOUTH AFRICA

Nicole Volavka-Close
Columbia University,
Earth Institute
Center for Sustainable
Urban Development
New York, NY

Darren Walker
Vice President
Foundation Initiatives
The Rockefeller
Foundation
New York, NY

Brenda Lee Wilson
Correspondent/Editor
National Public Radio
Science and Health Desk
Washington, DC

Godfrey B. Woelk
Professor
University of Zimbabwe
Dept. of Community
Medicine
Harare, ZIMBABWE

Eliya Msiyaphazi Zulu
Deputy Executive
Director
African Population &
Health Research Center
Nairobi, KENYA

GLOBAL SOUTH TRACK
**Urban Planning
and Design**

Andrew Amara
Student-Graduate
Architect
Makerere University
Dept. of Architecture
Kampala, UGANDA

Alejandro Aravena
Chilean designer behind
current housing policy
Santiago, CHILE

Nidhi Batra
Architect-Student
School of Planning &
Architecture
Urban Design
New Delhi, INDIA

Barry Bergdoll
Phillip Johnson
Chief Curator
Museum of Modern Art
New York, NY

Anna Brown
Research Associate
The Rockefeller
Foundation
New York, NY

Gabriella Y. Carolini
Columbia University
The Earth Institute
Center for Sustainable
Urban Development
New York, NY

437

John Cheshire
Producer
BC Video
New York, NY

Bill Cote
President
BC Video
New York, NY

Aline Couri Fabião
Global Studio Student
Universidade Federal
Urban Planning
and Design
Rio do Janeiro, BRAZIL

Paul Farmer
Executive Director
& CEO
America Planning
Association
Chicago, IL

**Joaquim Vieira
Ferreira Levy**
Secretary of Finance
Rio de Janeiro, BRAZIL

Harrison Fraker
University of Minnesota
Dean, College of
Architecture and
Landscape Architecture
Minneapolis, MN

Pietro Garau
Senior Researcher
University of Rome
Rome, ITALY

Amelia Gentleman
Journalist
International
Herald Tribune
New Delhi, INDIA

Gordon McGranahan
Head
International Institute
for Environment
Human Settlements
Group
London, ENGLAND

Gary Hack
Dean, School of Design
University of
Pennsylvania
Philadelphia, PA

Arif Hasan
Architect
Urban Resource Center
Karachi, PAKISTAN

Lenneal Henderson
Citistates Group
Baltimore, MD

Curtis W. Johnson
Citistates Group
Minneapolis, MN

Erminia Maricato
Formerly Deputy
Minister
University of São Paulo
Faculty of Architecture
and Urbanism
São Paulo, BRAZIL

Peter Joseph Matlon
Managing Director, ARP
The Rockefeller
Foundation
Nairobi, KENYA

Peter Musyoki Ngau
Professor
University of Nairobi
Dept. of Urban &
Regional Planning
Nairobi, KENYA

Nikki Ortolani
Administrative
Coordinator
Columbia University,
Earth Institute
New York, NY

Suha Ozkan
Director General
Aga Khan Award for
Architecture
Geneva, SWITZERLAND

Haixiao Pan
Professor
Tongji University
Urban Planning

Department
Shanghai, CHINA

Janice E. Perlman
Founder and
Executive Director
Mega-Cities Project
New York, NY

Edgar Arthur Pieterse
University of Cape Town
Dept. of Engineering &
the Built Environment
Cape Town, SOUTH
AFRICA

Richard Plunz
Professor
Columbia University
Graduate School
of Architecture,
Planning and
Preservation
New York, NY

**Kallyat Thazhathveetil
Ravindran**
Professor of Urban
Design
School of Planning
and Architecture
New Delhi, INDIA

Lars Reutersward
UN-HABITAT
Global Division
Nairobi, KENYA

Anna Rubbo
The University of Sydney
Faculty of Architecture
Global Studio
Sydney, AUSTRALIA

Joseph Sauve
Global Studio Student
Carleton University
Dept. of Architecture
Ottawa, CANADA

Elliott Sclar
Professor
Columbia University
New York, NY

Nan Shi
Secretary General,
Senior Planner
Urban Planning
Society of China
Beijing, CHINA

Joan Aiko Shigekawa
Associate Director
The Rockefeller
Foundation
New York, NY

Gaétan Siew
President
Union Internationale
des Architectes (UIA)
Lampotang & Siew
Architects, Ltd.
Port Louis, MAURITIUS

Justin P. Steil
Ph.D. Student
Columbia University
Urban Planning
Brooklyn, NY

Geetam Tiwari
Professor
Indian Institute of
Technology
Transportation Planning
New Delhi, INDIA

Nicole Volavka-Close
Columbia University
The Earth Institute
Center for Sustainable
Urban Development
New York, NY

Darren Walker
Vice President
Foundation Initiatives
The Rockefeller
Foundation
New York, NY

Ham S. Wesonga
Student
Jomo Kenyatta
University of Agriculture
& Technology
Nairobi, KENYA

Zhiqiang Siegfried Wu
Dean of the College of
Architecture and Urban
Planning, Chief Planner,
Shanghai Expo 2010
Tongji University
Shanghai, CHINA

U.S. TRACK
America 2050
Project

Eugenie L. Birch
Co-Director
University of
Pennsylvania
Penn Institute of
Urban Research
Philadelphia, PA

**Angela Glover
Blackwell**
Founder and CEO
PolicyLink
Oakland, CA

Edward James Blakely
Executive Director
City of New Orleans
Mayor's Office of
Recovery Management
New Orleans, LA

**Earl Francis
Blumenauer**
Member of U.S.
Congress
U.S. House of
Representatives
Portland, OR

**Jonathan Todd
Capehart**
Editorial Writer
The Washington Post
Washington, DC

**Armando Jose
Carbonell**
Chairman
Lincoln Institute of
Land Policy
Dept. of Planning and
Urban Form
Cambridge, MA

Ann M. Drake
Chief Executive Officer
DSC Logistics
Executive Dept.
Des Plaines, IL

**Frances Beinecke
Elston**
President
Natural Resources and
Defense Council
New York, NY

Barbara Lee Faga
Executive Vice President
/Principal
(FASLA)-EDAW
Atlanta, GA

Robert L. Fishman
Professor
University of Michigan,
Ann Arbor
Taubman College
of Architecture and
Planning
Ann Arbor, MI

Shirley Clarke Franklin
Mayor
City of Atlanta
Atlanta, GA

John Fregonese
Principal
Fregonese Associates
Portland, OR

Miguel Angel Garcia
Program Officer
Ford Foundation
Assets: Community &
Resource Development
New York, NY

Fred Philip Hochberg
Dean
New School University
Milano Graduate School
New York, NY

**Christopher
Harris Jones**
Vice President, Research
Regional Plan
Association
New York, NY

Bruce Jonathan Katz
Vice President and
Director
The Brookings
Institution
Metropolitan Policy
Program
Washington, DC

Robert Cross Lieber
President
New York City
Economic Development
Corporation
New York, NY

Sunne Wright McPeak
President and CEO
California Emerging
Technology Fund
San Francisco, CA

Neal R. Peirce
Citistates Group
Washington, DC

Farley M. Peters
Citistates Group
Tracy Landing, MD

Mark Anthony Pisano
Executive Director
Southern California
Association of
Governments
Los Angeles, CA

Shelley Ross Poticha
President & CEO
Reconnecting America
Oakland, CA

**Richard Marshall
Rosan**
President
The Urban Land
Institute
ULI Worldwide
Washington, DC

Catherine L. Ross
Director and Harry
West Professor
Georgia Technology
University, College
of Architecture
Center for Quality

Growth and Regional
Development
Atlanta, GA

Baiju Ramesh Shah
President and CEO
BioEnterprise
Cleveland, Ohio

Ronald Cordell Sims
King County Executive
King County, State
of Washington
Seattle, WA

Frederick Ray Steiner
Dean
The University of Texas
at Austin
School of Architecture
Austin, TX

**David Bradford
Thornburgh**
President and CEO
Alliance for Regional
Stewardship
Philadelphia, PA

Petra Erin Todorovich
Director, America 2050
Regional Plan
Association
New York, NY

Darren Walker
Vice President
Foundation Initiatives
The Rockefeller
Foundation
New York, NY

David Allen Warm
Executive Director
Mid-America Regional
Council
Kansas City, MO

**Thomas Knowlton
Wright**
Executive Vice President
Regional Plan
Association
New York, NY

439

Robert Dickson Yaro
President
Regional Plan
Association
New York, NY

U.S. TRACK
Blueprint
for National
Prosperity (U.S.
Transportation
Policy)

Sharon Leah Alpert
Program Officer
Surdna Foundation
Dept. of Environment
New York, NY

Scott Evans Bernstein
President
Center for
Neighborhood
Technology
Chicago, IL

David Gates Burwell
Senior Associate,
Transportation
Project for Public Spaces
Bethesda, MD

Anne P. Canby
President
Surface Transportation
Policy Partnership
Washington, DC

Timothy Yorke Ceis
Deputy Mayor
City of Seattle
Seattle, WA

Stuart Cohen
Executive Director
Transportation and
Land Use Coalition
Oakland, CA

**Engelbert Lütke
Daldrup**
State Secretary
Ministry for Transport,

Building and Urban
Affairs
Berlin, GERMANY

Shirley Ann DeLibero
Chair
DeLibero Transportation
Strategies
Milton, MA

**Thomas Michael
Downs**
President & CEO
Eno Transportation
Foundation
Washington, DC

Emil Hiram Frankel
Principal Consultant
Parsons Brinckerhoff
Washington, DC

**Jacquelyne Dolores
Grimshaw**
Vice President
Center for
Neighborhood
Technology
Chicago, IL

Steve James Heminger
Executive Director
Metropolitan
Transportation
Commission
Oakland, CA

Oliver N. Jones
Head of Board
Support Division
UK Dept. of Transport
London, ENGLAND

Bruce Jonathan Katz
Vice President and
Director
The Brookings
Institution
Metropolitan Policy
Program
Washington, DC

Tyler Colin Kinder
Policy/Research
Assistant
The Brookings
Institution

Metropolitan Policy
Program
Washington, DC

John F. Lettiere
Senior Vice President
Edwards and Kelcey
Newton, PA

Robert Leo Liberty
Portland Metro Council
Portland, Oregon

Pat McCrory
Mayor
City of Charlotte
Charlotte, NC

Mark Muro
Policy Director
The Brookings
Institution
Metropolitan Policy
Program
Washington, DC

Faye Alexander Nelson
President & CEO
Detroit Riverfront
Detroit, MI

Neal R. Peirce
Citistates Group
Washington, DC

Farley M. Peters
Citistates Group
Tracy Landing, MD

Karen Angeli Phillips
Commissioner
New York City, Planning
Commission
New York, NY

Marco Ponti
Professor of Economics
Politecnico di Milano
Dept. of Planning
(D.I.A.P.)
Milano, ITALY

Robert Joseph Puentes
Fellow
The Brookings
Institution

Metropolitan Policy
Institution
Washington, DC

George Alfred Ranney
President & CEO
Chicago Metropolis 2020
Chicago, IL

Martin Edward Robins
Director
Rutgers University
Voorhees Transportation
Planning Institute
New Brunswick, NJ

Joel Edward Rogers
Director
University of Wisconsin
Center on Wisconsin
Strategy
Madison, WI

William Donald Smith
Cherokee Investment
Partners
San Francisco, CA

**Christopher Thomas
Swope**
Associate Editor
Governing
Washington, DC

Petra Erin Todorovich
Director, America 2050
Regional Plan
Association
New York, NY

Richard Patrick Voith
Senior Vice President &
Principal
Econsult Corporation
Philadelphia, PA

Darren Walker
Vice President
Foundation Initiatives
The Rockefeller
Foundation
New York, NY

**Julie Katherine
Wagner**
Non Resident Senior
Fellow

The Brookings
Institution
Milano, ITALY

U.S. TRACK
Blueprint for
National Prosperity
(U.S. Metros)

**John Cartwright
Austin**
Vice President
Michigan Dept. of
Education
Lansing, MI

Richard David Baron
Chairman & Chief
Executive Officer
McCormack Baron
Salazar
St. Louis, MO

Mary Sue Barrett
President
Metropolitan Planning
Organization
Chicago, IL

Alan Michael Berube
Research Director
The Brookings
Institution
Metropolitan Policy
Program
Washington, DC

**Kimberley Jane
Burnett**
Program Officer
The Surdna Foundation
New York, NY

Richard Daley
Mayor
City of Chicago
Chicago, IL

Margaret Daley
First Lady of Chicago
Chicago, IL

**Robert Nicholas
(Rob) Daumeyer**
Editor
Business Courier
Loveland, OH

**Anika Susan
Goss-Foster**
Director of
Philanthropic Affairs
City of Detroit
Mayor's Office
Detroit, MI

**Vincent Gradford
Graham**
Founder
The I'On Group
Mount Pleasant, SC

**Jacqueline Lynnette
Heard**
Press Secretary/
Chief AIDE
City of Chicago
Chicago, IL

Bennett Lowell Hecht
President & CEO
Living Cities
New York, NY

James Arthur Johnson
Vice Chairman
Perseus, LLC
Washington, DC

Bruce Jonathan Katz
Vice President and
Director
The Brookings
Institution
Metropolitan Policy
Program
Washington, DC

Robert W. Kerslake
Chief Executive
Sheffield City Council
Sheffield, ENGLAND

Tyler Colin Kinder
Policy/Research
Assistant
The Brookings
Institution
Metropolitan Policy
Program
Washington, DC

Amy Liu Witmer
Deputy Director
The Brookings
Institution
Metropolitan Policy
Program
Washington, DC

Karen Gordon Mills
Managing Director
Solera Capital
Brunswick, ME

Mark Muro
Policy Director
The Brookings
Institution
Metropolitan Policy
Program
Washington, DC

Jeremy Nowak
President & CEO
The Reinvestment Fund
Philadelphia, PA

**Wolfgang Michael
Nowak**
Managing DIrector
Deutsche Bank
Alfred Herrhausen
Society
Berlin, GERMANY

Dan Onorato
Allegheny County
Executive
Pittsburgh, PA

Neal R. Peirce
Citistates Group
Washington, DC

Farley M. Peters
Citistates Group
Tracy Landing, MD

Reynard Ramsey
Chairman & CEO
One Economy
Corporation
Washington, DC

John Wallis Rowe
Professor
Columbia University

Mailman School of
Public Health
New York, NY

James Samuel Rubin
Partner
One Equity Partners
New York, NY

Mary Jean Ryan
Director
City of Seattle Office of
Policy and Management
Seattle, WA

Carey Consuelo Shea
Associate Director,
New Orleans Initiative
The Rockefeller
Foundation
New Orleans, LA

Greg David Sutton
Executive Producer
Brooklyn Community
Access Television
Brooklyn, NY

**Nicholas Raymond
Turner**
Managing Director,
Foundation Initiatives
The Rockefeller
Foundation
New York, NY

Joost van Iersel
Chairman Consultative
Com. on Industrial
Change
European Economic
and Social Council
The Hague,
NETHERLANDS

**Julie Katherine
Wagner**
Non Resident
Senior Fellow
The Brookings
Institution
Milano, ITALY

Darren Walker
Vice President
Foundation Initiatives
The Rockefeller
Foundation
New York, NY

Ronald L. Walker
President & Founding
Partner
Next Street Financial
Roxbury, MA

**Christopher Owen
Ward**
Managing Director
General Contractors
Association
New York, NY

Oliver Weigel
Head of Urban Policy
Division
Federal Ministry of
Transport, Building
and Urban Affairs
Urban Development &
Housing
Berlin, GERMANY

**Anthony Allen
Williams**
Friedman Billings
Ramsey (Former Mayor,
Washington, DC)
Arlington, VA

Robert Dickson Yaro
President
Regional Plan
Association
New York, NY

Nancy Lusk Zimpher
President
University of Cincinnati
Cincinnati, OH

GLOBAL SOUTH AND
U.S. TRACKS
Urban Research

Deborah L. Balk
Associate Prof.
Baruch College, City

University of New York
School of Public Affairs
New York, NY

Nefise Bazoglu
Head, Monitoring
Systems Branch
UN-Habitat
Nairobi, KENYA

Eugenie L. Birch
Co-Director
University of
Pennsylvania
Penn Institute of
Urban Research
Philadelphia, PA

Joel E. Cohen
Professor of Populations
Rockefeller and
Columbia Universities
Dept. of Populations
New York, NY

Haya A. El Nasser
Journalist/Reporter
USA Today
News Dept.
McLean, VA

Timothy Grant Evans
Assistant Director-
General
World Health
Organization
Information Evidence
and Research
Geneva, SWITZERLAND

Kendra Goldbas
Associate Director
University of
Pennsylvania
Penn Institute for
Urban Research
Philadelphia, PA

Kyung-Hwan Kim
Professor
Sogang University
Economics Dept.
Seoul, SOUTH KOREA

John D. Landis
Professor
University of California,
Berkeley
Dept. of City and
Regional Planning
Berkeley, CA

Shuaib Lwasa
Research Scientist
Int'l Potato Center-
Urban Harvest
Social Science Division
Kampala, UGANDA

Faith Macharia
National Director
Forum for African
Women Educaionalists
Nairobi, KENYA

Stephen J. Malpezzi
Professor
University of Wisconsin
Dept. of Real Estate and
Land Economics
School of Business
Madison, WI

Afaf I. Meleis
Dean, School of Nursing
University of
Pennsylvania
Dean's Office
Philadelphia, PA

Maritza E. Mercado
Research Associate
University of
Pennsylvania
Penn Institute for
Urban Research
Philadelphia, PA

**Amy Montgomery
Decker**
University of
Pennsylvania
Penn Institute for
Urban Research
Philadelphia, PA

Mark Montgomery
State University of
New York
Stonybrook, NY

Kilemi Mwiria
Assistant Minister
Ministry of Education
Government of Kenya
Nairobi, KENYA

Katherine Namuddu
Associate Director,
Africa Field Office
The Rockefeller
Foundation
Nairobi, KENYA

**Wilber Khasilwa
Ottichilo**
Director General
Regional Center for
Mapping of Resources
for Development
Kasarani Road
Nairobi, KENYA

Suzana Pasternak
Full Professor
Universidade de
São Paulo
Departamento de
Historia da Arquitetura
São Paulo, BRAZIL

Ronak B. Patel
Emergency Medicine
Physician
Massachusetts General
Hospital +B16
Center for Global Health
Boston, MA

Martino Pesaresi
European Commission
JRC IPSC
IPSC Session
Ispra, ITALY

Neal R. Peirce
Citistates Group
Washington, DC

Farley M. Peters
Citistates Group
Fairhaven, MD

Lynne B. Sagalyn
Prof. of Real Estate
Development and
Planning

University of
Pennsylvania
City Planning
(PennDesign) & Real
Estate (Wharton)
Philadelphia, PA

Karen C. Seto
Assistant Professor &
Center Fellow
Stanford University
Dept. of Geological and
Environmental Sciences
Woods Institute for the
Environment
Stanford, CA

**Stephen Charles
Sheppard**
Professor of Economics
Williams College
Dept. of Economics
Williamstown, MA

Marilyn J. Taylor
Partner
Skidmore Ownings
& Merril
Dept. of Urban Design
New York, NY

Vinod K. Tewari
Advisor
The Energy and
Resources Institute
Center for Urban
Systems and
Infrastructure
New Delhi, INDIA

Susan Wachter
Co-Director
University of
Pennsylvania
Penn Institute for
Urban Research
Philadelphia, PA

Darren Walker
Vice President
Foundation Initiatives
The Rockefeller
Foundation
New York, NY

Douglas Webster
Professor
Arizona State University
School of Global Studies
Tempe, AZ

Anthony Garon Yeh
Professor
University of Hong Kong
Centre of Urban
Planning &
Environmental
Management
Hong Kong, CHINA

Index

Photo Credits